INGMAR BERGMAN REVISITED

Ingmar BERGMAN
revisited

Performance, Cinema and the Arts

Edited by Maaret Koskinen

WALLFLOWER PRESS
LONDON & NEW YORK

First published in Great Britain in 2008
Wallflower Press
6 Market Place, London W1W 8AF
www.wallflowerpress.co.uk

A catalogue record for this book is available from the British Library

ISBN 978-1-905674-33-6 (pbk)
ISBN 978-1-905674-34-3 (hbk)

Book design by Elsa Mathern

Printed and bound in Poland; produced by Polskabook

CONTENTS

ACKNOWLEDGEMENTS

We wish to extend our cordial thanks to the Royal Opera, the Royal Dramatic Theatre, the Swedish Film Institute (SFI), Sveriges Television (SVT), Svensk Filmindustri (SF), the Theatre Museum of Sweden, and the Ingmar Bergman Foundation for permissions to use illustrations in this volume. On a more personal note, warm thanks to Margareta Nordström of the Ingmar Bergman Foundation, and film scholar and critic Michael Tapper, as well as Technical Director Bart van der Gaag and Doctoral student Christopher Natzén, both of the Department of Cinema Studies at Stockholm University.

Also thanks to the Swedish Research Council for generous financial support in the preparation of this volume.

NOTES ON CONTRIBUTORS

Thomas Elsaesser is Professor of Media and Culture, and Director of Research, Film and Television Studies at the University of Amsterdam. He is one of the most widely-published authors in the fields of film history, German and European cinema, media theory and digital aesthetics. His books include *New German Cinema* (1989), *Early Cinema: Space Frame Narrative* (1990), *Fassbinder's Germany* (1996), *Cinema Futures: Cain, Abel or Cable? The Screen Arts in the Digital Age* (1998), *Studying Contemporary American Film: A Guide to Movie Analysis* (2002), *Harun Farocki – Working on the Sight Lines* (2004), *The Last Great American Picture Show: New Hollywood Cinema in the 1970s* (2005) and *European Cinema: Face to Face with Hollywood* (2005).

Linda Harverty Rugg is Associate Professor of Scandinavian Studies at the Department of Scandinavian Studies at the University of California, Berkeley. Her research interests include autobiography and visual culture, particularly photography and film; comparative studies in literature and film, ecology and culture and whiteness studies; nineteenth- and twentieth-century Swedish literature and film, particularly Ingmar Bergman, Kerstin Ekman and August Strindberg. She is currently working on the book *The Auteur's Autograph: Cinematic Auteurism and Autobiography* and has previously published several articles and *Picturing Ourselves: Photography and Autobiography* (1997).

Erik Hedling is Professor of Comparative Literature and Associate Dean of Languages and Literature at Lund University. His main research interests are American, British and Scandinavian cinema and literature. He has been a British Council Fellow at the University of East Anglia, a visiting professor at the University of Minnesota at Minneapolis and a Fulbright Hildeman Scholar at the University of Colorado at Boulder. He is the author of *Lindsay Anderson: Maverick Film-Maker* (1998) and *Brittiska Fiktioner: Intermediala studier i film, TV, drama, prosa and poesi* (2001). He is the editor of *Blågult flimmer: svenska filmanalyser* (1998), and co-editor of *Interart Poetics: Essays on the Interrelations of the Arts and Media* (1997) and *Cultural Functions of Intermedial Exploration* (2002).

Stefan Johansson is Head of Dramaturgy of the Royal Swedish Opera. Originally a director, actor and dramatist, he is one of Sweden's foremost experts on opera and the history of the Royal Swedish Theatre. In 1969 he was a co-founder of the internationally renowned Teater 9, appearing at festivals and in collaborative work in Sweden, Poland, Italy, Germany and South America, from where he also brought a number of important theatre groups and productions to Scandinavia. Between 1988–94 he was Head of Drama and Documentary at the Swedish National Radio. Since the late 1960s he has published articles on film, theatre and cultural politics in journals, newspapers and anthologies, as well as having produced several hundred radio programmes.

Marilyn Johns Blackwell is Professor and Director of Swedish/Scandinavian Studies at the Department of Germanic Languages and Literatures at Ohio State University. She specialises in 19th- and 20-century drama and prose, feminist criticism and film, and has taught major courses on and written two books about the films of Ingmar Bergman. Her books include *Structures of Influence: Comparative Approaches to August Strindberg* (1981), *C.J.L. Almqvist and Romantic Irony: The Aesthetics of Self-Consciousness* (1983), *Persona: The Transcendent Image* (1986) and *Gender and Representation in the Films of Ingmar Bergman* (1997).

Maaret Koskinen is Professor of Cinema Studies at Stockholm University. Her articles on auteurs, intermediality, actors and popular film have appeared in a number of national and international film journals. She is the co-editor of *Swedish Film Today* (1996) and the author of two recent books on Bergman: *Ingmar Bergman: Allting föreställer, ingenting är. Filmen och teatern – en tvärestetisk studie* (2001) on relations between Bergman's films and his work in the theatre and *I begynnelsen var ordet. Ingmar Bergman och hans tidiga författarskap* (2002), which examines unpublished materials in Bergman's private archive focusing on his work as author of fiction. Her most recent book (co-written with Mats Rohdin), covers the writing and filming of *Fanny and Alexander* and is based on unpublished materials in the Bergman archive, including the director's private diary written during the shoot. She is also film critic for the national daily *Dagens Nyheter*.

Ulla-Britta Lagerroth is Professor at the Department of Comparative Literature at Lund University. She has published several books and numerous articles in the fields of literature, theatre and music, as well as specialising in interartial and intermedial studies. She is the author of *Körkarlen och Bannlyst: motivoch idéstudier i Selma Lagerlöfs 10-talsdiktning* (1963), *Regi i möte med drama och samhälle: Per Lindberg tolkar Pär Lagerkvist* (1978) and *Johannes Edfeldt: en författarskapsbiografi* (1993). She is the co-editor of *I musernas tjänst: Studier i konstarternas relationer* (1993),

Interart Poetics: Essays on the Interrelations of the Arts and Media (1997) and *Cultural Functions of Intermedial Exploration* (2002).

Paisley Livingston is Professor at the Department of Philosophy, Education, and Rhetoric at Copenhagen University and currently Visiting Professor at Lingan University, Hong Kong. His background is in film and literature, specialising in issues relating to aesthetics and philosophy. His books include *Ingmar Bergman and the Rituals of Art* (1982), *Literary Knowledge: Humanistic Inquiry and the Philosophy of Science* (1988), *Literature and Rationality: Ideas of Agency in Theory and Fiction* (1992), *Models of Desire* (1992) and *Art and Intention: A Philosophical Study* (2005).

John Orr is Emeritus Professor at the University of Edinburgh where he teaches film studies. His recent books include *The Art and Politics of Film* (2000), *Hitchcock and Twentieth Century Cinema* (2005) and *The Cinema of Roman Polanski* (2006, edited with Elżbieta Ostrowska). He has also published essays on Peter Greenaway, Derek Jarman, Terrence Malick, Carl Theodor Dreyer and Dogme95, Stardom in French Cinema and New Directions in European Cinema.

Janet Staiger holds the William P. Hobby Centennial Professorship in Communication at the Department of Radio, Television and Film at the University of Texas at Austin. She has published on the Hollywood mode of production, poststructural and postfeminist/queer approaches to authorial studies, the historical reception of cinema and television programmes, and cultural issues involving gender, sexuality and race/ethnicity. Her books include *Interpreting Films: Studies in the Historical Reception of American Cinema* (1992), *Bad Women: Regulating Sexuality in Early American Cinema* (1995), *Blockbuster TV: Must-See Sitcoms in the Network Era* (2000), *Perverse Spectators: The Practices of Film Reception* (2000) and *Media Reception Studies* (2005).

Birgitta Steene is Professor Emerita at the Department of Scandinavian Studies at the University of Washington. Throughout her career, she has done extensive research in the fields of comparative literature, cinema studies and Scandinavian drama and film. She has published books and numerous articles on, among other subjects, August Strindberg and Ingmar Bergman. Her books include *Ingmar Bergman* (1968), *Focus on the Seventh Seal* (1972), *August Strindberg: An Introduction to His Major Works* (1982), *A Reference Guide to Ingmar Bergman* (1982), *Strindberg and History* (1992) and *Måndagar med Bergman: en svensk publik möter Ingmar Bergmans filmer* (1996). A revised and enlarged edition of *A Reference Guide to Ingmar Bergman* was published in 2005.

Astrid Söderbergh Widding is Professor of Cinema Studies and Associate Dean of the Faculty of Humanities at Stockholm University. Since her dissertation on off-screen space in the work of Andrei Tarkovsky, she has published numerous books and articles on Nordic cinemas, art cinema and theology and film. She is the author of *Blick och blindhet* (1997), co-author of *Nordic National Cinemas* (1998), co-editor of *Moving Images from Edison to the webcam* (2000), and edited the volume *Konst som rörlig bild* (2006).

Liv Ullmann Actress/director Ullmann was already well-established on stage and film in Norway before her acting debut in an Ingmar Bergman film, *Persona* (1966). Since then she has acted in ten films directed by Bergman, including *Hour of the Wolf* (1968), *Cries and Whispers* (1972), *Scenes from a Marriage* (1973), *Face to Face* (1976), *Autumn Sonata* (1978) and *Saraband* (2003). Her work with Bergman made her known worldwide and she made numerous films both in Europe and the United States, as well as starring on Broadway, for instance in *Anna Christie* (1977). She has also won the New York Film Critics Award for Best Actress several times. In later years she has started a career as a director, beginning with *Sofie* in 1992; more recently she has directed *Private Confessions* (1998) and *Faithless* (2000), both scripted by Bergman. Ullmann has also written two books of memoirs, *Changing* (1977) and *Choices* (1984).

INTRODUCTION

Maaret Koskinen

It is now some years ago that the Swedish film director Ingmar Bergman (1918–2007) threw a question in my direction: 'Hey listen. There's a room here in my house on Fårö' (a small island in the Baltic, where Bergman shot many of his films, and where he lived in seclusion until his death at age 89). Continuing, he added: 'It's five times five square metres, and in it I've amassed all kinds of things. In fact, it's a hell of a mess. Would you like to take a look at it?'

As with almost everything having to do with Ingmar Bergman, questions like these, thrown out seemingly quite spontaneously, were in fact highly premeditated. True enough, his aim (I came to understand later) was to recruit someone who was well aquainted with his work to function as a kind of go-between and mediate with the powers that be, with the ultimate aim of securing his personal archive for the future. More specifically, the aim was to save his legacy from being squandered around the world and, as so often in cases like these, sold off to the highest-paying individual or institution abroad. Naturally, I did not mind being that someone, not least since it was a fantastic opportunity for me as a film scholar to suddenly get access to hitherto entirely unpublished materials, in this case dating as far back as 1937. Subsequently, parts of those findings were published under the title (in translation) *In the Beginning was the Word: Ingmar Bergman's Early Writings* (Koskinen 2002, see also Koskinen 2003).

More importantly this process eventually led to Bergman's subsequent donation of his (then) personal archive, and the formation of the Ingmar Bergman Foundation in 2002. Åse Kleveland, the former CEO of the Swedish Film Institute, whom I contacted soon after a first perusal of the content of this archive, became the creator and first Chair of the Foundation. However, an archive needs to be situated on the academic map as well, not least internationally. With this aim, in 2005 the Ingmar Bergman Foundation and the Cinema Studies Department of Stockholm University took a joint initiative in establishing the first international 'Ingmar Bergman Symposium'. The general theoretical framework for it was interartistic and intermedial, one obvious reason being the materials in this particular archive cover not only film but also theatre – it is often forgotten that besides a prolific career as director of more than fifty films, Bergman has staged about 130 plays, as well as creating works for television, radio, music/opera and literature. This approach gave ample opportunity for theoretical inquiry into intermediality as a field of research, as well as empirical studies, from the vantage point of each scholar's particular discipline and expertise.

Thus far the general background for the genesis of this book. However, let it at the same time be said that this volume is far from a mere collection of conference proceedings, but a much augmented work, theoretically as well as quantitatively, not least since several new writers have been commissioned. It almost had to be; after all, this is a book on a film director once considered among the foremost (if not *the* foremost) of auteurs, but whose international reputation over the last few decades has fallen into relative obscurity. The obvious question is: why?

One answer can be found in the notion of the auteur as such. For it is hardly by chance that Bergman's fall from grace occurred parallel to the post-structuralist demise of the idea of authorship. What, then, could be more natural than linking this revisitation of Ingmar Bergman's work to the resurging interest in recent years among film scholars in not only particular auteurs (see, for example, Gunning 2000) but in revisionist studies in authorship as a theoretical concept (see Gerstner & Staiger 2003)? Thus, in revisiting the specific auteur labelled 'Bergman', this volume does so with the view of opening up some traditional approaches in this field of studies, by attempting to refocus and recontextualise the (usual) matters at hand.

However, the complexity of these matters cannot be underestimated. For instance, since many of the contributors to this book have gained access to original sources in the Bergman archive (diaries and handwritten scripts), it should come as no surprise that some basic tenets of traditional auteur theory still linger, not least that irresistable urge to seek likeness and repetition, which in turn seems to provide a virtual guarantee of the individual author as the dominant source and origin of meaning. But to the degree that this is the case, it rather accurately reflects the state of things in present-day scholarship on authorship; after all, it still seems more or less mandatory to position oneself either in a post-structuralist, supposedly hardcore camp, or a more traditional, supposedly 'softer' humanist camp.

Yet, what this book will show is the extent to which such either/or terms are basically untenable, if for no other reason than by now it is simply impossible to retreat to a totally naïve and uninformed position *vis-à-vis* the notion of authorship. In other words, post-structuralist critique did in fact achieve what it set out to do, namely serve as a corrective to the idea of the author as a free agent, unhampered by wordly constraints like the conditions of production and various cultural discourses. In short, we have learnt to distinguish between the actual, biographical person and the author as his/her other, whatever, given the specific theoretical framework, we choose to call him/her/it: a textual construct, a biographical legend, a figure, signature, myth or implied author. What we see in the resurging interest in authorship, then, is not an author awakened from the dead to a condition of original glory, nor an unproblematically rehabilitated notion of authorship, but rather a comeback with substantial revisions.

At the same time we seem to have come out on the other end of the most extreme variants of post-structuralism, that is, those that declared the author absolutely dead and authorship as a mere de-personalised site of discourses. For, as Janet Staiger notes in *Authorship and Film*, 'the approach of authorship as site of discourses represents the biographical individual as a tablet for culture, without agency although potentially with individuality. The author may be a historically constituted subject that is the locus of social, psychological, and cultural discourses and practices; the author may no longer be a great person. But the author no longer seems to matter. Such a proposition dodges the material reality of human actions. Agency needs to be reconceived' (in Gerstner and Staiger 2003: 49). Also, as David Gerstner and Janet Staiger admit in the foreword of their volume, authorship is simply an enabling tool: 'Every scholar (even those who subscribe to the "death of authorship") speaks of going to a Robert Altman film. Coming to terms with our own ambivalence about the name of the author and the author-function is worthwhile' (Gerstner & Staiger 2003: n.p.). Perhaps the truth, they conclude, 'is that we don't think that the author is dead' (ibid.).

It is precisely such a fruitful yet critical ambivalence that can be found throughout the pages of this book. For while it at times may be worthwhile to regard the author as a linguistically or socially de-personalised, regulated function, there still lingers that odd feeling which Tom Gunning (2000) put his finger on in his study of Fritz Lang, namely that we as viewers, when watching a film, feel addressed – as if there indeed was a kind of organising, personalised principle behind it all, albeit more or less marked. In any case, as John Caughie has noted, 'recognition and expectation give the spectator a specific relation to the text, and, potentially, to the figure of the author' (2001: 199). Thus, the viewer's (pre-)knowledge of a particular director is part of the experience of watching the film. Ingmar Bergman's films, as well as other works, certainly belong to this category.

Equally complex is the concept of intermediality, which forms the second major theoretical strand of this book. It is, however, safe to say that when the term 'intermediality' is employed here, what is included as well is that which formerly was termed 'interart' perspectives, that is, the unwieldy field of study in which (virtually since Aristotle) literature and aesthetics have occupied a privileged position. However, since the visual turn of the humanities, and certainly the technologically-based medial and remedial turn of film studies (see Bolter & Grusin 2002), there seems to exist a consensus to use 'intermediality' as an umbrella term in order to cover the issues involved, including other terminologies – interarts, mixed media, media-dialogical (see Hedling & Lagerroth 2002; Fullerton & Olsson 2004).

In short, the intermedial concept is vague almost by nature, since it encompasses everything from strictly technological perspectives, mainly concerned with the medium as a physical and historically defined channel, to aesthetic perspectives, mainly concerned with the medium as a cultural practice (see Ekström *et al.* 2005). This is worth emphasising since here, as well, there tends to remain various demarcation lines between, on the one hand, studies directed towards traditional, work-oriented arts (with questions such as adaptation and authoring practices on the agenda) and, on the other, those dealing with strictly historical and/or technologically- oriented issues, which in the end tend to want to dispense with certain practices altogether. Thus, for instance, Friedrich Kittler's work (1999) is regarded as incompatible with the very idea of individual authorships, the essential factor in the sum of things being not authors but the *medium* or media as 'cause' and origin – the computer, the gramophone, the printing press.

Again, such absolute demarcation lines between 'traditional' humanist art perspectives and 'hardcore' technological ones are not a main concern here, since, as is so often the case, different perspectives more often than not are complementary rather than mutually exclusive. Rather, this volume has arisen from the conviction that there are more similarities than differences among scholars located on different, yet interconnected, places of the intermedial continuum. The majority of the contributors in this book can be located in either or both of two major theoretical frameworks – intermediality and various approaches to authorship.

This is why it is logical to begin with *Saraband*, Bergman's last film from 2003, since it so clearly belongs in both frameworks. In the first chapter I therefore make an attempt at delineating the influence and presence of various media in this work – in particular music, television, theatre and still photography – before discussing it from an auteurist perspective, tracing its very beginnings in the unpublished diaries and manuscripts of the Ingmar Bergman archive.

Ulla-Britta Lagerroth, as well, notes that Bergman is not only a recognised master within several media but, interestingly, also employs the possibilities of intermedialising them. He not only *theatricalises* his films, but *cinematises* as well as *pictorialises* his theatre productions. Furthermore, Lagerroth demonstrates to what extent and on how many various levels Bergman *musicalises* his theatre productions as well. She does so by a detailed analysis of four Shakespeare productions at the Royal Dramatic Theatre in Stockholm: *Twelfth Night* (1975), *King Lear* (1984), *Hamlet* (1986) and *The Winter's Tale* (1994). Since this aspect of Bergman's work is little known outside of Sweden, we are glad to be able to publish some rare photos taken, in the moment, during the rehearsal of one of these plays. Although not of the highest quality, these images are, needless to say, of great value and thus their importance outweighs their technical merit.

Bergman's work in opera is also little known outside of Sweden. In his very personal approach, Stefan Johansson traces the director's interest in this art form back to 1931 when a teenage Bergman became an avid Wagnerian, and then turns to the importance of his employment as an unpaid helper during the 1941–42 season at the Royal Opera in Stockholm. Johansson particularly stresses the fact that, at this time, the Royal Opera – including the ballet and the orchestra – had been separated from the Royal Dramatic Theatre for only a few decades. The fact that the theatre and the opera thus were one single institution, playing on two stages in a mixed repertoire, throws an interesting historical light on the intermedial issues under investigation in this book.

Marilyn Johns Blackwell, in turn, digs deeper into the many-faceted relations between Bergman's stage productions and his film career. Noting that this relationship offers a true 'embarras de richesses', she examines how Bergman transports and transforms a particular kind of privileged space from theatre to film, namely 'the platform stage' and variants of it, as well as their function as a kind of ritualised space, which focalises certain recurring thematic and visual clusters.

In the second section of this volume issues concerning authorship, self-fashioning and selfhood take centre-stage. Janet Staiger notes that authors employ certain recipes and codified exercises of agency in order to create the author function, thus producing their own descriptions of their authorship in order to re-create success in this area. Examining a number of motifs or generic formulae in Bergman's autobiography, *Laterna magica* (*The Magic Lantern*, 1987), Staiger also turns to the interview, a particularly privileged place to analyse self-fashioning by both authors and analysts of authorship, in this case most notably an interview with Bergman by the African-American writer James Baldwin, published in the 'gentleman's magazine' *Esquire* in 1959.

Linda Haverty Rugg approaches related issues, by focusing on different ways of imagining and representing selfhood in various media. More specifically, she examines the relationship between still and moving images in an intermedial as well as interdisciplinary light, relating the notion of self-projection in Bergman's films to recent ideas put forward by scholars working at the intersection of philosophy and neuroscience.

Paisley Livingston, also, takes an interdisciplinary approach by examining the possible connection between philosophy and cinema. Departing from Bergman's fairly well-known admission of having been impressed by the Finnish philosopher Eino Kaila's work *Psychology of the Personality* (1935) Livingston sets out to answer whether any of Kaila's specific philosophical propositions have made their way into Bergman's films and, if so, how they were transformed, adapted or revised in the process.

The third section of this volume enters into certain philosophical issues, but at the same time more socio-political territories. Thus John Orr traces the influence of

Nietzsche as well as classical Hollywood comedy in Bergman's work. Two unlikely bedfellows, certainly; however, Orr maintains that these two opposite sources of attraction can be traced virtually throughout Bergman's whole career, making use of, for instance, Stanley Cavell's concept 'comedy of remarriage', as well as intertextual contexts such as Strindberg, Thomas Mann and Weimar cinema.

Thomas Elsaesser further contextualises Bergman's work in a political direction by locating his contribution to the so-called 'retro-fashion' of historical films, made during the 1970s by many notable European directors. For like Visconti, Bertolucci, Pasolini and Fassbinder, Bergman in *Ormens ägg (The Serpent's Egg*, 1977) approached Europe's troubled past, specifically the phenomenon of fascism and Nazism, across show business and the mode of spectacle and excess. In this Elsaesser not only takes a closer look at a number of complexes in the representation of history in film, in order to indicate how one might extend, displace or simply re-affirm some of the dominant auteurist and aesthetic approaches to the work of Ingmar Bergman, but also in order to test a more theoretical proposition, which has to do with the cinema's relation to memory, both collective and individual.

Erik Hedling in turn scrutinises another neglected approach in traditional Bergman studies by focusing on the relationship between Bergman's films and the affluent Swedish welfare society in which they were conceived and received. Noting that while scholars have studied Bergman from many various perspectives, no one has really chosen to regard his films as a social critique of Swedish society, in the sense of, say, Godard of France, Bertolucci of Italy or Fassbinder of Germany. Consequently, Hedling sets out to do precisely this, mainly by drawing attention to landscape depiction in Bergman, comparing it to earlier Swedish film.

Astrid Söderbergh Widding offers both a review and a re-reading of earlier research into Bergman and religion, in particular theologians concerned with God, Lutheranism and the search for 'symbols'. Noting that as a rule the interpreter is successful in this regard, since Bergman's universe is so totally leavened with Lutheran tradition, she also concludes that what has been explicitly formulated in generally-accepted symbols does not tell us much about what meaning the Lutheran legacy gives to Bergman's filmic art. She therefore sets out to seek Christian traits in Bergman's aesthetics – in particular his facial close-up, which becomes a kind of ethical imperative – as well as the role of language, specifically speech, in his films.

In addition, we secured the participation of Birgitta Steene, the most prominent among Bergman scholars, who offers, in the form of an epilogue, both a salient review and a rich contextualisation of the issues and concerns of this book. Last, but certainly not least, Liv Ullmann, film director but perhaps best known as a world-famous actress in films by Bergman, agreed to contribute her opening address from the aforementioned symposium as a prologue to this volume. Needless to say, this speech was written while Ingmar Bergman was still alive, and since it is not only about Bergman but addressed in a very personal way directly to him, Liv's contribution is best read in the present tense, as it was spoken.

This is in fact perfectly apt and in accord with the spirit of this book, which has come about in celebration of that rich oeuvre and legacy labelled 'Ingmar Bergman'.

References

Bolter, J. D. and R. Grusin (2002) *Remediation: Understanding New Media.* Cambridge, MA: MIT Press.

Caughie, J. (2001) *Theories of Authorship.* London: Routledge.

Ekström, A., S. Jülich and P. Snickars (2005) *1897. Mediehistorier kring Stockholmsutställningen.* Stockholm: Statens Ljud och Bildarkiv.

Fullerton, J. and J. Olsson (eds) (2004) *Allegories of Communication: Intermedial Concerns from Cinema to the Digital.* Corso, Trieste: John Libbey/CIC Publishing.

Gerstner, D. and J. Staiger (eds) (2003) *Authorship and Film.* New York and London: Routledge.

Gunning, T. (2000) *The Films of Fritz Lang: Allegories of Vision and Modernity.* London: British Film Institute.

Hedling, E. (2001) *Brittiska fiktioner. Intermediala studier i film, tv, dramati, prosa och poesi.* Stockholm and Stehag: Symposion.

Hedling, E. and U.-B. Lagerroth (2002) *Cultural Functions of Intermedial Exploration.* Amsterdam and New York: Rodopi.

Kittler, F. (1999) *Gramophone, Film, Typewriter*, trans. G. Winthrop-Young and M. Wutz. Stanford: Stanford University Press.

Koskinen, M (2002) *I begynnelsen var ordet. Ingmar Bergman och hans tidiga författarskap.* Stockholm: Wahlström & Widstrand.

_____ (2002) 'Au commencement était le Verbe. Les écrits de jeunesse d'Ingmar Bergman', *Positif*, 497/498, July/August, 17–22.

_____ (2003) 'From Short Story to Film to Autobiography: Intermedial Variations in Ingmar Bergman's Writings and Films', *Film International*, 1, 5–11, available at http://www.filmint. nu/?q=node/82 (accessed 22 October 2007).

Ingmar Bergman, summer 2006, on Fårö (photo: Mats Bäcker)

PROLOGUE

Liv Ullmann

I wish Ingmar Bergman would have been here today. But he has made a decision: to stay on Fårö, and think those thoughts he may have missed during his life, thoughts concerning him and the people he cares for. Most of all he misses his actors.

He is 87 years old in a few weeks [14 July 2005]. And while walking around his island, those who are dead and those who are still here – the people he has touched – are all alive to him. They are all with him in that solitude he has chosen.

He listens, and he recognises. He reads wise books, sometimes with a magnifying glass. To read those heavy books is for him creative, he says. He has chosen isolation for almost two years now, but he bicycles around the island and still finds places that he has never seen before. He also finds things about himself he did not know.

'But I have a gift for love', he tells me on the phone. 'Don't you think so?' Oh yes, Ingmar – I do. 'I am also trying to find out where *music* comes from', he continues. I believe he will write about this some day. And today, on the occasion of the very first 'Ingmar Bergman Symposium', he sends you all his best wishes.

Now who am I? I have been his actress. His lover. We have a child together. He built the house on Fårö for the two of us. We have been the best of friends. Two of his film scripts (*Private Conversations* [1996] and *Faithless* [2000]), I directed.

I have been an actress in theatre and in films for almost fifty years. That is a lifetime, a very special kind of quality time. The particular quality of my profession includes the possibility of ever-rediscovering, grasping and revealing *reality*. That is, a reality often far away from where *I* lived – inside of me – and far from what I was brought up to understand and accept. So much of my knowledge, of my empathy, I found while watching a film in a dark movie-house, sharing the experience with other people. People I did not know. The fates and the movements and the voices on the movie screen became to me, as a young girl, something *more* real than reality.

One of my favourite films as a young girl was *Sawdust and Tinsel* [1953] by Ingmar Bergman. I saw it many years before I met him. I still remember all those people clutched to the cliff – glued to it, like birds – while watching the humiliation of that woman who had waded half-naked into the water. And then there was her lover, who waded after her, saving her, and carried her ashore: this young man, who was hiding his face behind a mask. I did not understand it – I could never have discussed it on a rational level – but I *recognised* it.

Later, I played Elisabet in *Persona* [1966], at 25 years of age. This young girl – me – *knew what Ingmar felt*. His pain was mine. Again, I did not understand, but I *recognised*. I *connected*. His loneliness ran through my body. His fear made my heart beat faster. His longing and his sadness – I knew I was playing *him*, and that can still bring tears to my eyes when I think of him that way, in *Persona*. Especially today. *To talk no more. To anyone.*

An image suddenly appears: Ingmar and I a long time ago at Copenhagen airport. He hates travelling and is apprehensive – all those people, all that noise. He panics, feels a strong urge to return home. The flight is delayed, and he takes an elevator to the men's room. I wait close by. After a while the elevator door opens and Ingmar comes out again. He has his beret on his head, and there is a faint smile of pride. Here is obviously someone who has overcome his phobia: gone first into a strange elevator, then into a strange toilet and finally made it back all by himself. He approaches me, his back stooped just a little. The faint smile has gone, but the anxious expression in his eyes is no longer so impelling – and I know that the trip will continue.

And then we are in Rome. He meets Fellini for the first time, and they become brothers within an instant. They embrace, laugh together as if they have lived the same life. They wander through the streets in the night, arms around each other; Fellini wearing a dramatic black cape, Ingmar in his beret and an old winter coat. I wonder if Fellini ever knew how endlessly vulnerable Ingmar was. Then again, perhaps Fellini was too. It is hard to know when you watch geniuses.

Indeed, I had the opportunity of watching and observing: being an actor, my material is the life I am living, the life I am watching, the life I am reading about and the life I am listening to. You know, that wonderful moment when a ballet dancer does a leap and stays in the air just a few seconds longer than seems possible – that is my aim as an actor. And that is what I look for in other actors when I direct: to suddenly see something that seems impossible. I wish to aim for that leap again and again, and I want to be regognised even when it fails.

I wish to express something about humanity in my work as an actor, or as a director or as a screenwriter; something which may come as a surprise, once identified. Also I wish to convey a message: that loneliness does not need to be, that it is a human right for people to belong. So that those of us who thought that we were on the outside, all alone, feel that we experience something together. For instance, in a dark movie-house – so good for shared feelings! It is all about recognising ourselves, even if only briefly. Recognising other people.

Most of my life I have been an actor. I have had a profession where I was always asked to share. As a child, when I acted, the only reality that existed was the pleasure of being in the world of make believe. I used to paint pictures. They just happened. And it never ocurred to me that people and trees and houses should be depicted in any particular way for others to recognise them and like them. My trees were violet and the sky was green. 'What is this?' the grown-ups would ask me. I did not mind because my grandmother always said, 'What beautiful dreams you make, Liv.' The pictures were *me*. Later the roles were me. And some would recognise them, just like my grandmother. What more do I want as an actor? I wanted to meet someone, a storyteller – like my grandmother – in my own field. And I met him: Ingmar. Though his stories were so different!

But he could see something – something that no one else recognised in me – and bring it forth.

You see, the limitation of an actor is to have only oneself as an instrument, and as a means of expression. For me it is impossible, and even without interest, merrily to go through a complete change of personality from role to role. Ingmar taught me to allow unknown *secrets* – so far within myself that I was totally unaware of them – to come forward, sparked by the shaping of my role, sparked by the experience of my life, sparked by the director. And most of all this happened with Ingmar.

Acting for me has meant stretches of happiness, when everything feels real. And even more so now that I am a director myself: this miracle in watching others offer their soul and their life and their observations of humanity and human beings. It is the truth of imagination, that truth that in a golden moment is revealed for the first time to an audience. *Because the actor recognised it, the audience will recognise it.* A performance that makes us realise truth – at least those truths that are given us to understand.

Being originally a theatre actress, I know that films have one thing that the theatre will never have: *the close-up.* For me it is like this: the closer the camera comes, the more eager I will want to show a completely naked face; show what is behind the skin, the eyes, inside the head; show the thoughts that are forming. Working as an actress in a film is to go on a journey of discovery within my own self. Throw away the mask and show what is behind it. The camera comes close, so close, and then there is the thrill in allowing it to capture what the eyes cannot see.

The human face is seen on the screen, closer to the audience than in any other medium. And the audience, in the moment of recognition and identification, should meet a real person, not an actor; meet himself, a face confronting his. A soul to identify with: yes, this is what I know about human beings, this is what I have experienced, this is what I have seen. This is what I would like to share. But this is no longer a question of make-up, of hair or beauty. It is an exposure that goes much further, because the camera does not simply show a face, but reveals what kind of life this face has seen and experienced; thoughts behind a forehead, something the face did not know about itself. But the audience will see and recognise. Privately, we long for exactly this kind of recognition: that other people will be able to perceive what and who we really are – deep inside.

This is what I love as an actor and as a director: that no one is uninteresting. Every one is special, in one excellent, golden moment. How were Ingmar and I interesting to each other – and why did we end up on Fårö? Here are a few paragraphs from my book *Changing*:

> We were making *Persona* on the island.
> It was hot. I was experiencing another human being…
> No summer since has ever been like that. Not like that. We went for walks along the shore and never spoke, made no demands, were not afraid.
> Once we wandered far from the others, discovered a small ridge of grey stones with barren, unfertile earth beyond. We sat and he looked at the sea, which for once lay completely still in the sunlight.
> He took my hand and said: 'I had a dream last night. That you and I are painfully connected.' On the spot where we were sitting he built his house. And that changed his life. And mine. (1977: 112)

> The island lies between Russia and Sweden.
> I could not remember having seen a place so barren. Like a relic from the Stone Age. But in the summer sunlight, moving and rather mysterious.
> At night we could see the ocean from our bedroom. And we imagined ourselves passengers on a journey. Lights from ships in the far, far distance we looked upon as mysterious messages to strangers down on our beach. We pretended we were in constant danger, because the house was so isolated and we only had each other.
> When I was a girl I dreamed of another kind of island. It had palm trees and fruits and warmth. And when it was night there, the animals of the forest kept watch over me. I never associated loneliness and eeriness with that.
> His island had gnarled spruce trees of strange green colours, most of them stunted and bent along the ground. Only the strongest managed to lift themselves upward. And when the dusk came, they looked in their vain longing toward heaven, like slender female dancers no longer able to stand on their toes.
> The most beautiful of all the trees grew outside our living-room window, and he told me it was mine. The winter after I left the island it blew down. That made me happy. He could not share it with somebody else. (1977: 116)

> It is a short love story that resembles so many others.
> It lasted five years.

When she had lived with him for a few years she began to observe him. She would sit quietly and experience him as an individual.

One who no longer existed only in relation to her.

Her understanding and respect for him grew.

The adoration disappeared. She noticed that his hair was grey; he was much older than she; he was wise and stimulating; he was vain and egotistical.

And she discovered to her surprise that this was love…

She tried to recall who she had been when she came to this island five years before.

Something had been crushed in her and something was more alive.

She had undergone a change…

But she would never be able to talk about it.

She had seen into another person and was full of tenderness for what she had found.

For a period of time they had taken each other's hand and had been painfully connected.

But only when it was all over did they become true friends. (1977: 130–1)

The last movie we made, while we were still living together, was *The Passion of Anna* [1969]. Here is another personal memory, related to one of the many things I learned

Scenes from a Marriage

from Ingmar: that a director, and sometimes an actor, in certain ways must 'act like a cannibal'. That is, you do not only *watch* other people, you *use* them. You 'eat' them.

I remember a diary he asked me to write one long Easter weekend that I spent with him on our island. Lonely it was. Isolated. I wanted to be seen. So my diary – knowing he would read it – kind of screamed out to him: 'Here I am – see me – listen to me.' Later, he ended up using parts from my diary in *The Passion of Anna*, as well as later in *Scenes from a Marriage* [1973], in the scene where Marianne reads from her diary to Johan – and he falls asleep! The diary is written exactly in the kind of childish language that I used in that Easter weekend diary that I wrote for Ingmar. You remember Nora in *A Doll's House*? Childlike, naïve, using the kind of language a woman uses, when she – just like Nora – dances for him. Because she wants to please him, being a doll in *his* doll's house.

Yes, it is painful to know that you have been 'seen' and 'listened' to – but not in the way you had hoped for. Oh, and all for the art – and the artist. This I know – but with a smile I know it. There are different soils from where an artist allows his roots to spread…

Another memory. Once we were travelling. Ingmar drove me to the airport, on that long road from our house on Fårö. We stopped on the way to buy newspapers. *The Passion of Anna* had just premiered, and Ingmar wanted me to read the reviews while he drove. Dreadful reviews! What should I do? I could not harm him. He had hoped, I thought, that the movie would be well received. Understood. And what does 'Nora' do? She makes up the reviews. In broad daylight she lies – every word was a lie – and he never understood it. He had to stop the car. He cried. Only twice before had she seen him cry. She never knew he had been so afraid. She boarded the plane, and caught a glimpse of his happy face – the one she had created.

They never spoke of this episode. And later they parted – it was over. But the memory would always be with her. 'Nora' dancing. 'Nora' lying. 'Nora' wanting everyone to be happy. Mostly him.

One day, not too long ago, I asked Ingmar: 'Why have we worked so much together? I mean – you had so many choices.' And 'Nora' tried her little lies again: 'You are such a genius, and I am – well I'm just me…' He looked at me and said: 'You don't understand, Liv. Don't you see that you are my Stradivarius.'

Making a film with Ingmar was not like working. To me he will always be like one of the *younger* directors. If I need a new way of thinking, I will go to him. I believe he kept young because he is always creative, and because he is amused by life. He kept us all inspired, because he showed us how *free* we could be in our profession.

The speeches of most presidents and prime ministers and generals will surely be forgotten. But I know Ingmar Bergman will change those who experience him, and will remain being part of them, awakening them to something within themselves

The director and his 'Stradivarius' (photo: Ingmar Bergman Foundation)

they were unaware of. It happened to me.

We know – at least until this present moment – that the images and the visions of the cinema from the most gifted creators will still fill people with hope that there is some dignity to life; that there are possibilities, opportunities. And the tragedy we filmmakers are facing, because of all the negative changes for creative workers in today's European policy-making is, in fact, a tragedy for *everyone*. Not least for the potential public. We have a world which to me seems to be governed by mindlessness. We, those of us who work in and with culture, may be facing the last moment when we still can make a difference. We can still lobby for greater issues, and be *heard*; issues that deal with the mind and the soul, and the compassion and dreams of human beings. Wars and TV-speeches will never do this. *But our acknowledgement of every person's uniqueness will. We are fighting for our identity.* Belonging one way or another to the world of the cinema, we have an obligation – because we are bearing witness to our times.

Thank you, Ingmar Bergman – for being. And for being one of those who will continue making cultural work – our work – more important than ever.

MUSIC, STAGE, FILM – BETWEEN THE ARTS

OUT OF THE PAST: *SARABAND* AND THE INGMAR BERGMAN ARCHIVE

Maaret Koskinen

It goes without saying that Ingmar Bergman's donation of his personal archive, now under the auspices of the Ingmar Bergman Foundation, is a virtual treasure of materials, and one that transgresses disciplinary boundaries: film, theatre, literature, music, television and radio.

Already in empirical terms, then, such material seems to call out for intermedial approaches, which focus on the multi-faceted relationships between various arts and media, including different forms of historic as well as present-day transgressional traffic between them. Naturally, such transgressional aspects can be found on a number of levels, both with regard to individual works as well as Bergman's entire oeuvre. Here, for instance, you can find a multitude of so-called 'visualisations' or 'theatricalisations' of written texts. A prime example is Bergman's autobiography *Laterna magica* (*The Magic Lantern*, 1987), of which the very title announces its close links to the idea of – literally – pictorialising memories. In equal measure, Bergman's work is saturated with examples of the opposite, that is, all kinds of 'literature-lisations' of the (arguably) mainly visual and aural arts of film. One example is his use of the theatrical *Kammerspiel*-form (which in turn has been transposed from a musical form), as well as his propensity for allegory or representational abstractions, and, not least, heavy reliance on well-crafted dialogue.

Take, for instance, the unpublished story from 1942 found in the archive material, which first was conceived as a literary *novella*, and a few years later was rewritten into a film script (unpublished and not filmed), which in turn was followed by yet another version in the shape of a stage play called *Dagen slutar tidigt* (*The Day Ends Early*), this time both published and staged (see Bergman 1948). Or, to take a more well-known example, think of *Scener ur ett äktenskap* (*Scenes from a Marriage*, 1973), which was first written as a script with decidedly literary qualities, then became adapted into a six-part mini-series for television, and later was cut down to half for cinema distribution – and eventually ended up being (re-)produced for the stage.

In short, it is safe to say that Bergman's practice forms an eminent, if not unique, example of a transgressional aesthetic project, as if made to be studied in the light of interarts or intermedia approaches.

However, besides close readings of *empiri*, the archive material encourages theoretical reflection on interartiality and intermediality as theoretical concepts and approaches as well. Thus it prompts one to ask, for instance, what issues are involved in the present-day influence of new media (like television and digitalisation) over the traditional arts? What, for instance, if a given manuscript is produced as a television series instead of as a film for the cinema? Consider the fact that the aforementioned *Scenes from a Marriage* first was produced as a television series, that is, for another medium as well as for quite different conditions of reception than those encountered in a darkened cinema. In addition, this series was consciously conceived and construed as a daytime soap opera (albeit in an ironic, modified fashion). Nonetheless, it was received as yet another masterpiece by Bergman the artist or auteur, that is, in line with those theoretical notions and contexts associated with 'high culture' that Bergman's work is almost exclusively (and sometimes quite erroneously) framed by, not least abroad. Needless to say, this in turn rather efficiently disposed of other relevant approaches such as melodrama or gender perspectives.

Saraband from an intermedial perspective

It is not by chance, then, that Ingmar Bergman's last film *Saraband* (2003) also lends itself to an intermedial approach.

One could, for instance, focus entirely on the fact that it was made for television, just as *Scenes from a Marriage*, with which it shares internal relations, mainly through the characters Johan and Marianne, here played thirty years later by the same actors (Erland Josephson and Liv Ullmann). Or one could focus on the fact that *Saraband* was shot digitally, which supposedly, according to what was reported in the press, was why Bergman refused to send it to the Cannes Film Festival in 2004, since he did not consider the technical standard good enough for a theatrical screening. But the real reason, I suspect, is that he sensed (just as, he told me, was the case with *Efter repetitionen* (*After the Rehearsal*) from 1984) that this particular story was not conceived for nor meant for the big screen, but rather for the medium of television and its much more intimate viewing conditions.

Alternatively, one could ponder the many-faceted relations between the aural and visual arts, through the use and function of *music* in *Saraband*. The centrality of music is of course already announced in the title, referring to the fifth suite for solo cello by Bach, which can be regarded as a kind of 'sublimated dance music' if one were to believe Bergman's own notes on the cover sheet of the first handwritten draft of the script. In the film, Bach is very much related to Anna, the woman who has died recently, and whom we never see (except in a photograph), but whose presence seems to be felt by the other characters in the story, in this case her daughter Karin, her husband Henrik, and her elderly father-in-law Johan. Indeed, at times Bach's music seems interchangeable with Anna, representing something of her presence for the people left behind: a sense of belonging, grace, perhaps a redemption of sorts. An obvious comparison, thematically as well as stylistically, is the way Bach's music functions in, for instance, *Tystnaden* (*The Silence*, 1963) and *Viskingar och rop* (*Cries and Whispers*, 1973), both in which the dialogue suddenly falls silent, as if giving in to music, and acceding to the deviousness and frailty of (spoken) language as a communicative tool.

Another example of the function of music in *Saraband* can be found in that strangely aggressive part (*scherzo*) from Bruckner's ninth symphony, which Johan at one point plays at highest volume, while alone in his room. As a Swedish music critic has noted, this is Bruckner's last symphony and what is more, dedicated to God (Nyström 2003). Now Bergman does not dedicate *Saraband* – by all accounts, *his* last work – to God, or any other otherworldly force. However, he does dedicate it to his wife Ingrid, who died in 1995, and thus arguably to the beyond in some kind of metaphysical sense. In fact, this beyond, or the hope and possibility of such a place or existence, is perhaps the most overriding theme in *Saraband*, to which I will return.

But let me first mention two other forms of intermediality at work in *Saraband*. Take, for instance the *theatre*, which is so present in almost anything that Ingmar Bergman has touched upon throughout his long career. It comes as no surprise to find that Bergman wrote *Saraband* while planning his last production for the stage, *Ghosts* by Henrik Ibsen, at the Royal Dramatic Theatre. This is confirmed by the work diary, which clearly states that Bergman started writing *Saraband* on 12 June 2001, that is, during the time that he translated, reworked and (some would say) rewrote the play, given the extensive changes and cuts in Ibsen's original text.

Not surprisingly, there are uncanny similarities between Ibsen's play and *Saraband*. An obvious one is the fact that Johan and Marianne (Johan's former wife, as well as narrator of the story) share a past, since they used to be married, just as Mrs Alving and Pastor Manders in *Ghosts* share a past. But not only the past but death, too, lies heavily on the characters, as is the case in the play. For, as mentioned, Anna has died, but remains (invisibly) present, and plays an important role in the lives of the other characters: her husband Henrik, who seems to have been reduced to a physical as well as moral ruin in her absence; her daughter Karin, whose young life is about to be smothered in the most horrific way by Henrik, her father; while Johan, this cynical old man, does his best to avoid any kind of insights into others or himself, including his own fear of dying. Another parallel between Ibsen's play and Bergman's film is the theme of euthanasia, as well as that of incest, which are clearly present in both works. In *Saraband*, there is of course the sexual relationship

Out of the past: shooting *Saraband* (photo: Bengt Wanselius/SVT)

between father and daughter, while in Ibsen's *Ghosts* there is the complex relationship between mother and son (one that, incidentally, was strongly emphasised in Bergman's own stage production of the play in 2002).

Let us, finally, turn to the role of *photographs* in *Saraband*. As is well known, photos have been put to various uses in Bergman's films. Just think of *Persona* (1966), and the famous picture of the Nazis surrounding a group of Jewish women and children, including the Jewish boy with his hands stretched up in the air. Or take the freeze-frame in the form of a photo-montage of Liv Ullmann and Bibi Andersson (often re-produced on the film poster of *Persona*), in which their faces form a kind of visual monster, expressing in a condensed fashion the film's self-reflexive meditation on its very means for existing.

In later years, however, Bergman's use of photographs have turned towards their relation to time and memory. As Linda Haverty Rugg puts it in her contribution to this book, still images in Bergman's work often become types of portals to the past or gateways into other worlds. Take for instance the autobiographical book *Laterna magica*, where this idea seems to be announced in the very title. On second thought, it is hardly surprising that a film director writing his memoirs would use the metaphor of a photographic machine, for what is writing an autobiography if not – literally – *writing the images* of memory?

If nothing else, the title of the book serves to remind us of the fact that writing always establishes a complex relationship to images. Or to put it another way, that images and language are intimately connected – just as 'real', physical images are intimately connected to inner, mental ones. If this is the case, the same can be said about the related issue of forgetting. In short, every memory revisited through writing may result in yet another layer of re-writing, so to remember is, paradoxically, also a way of forgetting. Or, to put it in yet another way: if for some writers (the writing of) fiction is constantly invaded by memories, with time memories can in turn become increasingly fictionalised (see Forslid 2000). This, it seems, is quite often the case with Ingmar Bergman's entire work, and one that is put to effective use in *Laterna magica*: here memory images at times seem to blur into (still or moving) cinematic images, while descriptions of films and the images of cinema bear striking resemblance to memory images from life proper.

Saraband from an auteurist perspective

I will return to memory and the internal 'memory-shots' in *Saraband* shortly, but let me do so by way of citing one of Bergman's diaries, in which he looks back on *Höstsonaten* (*Autumn Sonata*, 1978). Why bring in this film? Quite simply, because it is hard *not* to – just as hard as it is to avoid regarding *Saraband* in the light of traditional and naïvely 'uncorrupted', pre-structural auteur theory as well. For even if it is a fact that Bergman's work is certainly one of the most authorially overdetermined ever (and thus only can benefit from having some of its most basic tenets questioned and complicated through, for instance, intermedial issues), it is equally undeniable that Bergman, as writer for and director of film, has enjoyed a virtually unique creative freedom throughout his long career. In such a case, and when confronted with the wealth of materials such as those in the Bergman archive, it remains oddly intriguing to insist on looking for the usual matters at hand (patterns, similarities and so on), if for no other reason that, as John Caughie has noted, the viewer's (pre-)knowledge of a certain director is part of the experience of watching a film: 'recognition and expectation give the spectator a specific relation to the text, and, potentially, to the figure of the author' (1999: 129). This figure indeed looms large in *Saraband*, especially when regarded in conjunction with various unpublished, archive material, such as diaries and various versions of the script.

Indeed, there are striking similarities between *Autumn Sonata* and *Saraband*. Firstly, there is the prominent role of classical music. Secondly, there are the characters: strong parents; weak or mediocre children; in the case of *Autumn Sonata* a neurotic relationship between the mother, a world-famous pianist (Ingrid Bergman) and her daughter (Liv Ullmann), who, as everyone who has seen the painful piano-playing sequence of the film knows, will never be able to interpret Chopin as well as her mother. It is hard not to compare their relationship to the tortured goings-on between father and son in *Saraband*, and Johan's relentless contempt for his son Henrik's mediocrity, both as an individual and as a musician. (In this film, the conflict between the generations is also mirrored in the incestuous relationship between Henrik and his daughter Karin, both of them musicians.) Finally, there are in *Autumn Sonata* and *Saraband* those repressed daughters, who in both even seem to arrive in doubles. For in *Autumn Sonata* there is not only a middle-aged daughter caught in a power struggle with an overbearing parent, but also a younger sister who is (literally) disabled, hidden away on the upper floor of her older sister's house. In *Saraband*, in turn, Karin's predicament is mirrored in the fate of Johan and Marianne's middle-aged daughter, who is locked away in a mental asylum.

But besides such striking thematic similarities, there are passages in Bergman's diaries which are of great interest for our discussion of the role of photographs in his films. For, a couple of years after having worked on *Autumn Sonata*, Bergman wrote the following in a diary:

> I often think of Ingrid Bergman. I would like to write something for her that would not be too demanding, and I see a summer porch in rain. She is alone, waiting for her children and grandchildren. It is afternoon. The whole film is set on a veranda. The film will last only as long as the rain. Nature is showing her fairest face; everything is enveloped in this soft unceasing rain … She sees her reflection in the windowpanes – and can catch a glimpse of herself as a young woman … The porch in the summer – everything is enveloped in a soft chiaroscuro. In this piece there are no hard edges; everything must be as soft as the rain. A neighbour's child comes and asks for the other children. She has brought wild strawberries, and she is given a treat. (1990: 366–7)

This film with Ingrid Bergman was never realised. However, this particular scene on the porch did find its way into into the director's work, namely in *Fanny och Alexander* (*Fanny and Alexander*, 1982/1983), the television mini-series (later distributed as a feature film, cut down to almost half its original length), which Bergman in fact was in the midst of writing as he jotted down these words. The scene in question is the one in which Helena Ekdahl, Alexander's grandmother, is waiting in the indoor porch of her summer house for the rest of the family to return from a boat excursion, while a soft summer rain is falling outside the big picture windows. And clearly, the most important elements in the imagined film in Bergman's notes can be found in this scene: the elderly woman, the summer porch, the soft rain, even a child who brings wild strawberries. Also, just like the woman in the imagined film catches a glimpse of herself as young, Helena as well thinks of the past, and suddenly finds herself engaged in a conversation with her recently deceased son Oscar (Alexander's father), seeing him, just as clearly as the viewer sees him, sitting opposite her. 'Your wrist was so terribly thin,' she exclaims, while holding the grown-up man's hand in

Inside looking out: *Fanny and Alexander* (photo: Arne Carlsson/The Ingmar Bergman Foundation)

hers. 'See, that's just it,' she continues. 'One is old, and is a child, at one and the same time', obviously talking just as much about herself as her son's apparition.

In other words, children and childhood, the images of the past and the images of memory, all come together on this porch. Thus it should come as no surprise that Helena at one point ends up at a big table, with piles of family photographs spread out in front of her, which she is trying to organise into her bulging family album. It is precisely here, at Helena's table full of pictures, that the many similarities between Bergman's last film for theatrical screening and his last film for television become apparent. After all, *Saraband* begins, as well as ends, in a room very similar to the indoor porch in *Fanny and Alexander*. Here we find Liv Ullmann (as Marianne) seated at a big table with hundreds of photographs spread out in front of her, puzzling – just like Helena – over the riddle that is life, time and memories. And although her porch is entirely void of Helena's flowers, it is still suffused with a soft, summery, yellow light. Also, the fact that she directs her gaze in the direction of the viewer, as if to an intimate confidante, is reminiscent of Helena's conversation with her dead son: in both cases, boundaries of all kinds – those between imagined worlds and the exterior world – do indeed blur.

In any case, there is definitely something about summery porches in Bergman's work that seems overdetermined, layered with meaning; here place, memory and identity seem to merge. Also, should one wish to continue in this (auteurist) vein, one could go even as far back as *Smultronstället* (*Wild Strawberries*) from 1957, the film in which Isak Borg, the old professor (played by silent-film director Victor Sjöström) embarks on his sentimental journey though the summery landscape of Sweden, as well as the inner landscape of his reveries and reminiscences. Then, halfway, he decides to visit the old summerhouse where he spent his summers as a youngster, and where he is now whisked away to his very first daytime revery of the past. Interestingly this transition occurs as he is watching the house, and suddenly finds himself standing in the darkness of a kind of foyer, very much reminiscent of a porch, while peering into a brightly-lit room in which a scene from the past plays itself out. It is worth noting that this is where Borg remains, outside, in the dark, as he is never seen to enter into or be part of his own visions (for instance as a young man). He is indeed an outsider, and has cut himself off from personal relationships. As the teacher tells him in one of the film's nightmare scenes: 'A surgical masterpiece, Dr Borg. Everything has been removed. Nothing hurts, nothing bleeds or quivers.'

Something to that effect could be said as well about Johan in *Saraband* almost fifty years later. For just like Borg, he is a misanthropic and rather cruel old man, and just like his predecessor, Johan's relationship with his son is emotionally troubled. Also (at the risk of being repetitive), it is hard to refrain from pointing out exactly where Marianne finds Johan, as she meets him for the first time in several decades: on a porch, in this case a summer veranda outside a house, very similar to the one in *Wild Strawberries*. *Nota bene*, it is an *outside* porch, as opposed to the inside porches associated with Helena in *Fanny and Alexander* and Marianne in *Saraband*. One can,

Outside looking in: Victor Sjöström in *Wild Strawberries* (photo © AB Svensk Filmindustri)

Johan with Marianne on his veranda (photo: Bengt Wanselius/SVT)

as so often before, note the degree to which Bergman's fictional universe is (conventionally) gendered: women seem to have a privileged access to the inside (of things and themselves), while men tend to remain on the outside.

Thus, from *Wild Strawberries* in the 1950s to *Fanny and Alexander* in the 1980s to *Saraband* more than twenty years later: childhood, strawberries and porches; Helena and Marianne with their respective memories, snapshots and unsorted family pictures; and Isak and Johan, two old men who are forced to confront reality, although they both do their best to avoid it. Undeniably, a circle of sorts seems to have come to a close.

However, let me round off these observations on the role of photographs as gateways into the past, or nodal points where boundaries are transgressed, by drawing attention to a curious photograph that is shown towards the end of *Saraband*. Here Marianne has decided to stay the night at Johan's – her former husband's – house, and in the middle of the night he sneaks into her room, crawling into her bed like a frightened child. The two former spouses talk awhile before saying goodnight, agreeing to meet more often. At this point there is a cut-back to the present, the beginning of the film, with Marianne, now in her role as narrator, again seen seated by the big table with the photographs spread out in front of her. The point of interest in this context is exactly how this transition from the past to the present is executed,

Who took the picture? (photo: Bengt Wanselius/SVT)

namely through a freeze-frame shot of Johan and Marianne in bed, which then is transformed into a black and white photograph of the two, which Marianne now is holding in her hand, while addressing the camera. What is slightly peculiar about this photograph is this: who took it? It can hardly be a snapshot taken by Marianne herself, or even more unlikely, by Johan, given his state of mind – unless, of course, you imagine that this elderly couple suddenly were seized with the (very unlikely) idea of playing around with a camera in bed for one last frolic.

Rather, it seems, it is the director who at this point took one final chance to frolic. Indeed, what this improbable photo in *Saraband* seems to mirror, albeit in a clouded fashion, is the narrative experiment in, for instance, *Persona*. For just as the self-reflexive photo-montage of the faces of the actresses in this film contributes to its overall meta-narrative patterns, the black and white photograph in *Saraband* serves to draw attention to itself, as an image attributable to a third, invisible party – namely, that narrative position usually labelled with the director's name: 'Bergman'. If nothing else, this curious transition from the moving images of the elderly couple in bed, to a still photograph of that same event, adds a particular kind of distanciated humour to this already rather tragi-comic scene.

Out of the past: characters and spectres

But who, finally, is Marianne herself? Is she merely a secondary character, someone designed for the purpose of guiding the viewer into the characters' various pasts? Hardly, for after all her name is Marianne, which seems to carry particular weight and meaning in the context of Bergman's fictional universe. There is, as mentioned, Marianne in *Scenes from a Marriage*, who, at least if we are to believe the public relations department of Sveriges Television (SVT, the Swedish public service television corporation) is none other than a younger version of Marianne in *Saraband*. True, both Mariannes are played by Liv Ullmann and since both Johans in *Scenes from a Marriage* and *Saraband* are acted by Erland Josephson, it is certainly a good sales argument to raise the expectation of *Saraband* being a continuation of their story, thirty years later.

However, there are other Mariannes to be reckoned with. There is Marianne in *Faithless* (2000), scripted by Bergman and directed by Liv Ullmann. Finally, there is one more prominent woman with the same name in Bergman's film oeuvre: Marianne in *En lektion i kärlek* (*A Lesson in Love*) from 1954, acted by the formidable Eva Dahlbeck. But these four stories – *A Lesson in Love*, *Scenes from a Marriage*, *Faithless* and *Saraband* – are not only conceived for different media (film, television and, in the case of *Faithless*, only scripted by Bergman) but belong to different genres as well: *A Lesson in Love* is a comedy, designed for public success, by Bergman's own admission (in Björkman *et al.* 1986: 79), as was *Scenes from a Marriage*, whereas both

Faithless and *Saraband* are close to being tragedies. Further, there is no less than fifty years between the first and the last production. Given this, how could there be a common thread between all those varying Mariannes? Or, to rephrase it, why would it be of interest in the first place?

The connection may not be that far-fetched after all, since characters named Marianne always seem to surface in a context of intense self-scrutiny, especially in regard to questions of marital life, fidelity and, not least, that potent poison that Bergman, here as well as in his autobiography, has called 'retroactive jealousy'. Thus, in *Scenes from a Marriage*, Johan one evening, while seated on the edge of the marital double bed, suddenly tells Marianne that he is going to France with a newfound lover. Thirty years later, similar ingredients are found in *Faithless*, now with overtly autobiographical aspects. It is not by chance that the story revolves around an elderly writer named 'Bergman' (again acted by Erland Josephson), who one day is visited – or rather, is visited in his imagination – by a woman from his past called Marianne. Suddenly, she materialises in his study and starts telling a story of infidelity much reminiscent of the one in *Scenes from a Marriage* (involving a trip to France, as well as the theme of 'retroactive jealousy'), only this time the chain of events is told from her point of view. And as the story unfolds, it gradually becomes apparent that David, Marianne's lover with whom she runs off, is a younger version of the old man called 'Bergman', guilty of that destructive jealousy that she once, violently, became a victim of. Thus 'Bergman' and David become aspects of one and the same personality, mirroring each other across time.

Differently phrased, *Faithless* is about an ageing man who is trying to remember painful incidents in the past. But since there are places in the topography of that 'past-ness' where he dares not walk alone, he conjures up a female guide, Marianne. Meanwhile she herself at first seems to have only vague outlines, and indeed at one point asks the writer's guidance in 'creating' herself: she is a character in the process of emerging, and only gradually assumes an outline and a body. As such, Marianne is a remarkably suitable contribution to the kind of epilogue-writing that Bergman has devoted himself to in the latter part of his career, one that spans film, theatre and literature: Marianne is a role who finds a film director but who is also – to paraphrase Pirandello – a character in search of an author.

However, this still leaves Marianne in *A Lesson in Love* from the 1950s out of the equation. But on closer scrutiny some basic story elements of this film remain the same, for all its comic aspects. The most obvious ones are infidelity and jealousy between husband and wife, as well as a trip abroad. More importantly, however, there are those ever-returning names. For instance, it turns out that Marianne's husband's name in *A Lesson in Love* is none other than David. In other words, it is the drama of these particular lovers that seems to turn up in *Faithless*, spectre-like, almost fifty years later.

It comes as no surprise that the tenacity of this dramatic nexus at least in part is due to its strong personal undercurrent. Bergman himself has hinted as much in his autobiography, where he writes about his third wife, Gun Grut, and the 'life changing' trip they took to Paris together, both running away from their respective spouses. In this context he also admits that Grut served as an inspirational source for a number of his female characters in the films of the 1950s. She stood model, he writes, 'for many women in my films: Karin Lobelius in *Waiting Women*, Agda in *Sawdust and Tinsel*, Marianne in *A Lesson in Love*' (1987: 210). This seems to be corroborated by the material in Bergman's archive as well, since Gun Grut's name tends to resurface in the most unexpected places in the diaries – sometimes, it seems, unexpected even for Bergman himself. Thus, for instance, the following notation: 'Strong and strange dreams', Bergman writes. 'Meeting with Gun in the land of the dead. Violent and unreal feelings. A whole film really. The things you carry around with you!' The note book is annotated 'U.A.' (Utan År/No Year), but evidently (judging from its contents) was used and possibly also written while Bergman wrote *Faithless* at the end of the 1990s.

Equally suggestive is a short note that Bergman jotted down in the diary for *Fanny and Alexander*. 'While one is writing a film, other films always announce themselves', he notes. 'It is strange, but probably one's brain [the word used is 'hjärnkontor', 'brain-office'] works overtime during such periods. [I'd like] to raise an honorary memorial over G. I'd like to do this ... from her point of view. Narrated in first person.' Perhaps it is here, while Bergman was in the midst of writing the script for *Fanny and Alexander*, that the story which was to become *Faithless* germinated – fifteen years before its realisation. After all, *Faithless* ended up being narrated in first person, as well as from the woman's point of view. Indeed, perhaps *Faithless* finally became that 'honorary memorial' to this woman, and narrated in a way that, for both private and professional reasons, was not possible back in the 1950s, when it was disguised as a comedy in *A Lesson in Love*.

But finally, what has all this to do with Marianne in *Saraband*? After all, Bergman's last film is certainly not that 'continuation' of *Scenes from a Marriage* from thirty years earlier, however much the smart PR-machine set in motion by SVT promoted it as such. *Saraband* of course is not a story of marriage and infidelity, but rather about the overwhelming presence of the past, as well as the terrible void, in the absence of a dead woman, in the present. In that case, *Saraband* is perhaps also about the wish or hope that there exists a 'land of the dead', to cite Bergman's own expression when writing in his diary about 'meeting' Gun Grut. Thus one could ask to what degree Marianne in *Saraband*, as well, is not merely a woman who pays a friendly visit to her former spouse, but is recruited from out of the past in a more improbable manner? Indeed she can be regarded as a kind of older version not so much of Marianne in *Scenes from a Marriage* but of Marianne in *Faithless*. Although in this case she turns up not so much in order to help her former lover (as well as creator) to face painful memories, but rather, it seems, to watch over the ruins among those who are still living, perhaps in order to ease their entrance into that 'land of the dead'. For instance, it is worth noting that Marianne in *Saraband* no longer seems actively engaged in the drama of the living, but instead serves as a confidante or is simply content with watching and observing – somewhat like a conscience or guardian angel.

If this is the case, we seem to have arrived at the quintessence of *Saraband*, namely death, perhaps the main character of the story. In this context it is of interest to what degree Bergman experimented with different names for his drama, before naming it *Saraband*. One is 'Marianne's Journey', and here obviously she is (still) the focal point of the story. However, when the first handwritten draft was finished, the piece had been renamed 'Anna', and now the dead woman seems to have taken centre stage. It was in the final draft, labelled by Bergman himself 'the first unedited version', that the piece was first called *Saraband*. In this context it is of equal interest to cite from a diary dated summer 1998, with the title 'Analysis of a Situation' in Bergman's handwriting on the front cover, since it seems to bear a close relationship to, and perhaps even form the very beginnings of what was to become, *Saraband*. Here, one finds a cover sheet with a suggestive title: 'Dialogue with the Dead'. Indeed, Bergman continues, there are many dead to be reckoned with. 'I think', he writes, 'of my paternal grandfather and grandmother, two people I never met … but perhaps I will meet them now and we will speak. As well as mother and grandmother, uncle Ernst, uncle Johan, Siri and Alma, and grandfather. Those near, those far.' In other words, he adds, 'there are many people I will have to talk to.'

However, it is not only the theme of death as a state of mind or *locus* that concerns Bergman in this diary, but also the thought of the passage itself into an unknown place or form of existence. Thus, for instance, in a note dated 26 June 1998: 'I can suddenly experience myself as already dead.' Bergman then turns and twists this thought, as if testing its artistic validity: how should one represent the idea of gliding over into another state, without having noticed how it happened? This is of course something that Bergman had reason to ponder many times during his long career: the difficult art of showing (on film) such complexities in as simple a way as possible; think, for instance, of *Cries and Whispers*, where a woman dies but cannot leave the living behind, instead getting caught as if in limbo. It is precisely such creative difficulties that are interesting to follow throughout these diaries. Not least among these is Bergman's advice to his own creative self, which he addresses as if a second self or character, with whom he is constantly engaged in dialogue, as in the case of the following thought: 'There's no time and space, there's freedom. You create the prerequisites for your life without coercion, your dreamed rooms. And there you will meet, sometime there you will meet [the dead].' Or, as he puts it in his diary the same month: 'I have decided to embrace the thought that I will meet Ingrid again –

and since I now have turned towards the reality of death, it is only natural that I also turn towards the already dead.'

Another piece of advice to his creative self is the following:

Let your intuition come to your help in your listening. I say 'listening', since your hearing is always more sensitive and in better tune with your feelings than your seeing, which always registers and analyses and receives far too many impressions, whether you like it or not. Listen and you shall hear. It is your hearing that gives you your images, projections, imaginings. Do so. This is my advice (Diary dated June 1998–1 August 2001).

Thus, 'listening' and 'hearing' is pitted against 'seeing' and 'registering'. Perhaps it is from such rumination of the aural qualities of film (or television) that the role of music in *Saraband* grew.

However, this advice to the creative self is often quite amusing, in particular when this 'other', at times aptly named 'Bergman', is chided and addressed in acid tones. One example is the following eruption of impatience, when sentimentality threatens to enter the proceedings: 'Calm down, you will get nowhere with such an ear-deafening emotional hullabaloo. Let me tell you, Ingmar Bergman: what will surprise you is that you will not be the least bit surprised!' (Diary dated June 1998–1 August 2001). In short, in creating his last work, Bergman seems to have continued vampirising himself, but in this case not only his personal biography but professional history as well, including that *biographical legend* called 'Ingmar Bergman' – which, ironically, he himself has been the best propagator of.

By way of conclusion, let me return to the scene towards the end of *Saraband* where Johan crawls into Marianne's bed, afraid and naked like a forlorn child. Interestingly, the last scene in Bergman's stage production of Ibsen's *Ghosts* was infused with a similar idea. For here the mother, Mrs Alving, helps her son to die, and in doing so in a strange way seems to give birth to him all over again: the actor who plays the son is seen entirely naked on the stage, while snuggling up in his mother's lap.

Could it be pure chance that a similar image can be found in *Gycklarnas afton* (*The Naked Night/Sawdust and Tinsel*) from 1953? For at the end of the film Frost, the circus clown, tells a friend of a dream about his wife Alma that he had the night before. In the dream, he says, she asked him:

Wouldn't you like to rest a little? Yes, I said. Then I'll make you as small as a foetus, she said, so that you can creep into my belly and you'll be able to sleep really well. I did as she said and snuggled down into her belly, and there I slept so nicely, so sweetly, rocked to sleep like in a cradle. And so I got smaller and smaller, and in the end I was just a little grain of corn – and then I was gone.

To me, it is precisely this that forms the core of *Saraband*, as well: it is about gradual disappearance, but it is also about the hope for re-birth, after death. But in that case, no longer in the image of becoming entangled by the big and frightening black cape of personified Death, as in *Det sjunde inseglet* (*The Seventh Seal*, 1957), but rather in the image of gradually disappearing into the soft embrace of a woman.

As Ingmar Bergman himself has put it in the diary for *Saraband*: 'I stand at a border ... And I turn, listening and perhaps also seeing, toward a reality I find increasingly self-evident.'

References

Bergman, I. (1948) *Moraliteter. Tre Pjäser* [*Moralities. Three Plays*]. Stockholm: Bonniers.

_____ (1987) *Laterna magica*. Stockholm: Norstedts.

_____ (1990) *Images. My Life in Film*, trans. M. Ruuth. New York: Arcade.

Björkman S., T. Manns and J. Sima (1986 [1973]) *Bergman on Bergman: Interviews with Ingmar Bergman*, trans. P. B. Austin. New York: Simon & Schuster.

Caughie, J. (1999) *Theories of Authorship*. London: Routledge.

Forslid, T. (2000) *Fadern, sonen och berättaren. Minne och narrativitet hos Sven Delblanc* [*The Father, the Son and the Narrator. Memory and Narrativity in Sven Delblanc*]. Nora: Nya Doxa.

Nyström, M. (2003) 'Musiken spelar störst roll i Bergmans filmer' ['Music plays the most prominent role in Bergman's Films']. *Dagens Nyheter*, 30 November, Culture Section.

Unpublished notebooks and manuscripts in the archive of the Ingmar Bergman Foundation:

'Arbetsbok U.Å.' [Work book/diary/No Year]. Dated inside 1994–95.

'*Trolösa*. Partitur för en film' [*Faithless*. Musical score for film]. Manuscript dated 14 May 1997.

'Anna/Mariannes resa/Sarabande [sic]/Analys av en situation' [Anna/Marianne's Journey/Sarabande [sic]/Analysis of a situation]. Diary dated June 1998–1 August 2001.

'Anna. Scener för valfritt medium av Ingmar Bergman. Första versionen.' [Anna. Scenes for any medium by Ingmar Bergman. First version]. Manuscript, undated.

'Anna. Scener för valfritt medium av Ingmar Bergman. [Anna. Scenes for any medium by Ingmar Bergman]. Typed script, dated 18 September 2001.

'Sarabande [sic]. Åtta verkliga scener av Ingmar Bergman. Första oredigerade versionen.' [Sarabande [sic]. Eight Real Scenes by Ingmar Bergman. First Unedited Version]. Undated.

MUSICALISATION OF THE STAGE: INGMAR BERGMAN PERFORMING SHAKESPEARE

Ulla-Britta Lagerroth

Many theatre and film directors, past or present, can be studied from the viewpoint of intermediality. One of the best is Ingmar Bergman.

Intermediality, the particular relation between distinct media of expression, is given attention within the internationally expanding research field 'Intermedial Studies', formerly called 'Interart Studies'.[1] Intermediality may occur in any art or medium, and the intermedialising traffic between the arts and media can go in any direction and take varying shapes and forms. A recognised master within several media – film, theatre, music theatre (opera, operetta), TV-theatre and TV-opera – Bergman, interestingly, also employed the possibilities of intermedialising them. As discussed by Maaret Koskinen (2001), he *theatricalised* his films, as well as *cinematised* his theatre productions. In the volume *Ingmar Bergman and the Arts* (1998), Birgitta Steene (21–2) and Eva Sundler Malmnäs (34–45) demonstrate that he also *pictorialised* his productions, that is, excelled in figure compositions and colour and light effects fetched from the visual arts, even from specific paintings.

Furthermore, and the focus here, Bergman *musicalised* his productions. Much has been said about the use of music in his films, by himself and others. In television interviews, particularly in one conducted by Camilla Lundberg (2000), Bergman talked about his personal relationship to music, of music as an important source of inspiration in his professional work, of his specific choices of music for the films – even of his ideas that the task of a director is similar to that of a musical conductor, and that he himself could also have become such a conductor. With references to Bach, Schubert and Mozart, and to the ways in which their music is integrated into his films, he also confessed that music for him conveyed a message that other realities exist.

However, amazingly little is written on music's presence and function in his theatrical work.[2] For this purpose, I have chosen to look more closely at his four Shakespeare productions at the Royal Dramatic Theatre in Stockholm: *Twelfth Night*

(1975), *King Lear* (1984), *Hamlet* (1986) and *The Winter's Tale* (1994). It would be easy to find other musicalised stage productions of Bergman's to be discussed as well, but one reason for concentrating on the four mentioned is that Shakespeare (whose *Macbeth, Merchant of Venice* and *A Midsummer Night's Dream* were staged by Bergman in the 1940s) again presented a challenge to him in 1975, seemingly in connection with his work on the televised opera *Trollflöjten* (*The Magic Flute*). Besides, these four Shakespeare productions offer a fairly coherent group of study objects, motivating aspects of similarities or differences in the ways they are musicalised. In addition, I have the advantage of having personally seen a performance of each of those four productions in the past.[3]

Stage directions for music appear already in Shakespeare's plays, and much has been written on those directions, and on how music was performed on his own stage. But for my purpose here it is of less interest to consider whether Bergman was 'faithful' or not to directions for music in the written texts; my focus will be on music's presence and function *in the process of the performance*. A performance, based on Bergman's personal interpretation of the text, is the result of a total medial transformation from the written, mono-medial play into a multi-medial work, involving words, actors' bodies and movements, scenography, light, sound and also music. Considering this fact, by which criteria are we then entitled to speak of a Bergman performance as particularly 'musicalised'? Music has long been a medium of expression that has been involved in the signification of a given theatre performance. Obviously, if we want to claim a stage performance as particularly 'musicalised', we must look more closely into problems of how, to what extent, with which functions and in which cultural, sociopolitical and ideological contexts that music is present and foregrounded in the signification of that individual performance.

Stage music has not been 'theorised' to the same extent as film music. But in her book *Semiotics of Theatre*, Erika Fischer-Lichte makes some valuable suggestions regarding music as a potential theatrical stage sign (1992: 122–8). The meanings of music on stage can be related to many things, she says, to words, space, bodies and movements, to character, mood and emotions, even to ideas. As a theatrical sign music can originate naturally from two sources: from the actors' activity, such as singing or playing instruments, and from live musicians or technical facilities for music, situated either on-stage or off-stage. *Any* kind of music can be employed in a stage performance. To the crucial question regarding which meanings music may create on the stage, Fischer-Lichte answers that music is never assigned a fixed meaning in the theatre. Rather, it is employed in particular functions, which are intimately related to the other signs produced during the performative process. In summary, all depends on the *totality* of the performance.

Twelfth Night

Bergman's staging of *Twelfth Night*, opening at the Royal Dramatic Theatre on 7 March 1975, serves as an excellent example of how he turned music into a very dominant sign in a theatre performance.

The production was based on Allan Bergstrand's translation into Swedish, and a few cuts and rearrangements of the text were made by the director. The unit scenography was designed by Gunilla Palmstierna-Weiss. The play was acted on a low, square platform, erected in front of an encircling Tudor framework of beams and gables, suggestive of an Elizabethan playhouse or the interior of a private manor house.[4] On this platform, which was reminiscent of the Shakespearean protruding platform stage, the props were kept to a bare minimum, a chair or a bench carried onto or off the platform by costumed stage-hands. The main characters awaited their entrances onto this central platform in full view of the audience. Placing actors as spectators on the stage was a frequently-used device by Bergman for increasing audience involvement, since the audience as spectators are supposed to identify with the actors as spectators on the stage.[5]

The vital part which *music* was to play throughout the performance became immediately visualised in this scenography. The gallery at the centre of the back was turned into a musicians' gallery, and there six costumed musicians continuously performed music, while flickering lanterns along the line of the gallery further pointed to the presence of the music. By placing the musicians on stage, where they were not only heard by the audience

Musicians on stage: *Twelfth Night* (photo: Beata Bergström/The Theatre Museum of Sweden)

but also *visibly* present throughout the performance, Bergman made the music diegetic – an integral part of the entire spatio-temporal universe of the play.

The music was composed and arranged by Daniel Bell, at that time director of the theatre orchestra. For a couple of the songs he used music, or some bars from music, which has survived from Elizabethan times. But his own vocal and instrumental compositions were in the *style* of English Renaissance music.[6] Bell himself acted as one of the six musicians, playing the violin, while the other five, who belonged to the theatre orchestra, played instruments more or less associated with Renaissance music: a lute, a flute, a bassoon, a tambourine and a drum.

The performance also directly opened with a musicalised prologue, invented by Bergman. To some madrigal tunes composed by Bell, and played and sung from the gallery, a character with a Shakespeare mask entered onto the platform and in a few words, also written by Bell, enthusiastically welcomed the audience to the play. During this prologue, the characters of the play came whirling onto the stage, thereby introducing themselves to the audience, and then quickly withdrew to the sides. This musicalised opening of the performance was brief, lasting only for a couple of minutes. But it was an excellent example of what today is defined and discussed as a *frame*.[7] A frame, or framing, is considered to function as a key to communication, knowledge and understanding of the framed part. As is emphasised in intermedia criticism, a different art or medium is often employed to function as such a frame. In Bergman's theatre performance of *Twelfth Night*, the musicalised frame served as an initial meta-commentary to the performance. It provided an orientation for the spectators' reception, directing their attention to the fact that what they were going to experience and enjoy was the magic thing called theatre, a theatre in which *music* was of vital importance for the theatricalisation of the performance.

After this musicalised frame, a brief scene of the shipwreck followed, accompanied by some tones from the musicians which suggested waves of the sea. By then the audience had already seen Viola, charmingly played by Bibi Andersson. Not until then came the opening scene in Shakespeare's text, where the lovesick Duke Orsino, here played by Heinz Hopf, calls for music: 'If music be the food of love, play on,/ Give me excess of it.' Sweet but somewhat sad music, sung *a capella* from the gallery, now interacted with Orsino's words, signifying his melancholy character and underlining his tender words of love. Later, the same soft music from the gallery again supported Orsino's words, those beginning: 'Give me some music.'

Music was heard about thirty times during the performance, and not only when supporting the dialogue. Instrumental music indicated quick changeovers between scenes and locations. Fulfilling this function, music gave tempo and rhythm as well as mood to the action, and at the same time the music became associated with the different characters. For example, each time enchanting Olivia, played by Lil Terselius, appeared in what was imagined to be her garden, tender music from the gallery informed the audience that now the action will continue at *her* enchanting place.

The first scene with *vocal* music integrated on stage was, as indicated in Shakespeare's text, the one in which Sir Toby, Sir Andrew and the fool Feste, stunningly played by Ingvar Kjellson, join in a revel of drinking. For Feste's first song, which begins with the line 'O mistress mine', Bell had picked the two first bars of Thomas Morley's original instrumental work with this title. On the basis of those bars Bell composed new music to the whole song, as well as to the jolly catch song that followed. For Feste's later sad song 'Come away, come away, death', for which no Elizabethan music has survived, Bell's instrumental work strongly underlined Feste's melancholy weariness of life. According to several newspaper reviews of the opening night, his song had a tremendous impact on the audience who listened intently in absolute silence.

For the final scene, where all the identity mix-ups are resolved, Bergman invented a stunning musicalised epilogue. While the now happily-matched couples whirled around to a jolly jig composed by Bell, the music and the dancing suddenly stopped and the couples found themselves hand in hand with the wrong partner again! This added episode, functioning as a framing instance of reflexivity, signified that nothing had actually happened to the characters, nothing had really changed them.

Bergman's production of *Twelfth Night* was based on a more disillusioned inter-pretation of the text than is usually the case. He had turned the softer, bitter-sweet melancholy of Shakespeare's love comedy into a performance in which life as pain and hollow joy was emphasised. By courtesy of the Ingmar Bergman Foundation I have had access to his notes and promptbook for this production. And there, written in his own handwriting, I found the following statement, probably his basic inter-pretation of the play: 'Trettondagsafton är ett narrspel. Ett spel för narrar om narrar, som narrar andra vanliga mänskor att bli narrar.' Translated into English: 'Twelfth Night is a tomfoolery. A play for fools about fools, who fool other common people to become fools.'[8] The pessimistic mood was also strongly underlined immediately after the jig episode, when the fool Feste started to sing his sad 'Song of the Rain' to the original Elizabethan melody, with the added accompaniment of muffled drums. Now the stage was blacked out. A faint flickering light fixed onto Feste's head was the only visible spot the audience could follow, while in the darkness, still singing, he slowly moved upstairs to the musicians in the gallery. From this elevated meta-posi-tion, he turned towards the audience and commented upon the grim reality outside of the walls of the acting area, visible through some pointed glass windows: pouring rain and threatening dark clouds. Then Feste's light was finally extinguished, and the stage was completely darkened.

To sum up, this Bergman production must be defined as *musicalised* because of the extent to which music was employed. Although the music performed was fairly 'traditional', in the sense that it suggested Renaissance music, the use and function of the music was unique, with regard to: the musicians being visibly present and acting throughout the performance; the music interacting with the spoken words, signify-ing the speaker's mood or character, or the mood of the scene; the music indicating quick shifts of location for the action; and last but not least, the musicalised framing, in the opening as well as in the close of the performance, functioning for the audi-ence as a key to an understanding of what was going on in the stage world, and of how those events could be related to their own world.

King Lear

After eight years as director at the Residenztheater in Munich, where Bergman emi-grated in 1976 after a clash with the Swedish tax bureaucracy, he returned to the

Royal Dramatic Theatre in 1984, and this happy reunion with the Swedish public was celebrated by a new Shakespeare production, *King Lear*, which premiered on 9 March 1984.

In this production, based on a new translation into Swedish by Britt G. Hallqvist, and with several cuts in the text made by Bergman, a maximum of empty space was the basis for the abstract, unit scenography, again designed by Gunilla Palmstierna-Weiss: a huge red semi-circle or cyclorama, a red-carpeted stage floor and the walls covered with red cloth.[9] Once more the props were kept to an absolute minimum, for the most part replaced by the bodies of the extras. Acting as page boys, the extras bent to serve those in power as a chair, a throne, a catafalque and so on, striking visual signs of the prevailing violent oppression. As in *Twelfth Night*, actors stood waiting on the stage for their entrances.

Other striking visual signs were the costumes. King Lear, forcefully performed by Jarl Kulle, was dressed in saffron yellow. His two evil daughters, Goneril (Margareta Byström) and Regan (Ewa Fröling), wore low-necked fancy gowns in varying shades of shining red and orange, colours characterising other members of the court as well, while faithful Cordelia, played by Lena Olin in a much more modest dress, remained by the side of the front-stage as the suffering witness of the cruel events. A threatening line of tall warriors wore padded black uniforms and helmets, which some critics noted as more reminiscent of the film *Star Wars* (1977) than of the Renaissance.

But how did Bergman use music this time? In comparison with *Twelfth Night*, Shakespeare's *King Lear* has fewer directions for music: some trumpet sound, a couple of songs sung by the fool, music at the meeting between Lear and Cordelia in the fourth act, and a closing funeral march. For Bergman, however, the play communicated such a pessimistic 'panorama of our human existence', as he wrote in a preface to the new translation (1984: 5), that it necessitated a musicalised frame, an opening which immediately turned the audience's attention to the fact that they were going to understand the stage world as 'This great stage of fools', according to Lear's words in the play.

This prologue, invented by Bergman, began with the curtain open while the audience was still gathering. It lasted for some fifteen minutes and was dominated by music throughout. As in the production of *Twelfth Night*, all the music was composed and arranged by Daniel Bell. At first, couples belonging to Lear's court were seen ceremoniously dancing and singing to music in the Gregorian style. Then a flute and increasing drum beats accompanied the arrival to the court of lively performing acrobats and of noisy, jumping jesters who made music on their instruments. Finally, the group of jesters hurried up to the front stage. In a strongly ironic way they sang some threatening lines from the fool's ditty, which in Shakespeare's text does not appear until the third act. These lines prophesise that the realm of Albion shall 'Come to great confusion'. Not until after that song did Lear move forward on the stage, announcing his decision to divide his land between his three daughters.

With the fool's ominous song moved forward to this opening, which portrayed a court involved in superficial entertainment, the function of the song became fully evident. From the very start it directed the audience's attention to the mood of doom, which was going to prevail. This dark mood was later stressed further by, for example, sinister electronic music on a synthesizer, vibrating from under the floor of the stalls. This music signified the storm on the heath and in Lear's mind, and interacted with Lear's and the fool's dialogue during their roamings on the heath. Of particular importance in these scenes was the music to the words sung by the fool, a role memorably played by Jan Olof Strandberg.

While finally the crowd carried the deceased Lear in a procession over the

Bergman rehearsing *King Lear* with jesters (photo: Beata Bergström/The Theatre Museum of Sweden)

Singing the fool's ditty (photo: Beata Bergström/The Theatre Museum of Sweden)

stage, to the accompaniment of funeral music and soft singing, Bergman achieved a brief but shocking framing effect. As Albany and Edgar started a vicious fight over Lear's fallen crown – which had been lying on the forestage throughout the performance, fully visible to the audience – the stage world itself crashed down in ruins over the mourning crowd and revealed the naked theatre walls. This final chaotic image of the moral decay and collapse of the stage world served as meta-theatrical commentary to the Lear theme of this world as a stage of fools, giving the audience associations to our own cruel world as well.

As in his *Twelfth Night* production nine years earlier, Bergman in his *King Lear* stressed the importance of the music by inventing a musicalised frame – particularly so for the opening of the performance – a frame which again gave the audience a key to an understanding of the performance. But in contrast to the previous Shakespeare production, Bergman this time ventured to use such modernising effects as electronic music. This tendency towards fashionable modernising, not to say postmodernising, ways of employing music became still more evident in his third Shakespeare production two years later.

Hamlet

Ingmar Bergman's *Hamlet* at the Royal Dramatic Theatre opened on 20 December 1986. Again, a new translation into Swedish by Hallqvist, as well as some cuts in and rearrangements of the scenes by the director himself, supplied the basis for this Shakespeare production. The unit scenography, designed by Göran Wassberg, was nothing but an empty dark space surrounded by dark, high walls, and the actors were 'carved out' of the darkness and focused by changing light effects. As in Bergman's previous Shakespeare productions, actors remained on the stage when not acting, with Ophelia, played by Pernilla Österberg (now Pernilla August), even witnessing her own funeral in a passive spectator position after her death. Costumes derived from different epochs, somewhat confusing to the audience. On one occasion Hamlet (Peter Stormare) appeared in a modern black turtleneck jumper and grey trousers.

The music was this time composed and arranged by the new director of the theatre orchestra, Jean Billgren. The music displayed, like the costumes, a variety of clashing styles, bespeaking the moral disjuncture that Hamlet sees everywhere around him. The performance opened with a musicalised and indeed stunning frame, invented by the director. While the audience sat facing the red theatre curtain, which was further coloured by a red spotlight, the popular waltz from Franz Lehár's operetta *The Merry Widow* was heard on tape as played by Jean Billgren on an old square piano. Billgren played the waltz somewhat 'out of tune' in accordance with Bergman's instructions.[10]

This waltz music, connoting frivolous life in bygone days, functioned as an anachronistic reference to Queen Gertrude, who had remained a widow for only one month after the death of the former king, Hamlet's father. Consequently, when the audience saw Gertrude, played by Gunnel Lindblom, dressed in passionate red and, briefly but intensely, sexually active with her new husband – brother of the former king whom he killed, and now himself crowned as king – the waltz music still lingered in the audience's mind, and interacted ironically with her words. The opening waltz offered the audience a key to her character, and the realisation that her words and deeds should be doubted. In fact, the music became a guide to an understanding of the whole stage world as one of fraud and deception.

By means of musicalisation, in combination with other signs, the performance called attention to itself as performance from the outset. The Players of the play within the play in the third act came sweeping down the full width of the stage to the music of a fife and drum, and their following theatre performance was introduced by a wild torch dance. Rosencrantz and Guildenstern appeared as rose-coloured operetta dandies, chanting rather than speaking their lines. The gravedigger scene was acted out as part of a cabaret, with the gravedigger popping up from the grave as a clown-

Heavy metal: Fortinbras and storm troopers in *Hamlet* (photo: Bengt Wanselius)

ish figure in the company of a pair of masked Pierrots, armed with a trombone and a saxophone. Now and then this funny couple of musicians was seen strolling over the stage while making music.

Just as it began with a musicalised frame, the waltz music from *The Merry Widow*, the performance also ended with a musicalising effect. Shockingly to the audience, heavy metal music (composed and taped by a Swedish rock band) was roaring at the moment when Fortinbras and his followers, dressed in modern leather attire, like storm troopers, burst through an imitation back wall onto the stage, to the sound of their blazing machine-guns, and brutally killed Horatio, the last witness.[11] The same rock music forcefully interacted with Fortinbras's later words and violent actions, so obviously this kind of music was meant to function as a concentration of the sense of a corrupt society, also of our own society of today, dominated by guile and brutality.

The Winter's Tale

In spite of certain variations, music appeared and functioned in fairly similar ways in Bergman's productions of *King Lear* and *Hamlet*. In musicalised frames, and in interaction with the spoken words and the action, the music in both productions stressed the idea of the stage world, as well as our own world, as vain, false, brutal, bloodstained and chaotic.

However, Bergman's mode of musicalising a Shakespeare production took a new turn when eight years after *Hamlet* he staged *The Winter's Tale*, which opened at the Royal Dramatic Theatre on 29 April 1994, and immediately became such a tremendous success that the theatre was able to give more than one hundred performances during the 1994–95 season. A fresh translation into Swedish was made of Shakespeare's play by Hallqvist and Claes Schaar. More than a third of the text was omitted, and Shakespeare's five acts changed into eleven scenes (divided into two acts) by the director.

But directly sensational was the kind of frame which Bergman had invented this time. It was a *Swedish* frame, an early nineteenth-century Christmas party at a small castle in the countryside, involving entertainment, and with characters and music clearly linking the frame to the Swedish Romantic writer Carl Jonas Love Almqvist (1793–1866), and his works. Lennart Mörk's basic scenography displayed a semicircular room, a direct counterpart to the Royal Dramatic Theatre's beautiful *art nouveau* foyer.[12] Writes Egil Törnqvist: 'As a result, the audience found itself in a space between two areas mirroring one another, one meant for performances, the other for relaxation between the acts. The scenery in this way contributed to wipe out the borderline between stage and auditorium' (1995: 84).

Directions for music are sparse in Shakespeare's text, restricted to Autolycus's singing, the pastoral scene in the fourth act, and the scene in which the statue comes

Play mirroring the theatre's foyer: *The Winter's Tale*. (photo: Bengt Wanselius)

to life when Paulina calls for music. But in Bergman's production, on the contrary, music was employed throughout, both in the extensive frame and in the performance (within the frame) of Shakespeare's play. Jean Billgren, who arranged and composed the music this time also, informed me that Bergman considered the idea of a musicalisation of the entire performance to be absolutely essential from the very beginning of his interpretation and theatrical realisation of this play. By courtesy of the Ingmar Bergman Foundation, I have had access to his notations and own director's book for this production, too. In a little black notebook I found, written in his handwriting, expressions of his joy when the solution of how to do it all of a sudden had dawned upon him.[13] Later, in connection with the opening night, Bergman also told in an article how it was at a moment when he listened to music that he had found inspiration, and from Almqvist that he had taken the textually and musically very suggestive songs, the kind of *tableaux vivants*, which Almqvist called *Songes*. This had enabled him to envision the whole concept of the staging.[14]

While the audience was still finding their seats in the auditorium, the actors on stage were seen gathering for the party. As in *Twelfth Night* from 1975, music was foregrounded by being *visualised* throughout the entire performance. This visualisation again became a sign of the immense importance of music, also for the audience's understanding of the stage world. On each side below the stage stood a square piano, played by Billgren and Maria Wieslander, a member of the orchestra. The pianists were costumed, fully visible to the audience, and even spotlighted while playing music that interacted with the spoken word or accompanied the singing. Since Bergman had chosen to integrate the space below the stage into the performance, including the first row of the stalls where actors were seated waiting for their entrance, the two pianists and their music became diegetic – part of the performance proper. Further, as new characters listed first in the cast in the printed programme, Bergman had invented two singers who had special functions.

The pianists and the singers were already intimately involved in the extensively musicalised frame, inside which Bergman had placed Shakespeare's play. It was from Almqvist's ways of using a frame in his works that Bergman had struck upon the idea of a party at a castle. While the guests of the party were still gathering, the pianists began to play pieces of music for piano, composed by Almqvist, and soon the guests started lively dances in the style of ballroom dances from the Romantic period. As a beginning of the entertainment proper for the guests, one of Almqvist's songs, 'The Flower of the Heart', was beautifully sung by the female singer, Irene Lindh, who here acted as one of the guests at the party, upon which followed a duet between her and the male singer (Pierre Wilkner, who also acted in the role of the present guest Almqvist), succeeded in turn by a female choir, and finally flute music.

By means of gradual shifts in light, costumes and colour, the scenery turned into an amateur theatre performance of Shakespeare's *The Winter's Tale*, which then became the main part of the entertainment, a performance within the performance, witnessed by those guests on stage who did not participate as actors but instead turned into an audience. Acting in the leading parts of *The Winter's Tale* were Pernilla August as Hermione and Börje Ahlstedt as Leontes. Throughout this following performance, piano music, played by the two pianists, interacted with the spoken words of the characters, and signified shifts or moods of scenes by harmonious or disharmonious chords. The interplay between the tender words and a serene flute melody in the long dialogue between the young lovers Florizel and Perdita, a scene set in the context of a festive celebration of Swedish midsummer in Dalecarlia, had a particularly strong effect. Autolycus entered on a motorbike and offered his merchandise as an organ-grinder. He played the old 'cuckoo waltz', and the ensuing conversation between him, the clown and the couple Mopsa and Dorcas turned into a funny quartet.

Songs by Almqvist were also sung during the performance within the performance and functioned in a mood-setting way, indicating the development of the action. This was also the case at the magic moment when Paulina, played by Bibi Andersson, made the statue of Hermione come to life at her words 'Music, awake her!' The Almqvist song, first hummed *a capella* in the distance, was the same that was sung in the opening frame. This song, 'The Flower of the Heart', told how suffering in the way Christ suffered is the only way to atonement, and reflected Leonte's penance during the 16 years of separation from Hermione.

After the reunion between Hermione and Leontes, the happy ending of the play within the play, the scenery returned to the framing party, and music was heard accompanying a supper, to which the party vanished from the stage. But remaining to the right below the stage, Irene Lindh sang a concluding Almqvist song: 'O my Lord, how lovely is it,/To hear music from a holy angel's mouth./O my Lord, how lovely is it,/To die to music and the sound of song.'

This time, Bergman had employed music to an extent that brought the production close to the genre of music theatre. In my interviews with him, Billgren also compared his personal copy of the stage text to 'a musical score', in the sense that it is completely filled with his notations for Almqvist's music and for his own musical compositions and arrangements. Evidently, the thorough musicalisation of the performance aimed at turning it into an invitation to the audience to join in the happy festivities in the framing opening and closure, and, on the whole, to add to the audience's experience of theatre as a magical and enchanting event.

Or, to quote Billgren: 'Music became the wing of fantasy in the performance!'

In conclusion, it is obvious that the musicalisation of a stage performance was of vital importance in Ingmar Bergman's theatre poetics, and that this fairly neglected aspect of his stagecraft deserves more attention.

The words the actors speak were not enough for him. Music was needed to capture the audience's imaginative response, to direct the audience's understanding of the performance. Consequently, on the basis of a most personal interpretation – existential, social or political – Bergman transformed the written signs of the text into dynamising musical signs on the theatre stage.

We have every reason to believe Jean Billgren when he tells me that Ingmar Bergman was a 'thoroughly musical person', and 'the most skilful musicalising theatre director' he ever met or worked with, as we have every reason to believe Bergman himself when time and again he asserted that in all his life music has been one of his most important sources of inspiration.

Notes

1   For a theory of intermediality, see Wolf 1999: 35–50; Wolf 2002: 13–32; also cf. Lagerroth 2001: 26–35.
2   Bergman's opera and TV-opera productions, which belong to the genre of music theatre, have been dealt with in some publications.
3   Naturally, I have not trusted my memory only. Director of the Royal Dramatic Theatre (Dramaten) Staffan Valdemar Holm has kindly given me permission to use the theatre's own videotapes of the four productions. Thanks to Dag Kronlund and Vera Gowenius I have been supplied with copies of stage texts, programmes, stage photos, musical material, reviews and other kinds of relevant material kept in Dramaten's archives.
4   For further information on Palmstierna-Weiss's scenography, see Olofgörs 1995: 123–48.
5   In addition, the platform reflected Bergman's fundamental idea that actors are best located in a particularly focalised stage space, the space which he defines as the 'magnetic point' specific for each individual stage. See Marker & Marker 1992: 16.
6   In a couple of telephone interviews, which I conducted with Daniel Bell during April 2003, he provided me with valuable information on how and for which functions he and Bergman used music in this production, as well as in the 1984 production of *King Lear* (see below). For *Twelfth Night* also see Bell 1975: 28–30.
7   For a discussion of the concept of *frame*, cf. Wolf 2006.
8   The Ingmar Bergman Archives, Filmhuset, Stockholm, D: 019.
9   For a further discussion of the scenography, cf. Olofgörs 1995: 149–74.
10   In several interviews, which I conducted with Jean Billgren during April and May 2003, he generously informed me about his work with Bergman in general and their musicalisation of the *Hamlet* production, as well as of their production of *The Winter's Tale* (see below), in particular.
11   Interestingly, Bergman further intermedialised this musicalised scene by involving the television medium in a microphone interview with Horatio, aggressively conducted by one of the

brutal figures.

12 For Mörk's scenography, created in close cooperation with Bergman, see Florin 1998: 75–9.

13 The Ingmar Bergman Archives, Filmhuset, Stockholm, D: 047. This original vision is dated 'Torsd. 13 April '93'.

14 For this article, see Loman 2005: 91–3.

References

Bell, D. (1975) 'Shakespeare och musiken', *Dramaten*, 47, 28–30.

Bergman, I. (1984) 'Förord till en översättning', in *William Shakespeare. Kung Lear*. Stockholm: Kungl. Dramatiska teatern/Ordfronts förlag, 5–6.

Fischer-Lichte, E. (1992) *The Semiotics of Theatre*. Bloomington and Indianapolis: Indianapolis University Press.

Florin, M. (1998) '"Han talar och jag ritar...". Lennart Mörk om sina uppsättningar med Ingmar Bergman', in E. Näslund (ed.) *Lennart Mörk: retrospektivt 40 år i bild och teater*. Dansmusei skrifter nr 35. Stockholm: Dansmuseet, 65–78.

Koskinen, M. (2001) *Ingmar Bergman: 'Allting föreställer. Ingenting är'. Filmen och teatern – en tvärestetisk studie*. Nora: Nya Doxa.

Lagerroth, U.-B. (2001) 'Intermedialitet. Ett forskningsområde på frammarsch och en utmaning för litteraturvetenskapen', *Tidskrift för litteraturvetenskap*, 1, 26–35.

Loman, R. (2005) *Avstånd – Närhet: Ingmar Bergmans Vintersagan på Dramaten*. Stockholm: Carlssons.

Lundberg, C. (2000) 'Ingmar Bergman och musiken'. Swedish Television, channel 1, tx 25 December. Videotape owned by Camilla Lundberg, Stockholm.

Marker, F. J. and L.-L. Marker (1992) *Ingmar Bergman: A Life in the Theatre*. Cambridge: Cambridge University Press.

Olofgörs, G. (1995) *Scenografi och kostym: Gunilla Palmstierna-Weiss*. Stockholm: Carlssons.

Steene, B. (1998) 'Ingmar Bergman's First Meeting with Thalia', in A. Fridén (ed.) *Ingmar Bergman and the Arts. Nordic Theatre Studies 11*. Umeå: Association of Nordic Theatre Scholars, 12–33.

Sundler Malmnäs, E. (1998) 'Art as Inspiration', in A. Fridén (ed.) *Ingmar Bergman and the Arts. Nordic Theatre Studies 11*. Umeå: Association of Nordic Theatre Scholars, 34–46.

Törnqvist, E. (1995) *Between Stage and Screen: Ingmar Bergman Directs*. Amsterdam: Amsterdam University Press.

Wolf, W. (1999) *The Musicalization of Fiction. A Study in the Theory and History of Intermediality*. Amsterdam-Atlanta, GA: Rodopi.

_____ (2002) 'Intermediality Revisited: Reflections on Word and Music Relations in the Context of a General Typology of Intermediality', in S. M. Lodato, S. Aspden and W. Bernhart (eds) *Word and Music Studies. Essays in Honor of Steven Paul Scher and on Cultural Identity and the*

Musical Stage. Amsterdam: Rodopi, 13–34.

_____ (2006) 'Introduction: Frames, Framings and Framing Border in Literature and Other Media', in W. Wolf and W. Bernhart (eds) *Framing Borders in Literature and Other Media: Studies in Intermediality I*, Amsterdam: Rodopi, 1–40.

INGMAR BERGMAN AT THE ROYAL OPERA

Stefan Johansson

As Head of Dramaturgy (*Chefdramaturg*) at the Royal Swedish Opera, I have chosen to focus on Ingmar Bergman's relationship to the opera house of his childhood and youth, an aspect so far strangely neglected in Bergman studies. In this, I will dwell on points in his career that have been very sparingly dealt with, apart from what he himself has written in his autobiography, *Laterna magica* (*The Magic Lantern*) where he describes many of his experiences at the opera in a loving and sometimes intriguing manner (Bergman 1987: 127, 166–7, 244–51). What I hope to achieve is to open up a box, perhaps a magic one, through which future researchers might catch glimpses of two important periods in Bergman's formative years, until now not much investigated.

However, my personal connection with Ingmar Bergman was not very significant, and I am definitely not a Bergman scholar. Furthermore, most Swedish artists of my generation – directors, actors and writers – did not in fact acknowledge any very great debt to Bergman during our formative years. But, growing up in Stockholm from the 1950s and onwards, in a milieu of a certain culture, one could hardly avoid coming into contact with his productions at the Royal Dramatic Theatre and those at the Royal Opera – two of them – and, of course, with his films. Still, it was strange, in our youth, to encounter young artists from other parts of the world who always expressed deep admiration for all of his films and – if they had a chance to see it – his work for the stage. For their part, they were very surprised that we, Scandinavians, usually did not share this veneration. As Head of Drama of the (national) Swedish Radio, I was of course now and then Bergman's employer. This points to another neglected field in Bergman research, that of Ingmar Bergman and radio drama, of which he has produced over fifty works. At the end of this intervention, I will nevertheless tell something about my own, sparse, connection with Bergman, the person.

Usually, thinking about Ingmar Bergman and opera, in this case synonymous with the Royal Swedish Opera, one would mention three productions, of which one does not belong there at all. You may think of *Backanterna* (*The Bacchae*) by Daniel Börtz, which Bergman co-authored and directed at the Royal Opera in 1991. You will think of the television production of Mozart's *Die Zauberflöte* (*Trollflöjten/The Magic Flute*) from 1975. Finally, you will think of *Rucklarens väg* (*The Rake's Progress*) by Igor Stravinsky, Bergman's first opera production, a great success in 1961, later brought on tour by the Royal Opera to Montreal, Canada, in 1967.

The second of the three, *The Magic Flute*, perhaps the most famous of television opera productions ever, which has kindled an interest in opera in so many people all over the world, does not belong in any opera house at all. However, there were rumours at the time that it was to be co-produced by the Royal Opera and possibly staged at the Drottningholm Court Theatre, which shared the same general manager, but this was never really true. Ingmar Bergman's *The Magic Flute*, conducted by Eric Ericson, with chorus and orchestra from the Swedish Radio, stylistically and musically wanders on paths very far from the way Mozart was performed in the 1970s at the Royal Swedish Opera and its very different Mozart tradition, which in fact goes back to the years just after Mozart's death.

But Bergman's connection or infatuation with the Royal Swedish Opera started much earlier. In 2003 I heard him, on the popular radio programme 'Summer', describe his first night at the opera, supposedly on 8 August 1931. It was a new production of Richard Wagner's *Tannhäuser*, with Brita Hertzberg as Elisabeth, with whom he fell in love, at the same time as he became a Wagnerian. I thought Bergman was mistaken, as in the 234 seasons of our opera house the season has seldom started so early in August. But Bergman was right and I was wrong. In our archive, I found a playbill for *Tannhäuser* on 8 August 1931. In the cast, incidentally, among the lesser *Minnessänger*, one finds the world-famous tenor Jussi Björling, at 21 years of age in his second year as a soloist.

Most of the Wagner productions at the Royal Opera at the time were old, from the turn of the century. But photos from the new *Tannhäuser* production of 1931 show a fairly modern Wagner style, at least for Scandinavia. In *Laterna magica* Bergman tells us that after this event, he regularly sneaked away from his parents' house to go to Wagner performances. A 'sneak-away' to *Ragnarök* (*Götterdämmerung*) meant, of course, six hours of liberation from the parental yoke. Young Ingmar's great love at the Opera was *jugendlich-dramatische* soprano Brita Hertzberg, mentioned above, for thirty years very popular with opera audiences in Sweden, later active in operetta and as an actress. Sadly, we do not have any recording of her Elisabeth, as we have of her Isolde and her Elsa in *Lohengrin*. The only singer from Bergman's first encounter with opera, whose interpretation is preserved, is Einar Larson as Wolfram singing the song to the evening star in the third act of *Tannhäuser*.[1]

As one can hear from this recording, Wagner is sung as belcanto, a special Stockholm tradition. The artists of the Royal Swedish Opera were, already by the middle

The force of Wagner: Bergman's first visit to the opera

and late nineteenth century, in working contact with Wagner's own singers,[2] and some of them even worked with him.[3] Hence they managed to avoid what, in other circles, was called 'the Bayreuth bark', a typical Germanic way of singing Wagner, much in favour on the continent, with very much stress on text and an explosive pronunciation of consonants. Instead, Larson's lyrical baritone reminds one of the voice of the Swedish baritone Ingvar Wixell and a whole tradition of later singers. This voice was surely one of those which magically drew young Ingmar into the world of opera at the age of 13. Another example of this lyrical tradition, typical for Scandinavian Wagner singing, can be heard in a recording of Brita Hertzberg from

Wagnerian star: Brita Hertzberg

Lohengrin, one or two years after the *Tannhäuser* performance and recorded live from the stage for the radio, one of the oldest transmissions from the Royal Swedish Opera to be preserved. As Bergman describes himself as a Wagnerian already in his teens, he most probably also saw and heard this production.

The young stage hand in the 1940s

In 1939 the then 21-year-old Ingmar Bergman went to the Royal Dramatic Theatre to look for work or at least to get into the theatre to see what it was like (Bergman 1987: 244). He was, however, turned away by Pauline Brunius, actress and at the time general manager of that theatre. She would not even give him an unpaid occupation and told him that academic studies were mandatory for an aspiring stage director. So Bergman instead went to the Royal Opera, where he was accepted by the general manager Harald André and employed as an unpaid helper for the season 1941–42. Sometimes he worked as an assistant stage manager, sometimes even as a prompter, as for the production of Offenbach's operetta, *Orphée aux Enfers* (*Orpheus in the Underworld*). In those days, the stage manager could not signal the stage hands and light-technicians, as today, by electronic means. Bergman, who could read a piano score well enough, was sometimes positioned to signal, with whistles and lights, the different moments at which the stage hands were supposed to change the sets.

What was the Royal Swedish Opera like in 1941–42? Bergman has described it eloquently in *Laterna magica*, but some further points can be made. The creations of the season were the world premiere of jazz pianist Peter Kreuder's opera *Lips*, the first Swedish production of Mussorgsky's *Khovanshchina* and the world premiere of Swedish composer Natanael Berg's *Birgitta*. There were also new productions of Mozart's *Don Giovanni*, Gounod's *Faust* and Offenbach's *Orphée aux Enfers*. This single season's repertoire consisted of 41 operas and operettas and eight ballets – the ballet of course also appearing in several operas and all operettas. Yet Bergman had a hard time finding anything worthwhile to do in the opera house. He was often suspected of other objectives than artistic curiosity, such as when he wanted to follow the ballet's daily training. The female dancers told him in no uncertain terms to get lost.

Because of World War Two, the Swedish borders were more or less closed off to the rest of Europe. Theatrical Stockholm, however, was still a safe haven for some Jewish or left-wing directors and conductors. Among them was Fritz Busch, German expatriate and opponent to the Nazis, who in 1940–41 conducted a famous production of Mozart's *Così fan tutte* with his son Hans as director. There was Leo Blech, who, in spite of being a Jew, was *Generalmusikdirektor* of the Berlin State Opera until 1938, but from 1941 permanently living and working in Stockholm. Herbert Sandberg, Blech's son-in-law, and Kurt Bendix, both German-born Jews, were the house conductors for decades. Finally, there was Issay Dobrowen, a highly important Jewish-Russian director and conductor, with whom Ingmar Bergman remembered having had some important conversations. With a wide repertory, Blech and Dobrowen both spurred the Royal Opera and Royal Orchestra to a high level of musical excellence. Of Dobrowen's Stockholm productions, the most important was certainly

Bisexuality and insults: opera star Leon Björker

Khovanshchina, of which Bergman wrote a great deal. The only sound fragment preserved from this famous production is a chorus from the fourth act. The Royal Opera Chorus also sounds different from today, with strong expression but with wider vibrato and the intonation not always spot on. However, the disciplinarian Dobrowen had worked them hard to sound authentic, not necessarily Russian in some 'exotic' sense but as he recognised it from his own childhood. Russian operas, as almost everything else in the repertoire – except *Così fan tutte* – at that time were sung in Swedish to an audience used to following the story through the action and the sung or spoken words.

The Royal Opera in those days also performed much classic operetta. In the 'roaring twenties' Stockholm had seen a world famous production of *Orpheus in the Underworld* by Max Reinhardt. In 1942 the same work was recreated by Danish choreographer/director Svend Gade, in a very different style. In this production, Gunnel Broström, later a Royal Dramatic Theatre actress under Ingmar Bergman's *aegis* but at the time a student of its theatre school, made her debut as Cupid. More than forty years later, she described to me in conversation how Bergman worked as a prompter in this production, living at the same time with one of the dancers. No recording has preserved this production, but to get an idea of the style – a most refined kind of operetta-singing interspersed with dialogues in the comedy style of the era – one can listen to excerpts from the following year's *La belle Helene*.[4] This was directed by the Danish comedian Max Hansen, with the same first couple, soprano Rut Moberg and Einar Beyron, tenor husband of Brita Hertzberg.

In *Laterna magica* Bergman complained about the drudgery of most of his work at the Opera, but he did get an opportunity to listen to some very good music-making. And whatever he wrote about prompting operetta dialogues, Bergman never despised the lighter genre. Good examples are his productions of Lehár's *Die lustige Witwe* (*The Merry Widow*) in 1954 and of Dahlgren's & Randel's 'folk-play with music', *Värmlänningarna* (*The Vermlanders*), on stage in Malmö in 1958 as well as on the radio. The latter piece belonged to the regular repertoire of the Royal Swedish Opera since 1846 so Bergman would have been exposed to it, both as a child in the 1930s and in 1941–42 during his season as an unpaid assistant.

In *Laterna magica* there is a moving description of a rare and unusual conversation between the unknown Ingmar Bergman and the famous Issay Dobrowen about *The Magic Flute*. The older director/conductor explains his love and fear for a masterpiece which later would play such an important part in Bergman's creative life, as, for example, in a film like *Vargtimmen* (*Hour of the Wolf*) from 1968. It seems as if Dobrowen's views also had many affinities with the interpretation that Bergman would give to *The Magic Flute* in his famous film of 1975. But in 1941–42, it was not easy for the awkward and shy young Bergman to get on speaking terms with the important artists of the opera house; the opera was a strict hierarchy.

'Why do you look so arrogant, are you a bum-boy too?' This insult was thrown at Bergman one day in a corridor by the great bass singer Leon Björker, the magnificent old Prince Khovansky in Dobrowen's production of *Khovanshchina*. The younger man did not understand at all. Impressive live recordings show Björker as a tender soul for a bass, but he was angry with Bergman, who passed him every day without greeting. Bergman, of course, did not understand why he was accused of being a passive sodomite. Somewhat later he found out that the director, to whom he had finally managed to become the assistant, was bisexual. The director, who was doing a new *Faust*, was Ragnar Hyltén-Cavallius, despised, disillusioned and immensely experienced. Born in 1885, he was a pupil of Signe Hebbe and Max Reinhardt, started out as an actor, wrote and directed plays and films, and worked as a stage director at the Royal Opera from 1928 well into the 1950s. Bergman writes affectionately about this man, nicknamed 'Fiametta' by some colleagues, as a thorough practitioner of the art of the theatre, worthy of much respect, even if his artistic ideas were rather conventional.

This production of *Faust*, the only one that Bergman managed to assist practically, was premiered on 8 April 1942. Pictures from the production, designed by Sven-Erik Skawonius, clearly point forward to Bergman's staging of his own play, *Trämålning* (*Wood Painting*) in 1955, as well as to some scenes in his film *Det sjunde inseglet* (*The Seventh Seal*, 1957). I must of course stress that this is an opinion, founded on speculative observation rather than on proper research. However, it has been noted by others that there are similarities between this film and Bergman's own staging of *Ur-Faust* in Malmö in 1958 (see Koskinen 2001).

Transgressing borders

In this context, one must also keep in mind that the Royal Swedish Opera, long referred to as the Royal Theatre, was not only an opera house. At the time of Bergman's first visit in 1931, the Royal Opera – including the ballet and the Royal Orchestra – had only been separated from the Royal Dramatic Theatre for 45 years. Many people then still alive remembered having worked at or been in the audience when the Royal Dramatic Theatre and the Royal Opera were one single theatre institution, playing on two stages in a mixed repertoire. This had been the case until 1887, which seems long ago but in theatre history is only a moment – a shorter time-span, in fact, than between now and my first visit to this opera house in 1956.

When Bergman started to visit the Royal Opera, and when he worked there as a young man, the Royal Dramatic Theatre and the Royal Opera still made joint productions of a kind that is almost forgotten today. Shakespeare's and Mendelssohn's *A Midsummer Night's Dream*, Ibsen's and Grieg's *Peer Gynt* and Daudet's and Bizet's *Girl from Arles* were frequently given at the Royal Opera in the tradition of the nineteenth century. Actors and singers of both theatres mixed on stage with full orchestra and chorus, the ballet also participating, in a kind of spectacle which is hardly produced anywhere anymore. In his memoirs, we follow Bergman celebrating this kind of show much later in Paris as he goes to see *L'Arlésienne*, performed by the actors of Comédie-Française to the music of Georges Bizet. One may well imagine that here Bergman was looking for a kind of theatre he had experienced at the Royal Theatre in Stockholm in the 1930s and 1940s. Indeed, perhaps this found its reflection several decades later in his own spectacular and musically-inspired recreation of Shakespeare's *The Winter's Tale* (1994).

Thus, when Bergman directed *The Rake's Progress* at the Royal Opera in 1961, he redefined a link between legitimate theatre and opera, which really, in Stockholm, had never been totally cut off. In the *Bacchae* of 1991, as well, Bergman sabotaged the century-long official separation of the Royal Opera and the Dramatic Theatre with a mix of singers, dancers and actors from both ensembles. But these borders are also transgressed in the very content of the work, in its celebration of the Dionysian ritual as a profound and violent archetype, a theatre of blood. But even more, Bergman's internationally renowned production of *The Rake's Progress*, praised by the composer himself, had an importance far above his later excursion into opera. I myself remember the premiere as a young spectator, almost as young as Bergman at his first visit to the same opera house, and sitting with my mother – a passionate admirer of the 'rake', Ragnar Ulfung – in the very last row of the stalls. To my great pleasure and embarrassment we were seated beside a devastatingly beautiful Kjerstin Dellert – Mother Goose in the second cast – in an almost transparent silver dress. I remember the excitement of the occasion and, like other members of the audience and artists of the time, the shattering impact of that performance. In the annals of Swedish opera of the late twentieth century, the production of *The Rake's Progress* was only comparable to the world premiere of Karl-Birger Blomdahl's space-opera *Aniara* two years earlier. In fact, the people in the opera house still remember the stories of doors which had to be shut, the non-admittance to rehearsals of outsiders, the signs asking for silence in the corridors, as well as that special concentration, so new and rare, testifying to a deep respect for the work – and the director.

So far, I have tried to point out some influences from the world of opera, experienced by Bergman as a boy and as a young man, which we may have not been able to identify in his films and theatre productions because the key material up to now has been largely unexplored. Researchers have, as far as I know, made very little of these periods of his artistic development. First the 1930s, during which the teenaged Ingmar ran to the Royal Opera as often as he could to see all those Wagner performances, at a tender and formative age when he must have been strongly influenced by what he saw, heard and experienced (albeit Bergman, when writing about it years later, sometimes took a somewhat ironic view). Then there is the season of 1941–42, when the 23-year-old Ingmar was barred from producing professional theatre himself but instead was exposed to all that was going on in an opera house, where strange conventions and great traditions still held sway, but also under strong influence from some of the most radical figures in contemporary opera like Busch and Dobrowen. In the archives of the Royal Swedish Opera and the Swedish Radio rests much material that can be used to understand better how Bergman's theatrical universe was formed, very different from the more well-explored influences from contemporary film and theatre. There are ten years between Bergman's first visit to the opera in 1931 and his first working period here in 1941. Then there are twenty more years to *The Rake's Progress* in 1961 and thirty years between that production and *The Bacchae* in 1991. I repeat that I find it strange that so little has been written about these periods in Bergman's life.

Personal encounters

My own – very slight – personal connection with Ingmar Bergman began only in 1969. While making theatre more or less without money (at Theatre 9, one of the independent theatres in Stockholm during the 1970s and 1980s), I earned my living doing radio programmes about theatre and film. I was used to always being presented with sound clips from the big companies to illustrate my criticism of films by Truffaut, Hitchcock, Fellini and others. In the case of Bergman, I was told that in order to use a sound clip from one of his films, I had to ask his personal permission. I was given his number and told to phone him at a certain hour at his home on the island of Fårö. I still remember standing in the back-room – combined workshop, office and dressing-room – of the first Theatre 9 at Regeringsgatan 9 in Stockholm, trying to hush down members of our group. They showed little interest in my phoning the man who was arguably the world's most famous film director of the time. Bergman asked me what I wanted and I answered that I wanted to use some dialogue from *En passion* (*The Passion of Anna/A Passion*, 1969), which premiered that same year, in my review. Surprising to me, Bergman asked me what I thought of his film. Far from flattered, I felt as if he was trying to intimidate me. ('Who is this man who wants to know in advance what I'm about to say to the radio listeners about his film, is he trying to influence me?') I answered that my opinions about his film were very mixed and that I did not want to discuss that. Suddenly the fifty-plus Bergman's voice changed into a kind of almost pubescent teenager's voice. I was too nervous myself to understand his anguish, while he almost screamed: 'So you think I would accept having a part of my film being used on the radio to ridicule or humiliate me?' I said something to the effect that in that case we had nothing further to talk about, and hung up.

Let us then move forward, almost 18 years, to the late 1980s. I was then working both with Theatre 9 and as a dramaturgical adviser for Radio Drama at the Swedish Radio, with which I was associated until 1997. At a theatrical birthday party at a young actress's house, guests started to discuss the much-debated future of radio drama. At the time the Head of Drama, my immediate predecessor Per Lysander, was under great pressure from Ove Joanson, general manager of the Swedish Radio, to cut down the production of serious radio drama in favour of popular series, mini-plays, soap operas or worse. The film director Agneta Elers-Jarleman, sometimes a collaborator at Theatre 9, asked me 'Don't you think Ingmar Bergman loves radio drama?' 'Yes, perhaps', I answered, 'at least he has worked there a great deal.' 'Do you know him?' she continued. 'No, absolutely not, I hung up on him once, years ago, but that is all.' Elers-Jarleman then suggested that I write Bergman a postcard and ask him to appear in defence of my superior, Per Lysander, and the art of radio drama. I answered that I could not do that because I probably was in what was already then known in artistic circles as 'Bergman's blacklist'. But after a while, when the wine had gone to my head, I relented. A postcard was produced, with a stamp, and I wrote something like 'Highly esteemed colleague, I know you have directed much radio drama during your career and as far as I understand you feel strongly for this art form. Please do something to defend its future, which is in great danger.' The card was posted the same night.

I do not know the exact connection between this postcard and what happened then. But about a week later there was a whole page in *Dagens Nyheter* – the most important Swedish daily – where Bergman was interviewed coming out in the strongest way possible for the continued production of serious radio drama and culture programmes on the radio, telling Ove Joanson in no uncertain terms to quit his job or change his policy. When I returned home that day, there was – on the very first answering machine I had recently bought and installed – to my great astonishment a well-known voice, asking somewhat sarcastically 'Are you satisfied now?' I could not believe my ears. The voice continued to say that if I wanted to, I was welcome to phone a certain number. My first thought was, should I really do this? I was a great admirer of some of Bergman's work, but I did not want to discuss *The Passion of Anna* once more. But I did ring him up and found Bergman very satisfied with what he had achieved, while still seeming to ask for a kind of confirmation. I was even more surprised when he asked for two tickets for my current production of Heiner Müller's *Kvartett*, then playing at Theatere 9 with Gunnel Broström as Merteuil.

Excited, I offered to reserve two tickets for him and his wife, even if it was sold out. When they arrived at the matinee performance, Bergman asked if I could let them into the auditorium earlier as he did not really care to wait outside with all those people. I reassured him that in our small theatre there were only a hundred seats; we expected 98 persons apart from him and his wife. Anyhow, it would not work because the actors were already practising on stage before the audience entered. 'Oh, that kind of production', Bergman muttered. I thought his old leading lady from the Royal Dramatic Theatre, Gunnel Broström, might be aghast if she saw him sitting there alone before the rest of the audience was let in. However, I promised to smuggle them in while Bergman and his wife in their turn promised to be as quiet as mice. He also suggested that they enter the dark hall with their backs towards the stage, his solution for not disturbing the actors with his presence. Of course, I had already told three of them, but not Broström. I suddenly realised how hilarious the situation was, saying to myself: 'Stefan, you are now leading by the hand, into our little theatre, with their backs towards the stage, the world's most famous film director and his wife...' Suddenly I caught the eyes of Broström, sitting there in a wheelchair, heavily veiled in black and baubles, preparing to launch her great initial monologue, loaded with sexual metaphors. Afterwards she told me her reaction: 'Why on earth are Stefan and Ingmar and Ingrid entering in such a ridiculous fashion, their backs towards us – have they gone mad?'

After the performance, I was overwhelmed by the generosity of this man, who ninety minutes earlier wanted to hide from the rest of the audience. He placed himself strategically by the staircase where everyone would see and hear him, showering us and our work with praise. Some days later Gunnel Broström said 'Ingmar phoned me, he liked the performance very much.' 'What did he say?' I asked. 'You know, I hung up on him eighteen years ago.' 'Oh yes, he told me about that', said Gunnel, 'and calls you a devil, but he respects that.'

Later, I have many times shared actors with Ingmar Bergman in radio productions, which were supposed to start at three o' clock sharp, exactly as his rehearsals at the Royal Dramatic Theatre were supposed to end. The actors always reminded me in advance that I 'must understand, we might be a little late as we have to work with Ingmar exactly until three sharp and then we rush here'. Sometimes somebody added not to 'expect some of us until three-thirty; somebody must stay to have tea with him...' But by some magic most of them were transferred, sort of spirited away, in no time from the Royal Dramatic Theatre to the radio studio, hardly ever appearing later than ten past three. Also, they were always happy when they arrived, because they came from rehearsals which they appreciated, even loved, which put high demands on them and paid great dividends, spilling over to his fellow directors.

I have been fascinated by many of Ingmar Bergman's stage productions and learnt to appreciate a number of his films. But perhaps the most easily appreciable and least controversial part of his life's work, where very little interpretation is needed and from which we all have profited – as spectators or as colleagues and fellow artists – was his work with his actors, on stage, in the theatre, in film and television, and also at some very special moments at the Royal Swedish Opera. However, in my early years as a young Swedish theatre-maker of my generation I was rather fed up with Bergman. Back then I would never have envisaged that I would once be writing this homage to him. Back then we tended mistakenly to consider him as already canonised by the establishment – which, in fact, never really accepted him either. We made the grave mistake of thinking that we had to agree with the 'ideas' more or less clearly expressed in his works. Now we should be able to see his greatness as, first and foremost, an ingenious director of actors, in film, in theatre – and in opera.

Notes

1 In Swedish, on a commercial disc from 1938.
2 Wagner's first Rienzi and Tannhäuser, Joseph Tichatschek, appeared in Stockholm in the 1860s, and his Bayreuth pioneers Lilli Lehmann and Franz Betz in the 1870s.
3 For example, tenor Leonard Labatt in the 1870s, at the Court Opera in Vienna, and bass (later stage director) Johannes Elmblad at the first Bayreuth festival in 1876.
4 In the Swedish Radio Archive.

References

Archive material (posters, photographs, sound and music recording and so forth) at the archive of the Royal Opera, Stockholm, Sweden.

Bergman, I. (1987) *Laterna magica*. Stockholm: Norstedts.
Koskinen, M. (2001) *Ingmar Bergman: 'Allting föreställer, ingenting är'. Filmen och teatern – en tvärestetiskt studie*. Nora: Nya Doxa.

PLATFORMS AND BEDS: THE SEXUALISATION OF SPACE IN INGMAR BERGMAN'S THEATRE AND FILM

Marilyn Johns Blackwell

The relationship between Ingmar Bergman's stage productions and his film career offers the film and/or theatre critic a true *embarras de richesses*. These 'riches' are various indeed and have given rise to a number of studies of motifs, themes, characters and influences (of both author and work), as well as various other facets of production. But to state the self-evident, these two media share one overwhelming and inescapable condition – they take place in space. This factor impinges on virtually every aspect of the theatrical and filmic experience for the choices made in this area either naturalise or problematise in some way or another the 'reality' of the look of the production and thus the ways in which spectators are encouraged to engage with the work in question. In what follows I should like to examine how Bergman transports and transforms a particular kind of privileged space from theatre to film, namely the platform stage and variants of it, and then to explore the kinds of dramas that are enacted there.[1]

Leif Zern has said of Bergman's characters: 'De befinner sig verkligen mellan himmel och jord' ('They really do exist between heaven and earth') (1993: 45; my translation). The truth of this statement is, I think, not merely metaphorical but also quite literal as it is manifested in the platform stages that appear in so many Bergman productions.[2] It is, of course, true that not every instance of an elevation of stage space is particularly laden with significance. For instance, directors and set designers often need to find ways in which to vary and add dimension to the naked stage or to develop strategies to ensure that actors do not block the spectators' sight-lines; platforms are clearly one solution to these staging problems. Also, one should note that some of Bergman's Molière productions such as *The Misanthrope* from 1973, *Tartuffe* from 1979 and *Don Juan* from 1983 were set on raked stages, the function of which almost surely was to reflect a kind of historical verisimilitude since these dramas were first played on such stages. Bergman had yet another reason for using platforms during his tenure at the Malmö City Theatre during the 1950s. Working on a stage that was fully 117 feet wide which he described as '[en] vridscen som går halvvägs till Ystad' (a 'revolving stage that extends halfway to Ystad' – a small town on the southernmost tip of Sweden) (1987: 208; my translation)), Bergman not surprisingly used platforms to help carve more manageable acting spaces from the immense void that was his performance area.

The platform: 'Ur'-theatre and focal point

But practical considerations, historical verisimilitude and problem-solving are clearly not the only reasons Bergman so consistently chose platform stages. In a conversation with Frederick and Lise-Lone Marker, Bergman stated:

> Yes, I like [the low platform stage] very much because when the actor is standing outside the platform, he is private. The moment he takes a step towards the platform, he is an actor playing a part … It's a great magic … The platform is ancient. The platform is absolutely the archetypal theatre, the very oldest form of theatre. You have a wagon or a platform on the steps of a church or some stones on an elevation or some sort of an altar – and the actor standing there waiting … And then they climb up onto the wagon or platform or whatever it is – and suddenly they are powerful, magical, mysterious, multidimensional. And that is absolutely fascinating. (1992: 24–5)

This sense of the platform as a privileged space, a magical space, a kind of 'ur-theatre', a space of ritual, was for Bergman enhanced when he allowed the actors to remain on stage, just a few steps from the acting space and fully visible to the audience, a practice addressed by both Maaret Koskinen (2001: 129–30) and Egil Törnqvist (2003: 81). Certainly this metatheatrical practice parallels the metafilmic devices in his cinematic production, the most obvious examples of which we find, of course, in *Persona* (1966). But Bergman's use of the platform stage was also connected to his notion of a theatrical *brännpunkt* (focal point). He explained to Henrik Sjögren:

> Every scenic space has its specific focal point, in relationship to the stage and auditorium. So the first and most important thing is to try to locate it, before you can even start the blocking. Then you often construct the staging around this point, in purely technical terms … This is one fundamental fact that you figure out before you start; where is that magnetic point? Where does the actor stand in this scenic space, in relation to the auditorium? (1968: 291; my translation)

The platform stage, then, functioned for Bergman as precisely the kind of constricted space of which he is speaking here.

The raft-like space of *Long Day's Journey Into Night* (photo: Bengt Wanselius)

We also find theatrical platforms in Bergman's films. The most obvious 'real' platform stage is, of course, the one on Jof and Mia's wagon where they perform their simple theatrics in *Det sjunde inseglet* (*The Seventh Seal*, 1957). But the table on which Jof is forced by a hostile public to dance like a bear is also very much a performance platform. The same is true, as Maaret Koskinen has noted, of the platform on which Karin and Minus perform for their father in *Såsom i en spegel* (*Through a Glass Darkly*) from 1960 (1993: 224) as well as the chancel from which Tomas intones his empty ritual in *Nattvardsgästerna* (*Winter Light/The Communicants*) from 1963 (2001: 67).

A particularly interesting variant of the Bergman platform stage is the raft-like space, an example of which we find in his production of *Long Day's Journey into Night* (1989). Sjögren describes it: 'Allt på en något upphöjd plattform. Skådespelarna sköts som på en bricka ut mot publiken. Sverker Andersson in GP såg detta som "en spelplats för syner" mer än ett realistiskt rum: "en flotte i en mardröm"'. ('Everything takes place on a somewhat elevated platform. The actors were pushed forward towards the audience, as if on a tray. Sverker Andersson in GP [a reviewer in a major daily newspaper] regarded this as "a playing space for visions" more than realistic space: "a raft in a nightmare"') (2002: 387; my translation). This raft configuration also appears in the production of Ibsen's *Peer Gynt* from 1991 as 'a simple, totally flexible, rectangular platform, capable of being raised or lowered or tilted on edge [and become], at will, a precipitous cliff or a banquet table, the forbidding wall of a madhouse or the pitching and rolling deck of a ship in a storm' (Marker & Marker 1992: 279).

The sacrificial site of *The Bacchae* (photo: Bengt Wanselius)

Bergman also used platforms to suggest a delimited space of ritual. Examples of this kind of ritualisation of platform space occur throughout his career: the 1945 and 1958 productions of the Swedish play *Sagan* (*The Legend*), the 1955 production of Bergman's own play *Trämålning* (*Wood Painting*) and the 1996 production of *The Bacchae* all have a stylised quality that suggests either an altar or a sacrificial site. In-

Connotations of the Last Supper in *To Damascus…* (photo: Beata Bergström/The Theatre Museum of Sweden)

terestingly, in *The Bacchae*, as in the 1970 production of Strindberg's *Ett drömspel* (*A Dreamplay*), actors moved forward to place onto the metaphorical 'altar' items coded with particular meanings, an action which suggests some kind of ritualised closure or resolution, however negotiated. Indeed, as Paisley Livingston has demonstrated (1998), Bergman's understanding of art was very closely linked throughout his career with ritual, an argument to which we shall return later.

Another variation of this ritualised platform occurred in the various stagings of scenes connotative of the Last Supper. These scenographic configurations recur in both Bergman's theatre and his films: the 1974 production of Strindberg's *Till Damaskus* (*To Damascus*) and the 1995 production of Gombrowicz's *Yvonne, Princess of Burgundy* share such imagery with an early establishing composition in *Jungfrukällan* (*The Virgin Spring*, 1960). We note that this religiously-coded image occurs at the beginning of the film before the daughter is raped and murdered, while a later meal with the robbers present is shot in alternating close-ups and medium shots that prevent the iconisation of image that the earlier long shot fostered.

Bergman's films, however, contain relatively few images of platforms as such because, I would suggest, the function of carving out a smaller space within a space in order to highlight and theatricalise certain dramatic events, is in the films often transferred to images of beds. An examination of Bergman's use of beds demon-

... and again in The Virgin Spring (photo © AB Svensk Filmindustri)

strates that they are sites of the intersection of a number of the most central issues in his work. In regard to *Tystnaden* (*The Silence*, 1963), Leif Zern points to the bed as 'en av de centrala symbolerna ... om man nu kan kalla en spelplats med så många olika innebörder för en symbol' ('one of the [film's] most important symbols ... if it is possible to call a stage space with so many connotations a symbol') (1993: 142; my translation).

Beds and *Lits de Parade*

Throughout his later work as well, Bergman used beds on a number of occasions. Perhaps the most notable instance of a sexualised bed on-stage occurred in his production of *Nora* in which the final scene took place in the Helmers' bedroom with Torvald asleep and naked in their large brass bed. The Markers describe the drama of this moment: 'The utter vulnerability of his nakedness [was] accentuated by a single piercing shaft of light that turned his figure and the bedclothes into a blaze of white' (1992: 242). But while this may be the most memorable instance of Bergman using a bed on-stage, it is by no means the only one. Beds have also appeared on-stage in productions of *The Castle* in 1953, *Cat on a Hot Tin Roof* in 1956, *Tartuffe* in 1979, *Don Juan* in 1983, *A Dreamplay* in 1986 and *The Misanthrope* in 1995. Again, while

The vulnerability of nakedness in *Nora* (photo: Bengt Wanselius)

some of these beds are certainly diegetically motivated, this cannot be said of all these instances.

The connection between bed spaces and platform spaces is also intimated by Bergman's sense of the fundamentally sexual quality of stage space. For instance, when he was directing *Woyzeck* in 1969, he asked rhetorically: 'Finns det något mera erotiskt upphetsande än detta: att avgränsa själva spelplatsen?' ('Is there something more erotically exciting that this: to delineate the stage space itself?') (in Sjögren 2002: 361; my translation). This connection is also suggested by Harry Schein's interesting assertion of 'Bergmans demonstrativa likgiltighet inför varje socialt sammanhang utom sex och teater' ('Bergman's demonstrative lack of interest in anything social other than sex and theatre') (in Koskinen 2001: 25; my translation).

Just as a bed is part of an image connoting Nora's self-realisation, so too can these images function more and less subtly. On the less subtle end of the scale, we find beds that define women in terms of their pregnancy, as is the case literally in *Fängelse* (*The Devil's Wanton/Prison*, 1949) and *Nära livet* (*Brink of Life/So Close to Life*, 1958) and metaphorically in later films like *Viskingar och rop* (*Cries and Whispers*, 1973) and *Fanny och Alexander* (*Fanny and Alexander*, 1982/1983). But many of the films situate epiphanic, life-changing moments in beds. In *En lektion i kärlek* (*A Lesson in Love*, 1954), Marie thrashes about on a bed as she confesses that she loves David and thus cannot go through with her previously arranged wedding. In *Gycklarnas afton* (*The Naked Night/Sawdust and Tinsel*, 1953) the relationship between Albert and

The sexual spectacle in *The Silence* (photo © AB Svensk Filmindustri)

Anne is already delineated in the first shot of them asleep in their bed. We first see Albert in a foreshortened, upside-down close-up in which his face is located along an upper-left-to-lower-right axis and then, as he gets up, the camera pans to a shot of Anne also in a foreshortened, upside-down close-up but this time the image is situated in the frame along an upper-right-to-lower-left diagonal. The juxtaposition of these two shots clearly suggests that the two characters are deeply connected, almost doubles of a kind, but doubles who at that moment are in a state of opposition. It is only through the course of the film that this opposition is resolved.

As Bergman's career progresses, we note five different beds in *Sommarnattens leende* (*Smiles of a Summer Night*, 1955), perhaps not surprisingly given that it is a comedy of manners based on love triangles. In *Smultronstället* (*Wild Strawberries*, 1957) virtually the entire burden of the film, the resolution of Isak's psychological conflicts, takes place as he dreams in his beds and in the car. In *Ansiktet* (*The Magician/The Face*, 1958), we learn the truth of Vogler's and Manda's lives only when they have removed their disguises and lie in bed sharing an intimate conversation. Beds continue to appear as sites of self-awareness or self-confrontation throughout Bergman's career, including the bed which Sebastian sets aflame in *Riten* (*The Ritual/The Rite*, 1969), and those in *Scener ur ett äktenskap* (*Scenes from a Marriage*, 1973), all of which conflate sexuality, self-awareness and the lack thereof with role-playing and the difficulty of achieving authentic subjectivity.

In conjunction again with *The Silence*, Leif Zern points out that there are 'två

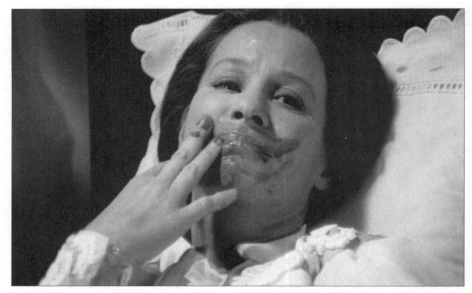

Death/disease and sexuality in *Cries and Whispers* (photo © AB Svensk Filmindustri)

sorters sängar: sexualitetens och dödens' ('two kinds of beds: one of sexuality and one of death') (1993:142; my translation). Ester is quite literally on her death bed and Anna leaves the sexualised bed that she shares with her son to join an anonymous waiter in another bed where they have joyless, violent sex. But Bergman's bed-stages are not completely binarised. Ester's bed is a case in point; not only is she dying in this bed but she also experiences here her albeit unsatisfying masturbation. Beds also function as sites of the very intersection of death/disease and sexuality in *Cries and Whispers*, as is evident in the terrible irony of the innocent Agnes dying of cancer of the uterus.

Interestingly, however, both films represent not only the convergence of death and sexuality but also the very theatricalisation of them on sexually configured *bed stages*. Anna provides a 'show' for her sister Ester on a bed. She hears her at the door to the room she shares with the waiter, quickly turns off the light and then, once Ester is in the room, turns the lamp on, consciously exhibiting herself and the waiter in a sexual pose, thereby creating a sexual spectacle upon the bed-stage. In *Cries and Whispers* the same dramatisation of death/disease and sexuality occurs; on her bed Karin dramatically *exhibits* her mutilated genitalia to her odious husband. And Agnes' bed also becomes a stage insofar as the very theatrical drama of her death takes place on it and the film's other characters are drawn (sometimes unwillingly) to it, hover around it and even sit upon it. Finally, the notion of her bed as a stage space culminates in the dramatic *pietà* tableau that so often serves as the visual icon for the film.

The dramatic tableau in *Cries and Whispers* (photo © AB Svensk Filmindustri)

The convergence of death, sexuality and theatre achieves striking visualisation in an image that recurs across Bergman's works – the *lit de parade*, an image usually in silhouette of a dead person laid out on a raised platform for the visual consumption of a spectating public. While a number of these images do not seem to be specifically sexually coded, others – as we shall see – certainly are. In connection with the issue of sexual coding, one might keep in mind several points: (i) these *are* after all called '*lits*' *de parade*; (ii) the objectification inherent in this kind of specularisation is, many contemporary film theorists would argue, *ipso facto* gendered; (iii) there is a kind of exhibitionism implicit in a *lit de parade*; and (iv) the delimitation and constriction of specular space is, for Bergman, in its very essence sexual.

We find at least three *lits de parade* images in Bergman's theatre work, one in the 1952 staging of Strindberg's *Kronbruden* (*The Crown Bride*), one in the 1983 production of *Don Juan* where the protagonist, according to the Markers, lay like a corpse on a 'bier-like bed' (1992: 150) (note the explicit sexuality in this description), and lastly one in the 1986 *Hamlet* production which ended with Hamlet's corpse 'placed on a high [platform] stage beneath an inferno of glaring lights' (Marker & Marker 1992: 261).

The silhouetted *lit de parade* image of the confluence of death and theatre presumably appears more extensively in Bergman's films than in his theatre work because in film he was not restricted to an already-authored text. One early instance of this composition occurs in *Smiles of a Summer Night*, where we find a shot of Fredrik rigidly positioned, asleep beside his virgin bride Anne while they take a nap before

The confluence of death and theatre in *Smiles of a Summer Night* (photo © AB Svensk Filmindustri)

going to the theatre, a composition in which he and his wife resemble two faces carved onto a sarcophagus. In *The Silence*, too, after Ester expresses how repulsed she is by the smell of semen and the smell of her own body when she was pregnant, her last suffocating attack ends with a long shot of her in profile on her bed, a sheet pulled over her face. Only when Johan returns and lifts the sheet do we even realise that she is still alive. A very similar explicitly sexually-coded *lit de parade* shot appears in *Vargtimmen* (*Hour of the Wolf*, 1968) when Johan rushes to see his beloved Veronica Vogler who is laid out upon a bier with a sheet over her. Like his younger namesake, Johan removes the sheet seemingly awakening the dead. The inherent sexuality of this image becomes even more overt when Johan begins stroking Veronica's naked body. Only after she begins to laugh does Johan notice that the entire demonic von Merkens clan is at the end of the room, some of them even perched up in the rafters watching them, the element of voyeurism heightening further the sexuality of the scene.

The long-shot profile of a sheet-covered figure appears yet again in the prologue of *Persona* when we see the form of a boy, motionless, and, to judge from the context of the surrounding shots, dead. This boy also acted the part of Johan in *The Silence* so the *lit de parade* association there is extended into this film as well. In *Cries and*

The sexually-coded *lit de parade* in *Hour of the Wolf...* (photo © AB Svensk Filmindustri)

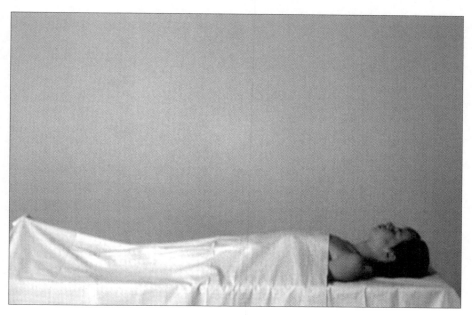

...mirrored in Persona (photo © AB Svensk Filmindustri)

Death and sexuality in *Peer Gynt* (photo: Bengt Wanselius)

Whispers we see a similar image, a medium-long profile shot of the dead Agnes. And finally in *Fanny and Alexander* we see several *lits de parade*. In an especially striking shot, Oscar's drastically foreshortened dead body is visible through a vertical slash of space between two pocket doors while Emilie paces back and forth howling like a wounded animal as her children look on in fear. Shortly thereafter Oscar's coffin, another *lit de parade*, is borne out of Uppsala Cathedral in a procession that is truly high theatre, complete with musicians and a cast of hundreds (see Törnqvist 1993: 120). Here death and theatre, as in all the aforementioned beds, do converge, a point that is underscored when towards the end of the film we are confronted with the image of a mummy who, despite having been dead for 4,000 years, is still breathing. The sense in which this is a body on a playing space is intensified when the breathing mummy turns to confront the spectatorial gaze.

But as Bergman's work continues, images of bed/platforms and bed/stages become even more multivalent. As a case in point, the staging of *Peer Gynt* suggests the direction in which Bergman's film work had already taken him. Although the Ibsen play calls for Åse's bed to be present only in Act Three, Bergman put it on-stage as a part of the initial scenography. Indeed, the production began with Åse, immediately followed by her son Peer, climbing out of her bed. In connection with this unusual directorial choice, the Markers argue: 'It was instantly clear that the point here was not incest, however, but the warmth and companionship that these two inveterate dreamers shared' (1992: 281). Mother and son both lose themselves in escapist fantasies, but the sexual imagery here is so obvious that it cannot be completely dismissed. For a connection between sexuality and maternality pervades virtually Bergman's entire production. His consistent polarisation of women into, on the one hand, good but asexual mothers and, on the other, bad but sexually active ones like Anna in *The Silence* suggests that the image of Peer and Åse emerging from the same bed is not so uni-dimensional as the Markers maintain. Rather, as is almost always the case with Bergman, the maternal and the sexual are deeply enmeshed.

The first words of the play are (in the Swedish translation) 'Peer, du ljuger!' ('Peer, you're lying') – a privileged line (by virtue of its position in the drama) that introduces the notion of artifice. This issue is, of course, the focus of the first three acts. Its association with death and sexuality culminate in Act Three when Peer, sitting at the foot of Åse's bed, tells a tale of their trip to Soria Moria castle ostensibly that he might ease her way into death. We then have an image of childhood and death on a bed, a sexual space that is also configured as a theatrical playing space. But this is just the second of such spaces, for the conjunction of sexuality and childhood on a bed-formed playing space already appeared in *Nora* in 1981 and 1989 where the Helmers' brass bed in the last act was a replica of a small toy bed from the first scene (Marker & Marker 1983: 20).

Certainly, child characters and the motif of childhood recur throughout Berg-

The porn performance stage in From the Life of the Marionettes (photo: Ingmar Bergman Foundatior

man's career, but in the earlier works, although injustice and cruelty often enter into it, childhood is generally represented as a time of awakening and discovery. But later in his career childhood became increasingly linked with the complex of death, sexuality and theatre that is standard Bergman fare. This development is perhaps not to be wondered at since Bergman was, after all, ageing and looking back on his life and, at the same time, contemplating the course of human life in general. Specifically these issues are increasingly played out upon theatrically configured beds or bed-like spaces that have a certain ritualistic character. Since beds do function as ritual playing spaces for Bergman, as images of sexuality, it is not surprising that the beds in later films are more heavily coded as signifiers.

Of all Bergman's films, it is perhaps *Ur marionetternas liv* (*From the Life of the Marionettes*, 1980) that provides the most striking image of the acting out and the playing out of childhood, sexuality and death on a bed-like platform stage. Both the beginning and ending of the film are dominated by an image of what appears to be a huge red bed but is actually a porn performance stage draped in brocade with pillows on it. Above it are hung spotlights whose function is to render the sexual spectacle all the more visible to those who voyeuristically watch the performances through peepholes. This bed image not only fills almost the entire screen, it is also shot from a low angle so as to give it yet more visual weight. The first action of the film then occurs when Peter Egermann murders and then sodomises the prostitute Ka on this plat-

The naked pietà in *From the Life of the Marionettes* (photo: Ingmar Bergman Foundation)

form/stage/bed. Here we have the quintessential articulation of the death/sex/theatre matrix. Significantly, the prostitute first took Peter to her *bed* and offered to have sex with him there, but he refused, insisting that they go back out to the platform. The end of the film then replays the murder and sexual attack on the platform bed but then shortly thereafter shows us Peter's wife Katarina peeping at him through a small window in the door to his cell where he compulsively makes his bed upon which he lies down clutching his childhood teddy bear.

This platform stage/bed becomes a sacrificial, ritual altar, and what happens upon it is a ritual slaying. This image is reminiscent of the altar in the 1996 production of *The Bacchae* where Agaue holds aloft the bloody head of her son Pentheus. The notion of Ka's murder as a ritual killing is also implicit in Stig Björkman's designation of the two characters as 'offer och bödel' ('victim and executioner') (in Assayas & Björkman 1993: 139). That Peter is indeed engaged in a ritualistic revenge murder is also clear in that it is only after he learns that the prostitute's name is Ka, a diminutive of his wife's name, that he sets out to kill her. But there are other moments in the film which reinforce the ritual subtext. His holding, in one of his dreams/fantasies, a knife against his wife's throat also connotes ritual slaying. Also, the life experiences of these characters are pervaded by the kind of humiliation that Paisley Livingston addresses and which he rightly connects to ritual. He notes the role humiliation plays in Bergman's conception of the artist but continues on to note that 'humiliation and victimage are models of interaction in no way limited to artistic activity, but Bergman suggests ... that artists somehow have a strong affinity for them' (1998: 59). The pervasive humiliation in which these characters lead their lives is apparent elsewhere in the film. We note, for instance, that Tim compulsively engages in sex acts that he finds extremely degrading and that Peter, after killing Ka, sodomises her dead body on the platform stage.

The prominence of humiliation in this film is not surprising given Livingston's observation that ritual is about social identity formation (1998: 50–7); for the however-subconscious goal of Peter's ritual slaying of the prostitute is to assert himself as both an authentic human being and as a powerful sexual male. Both of these hopes are, in the context of this film, futile, for the only identity that can be achieved in this society of grey traffic and greyer people is that of marionette or child. This point is foregrounded in the dream image of Katarina embracing the naked Peter in a *pietà* position, an image that clearly figures the same regression to childhood that is embodied in the shot of Peter holding his teddy bear at the end of the film. A ritual drama of sexuality, childhood and death is enacted on a platform/bed playing space.

The late Bergman: childhood and death

Bergman's self-avowedly 'last' film, *Fanny and Alexander*, is veritably teeming with beds on which sundry dramas of childhood, sexuality and death are acted out. The first image of a bed in the film occurs when Alexander throws himself on and tries to hide in his grandmother's bed in the opening sequence. This image is significant because it is she and the forces associated with her that prevail in the film; the congruence of theatre and maternality that are embodied in her character represent the film's redeeming values. We further encounter beds in the nursery where the children play and sleep, in Maj's room where she and Gustav Adolf have boisterous sex, and in Gustav Adolf's and Alma's bedroom where the sex is also ultimately if not initially lusty and rolicking. Interestingly the latter scenes represent two of the very few instances of happy, genuinely enjoyable sex in the entire Bergman canon. But it is important, I think, that the first beds we see are associated with the children because these stages establish the film as centering on their dramas and also because they are associated with Alexander and his magic lantern. These and the 'sexual' beds reinforce the sense of joy that Bergman posits as a central feature of 'the small world'. It is, of course, true that the bed platforms that stage this joy are interspersed with the scene on Carl and Lydia's bed where we witness a drama of self-loathing, suffering and existential angst. The marked distinction between this and the preceding scenes can, I think, be attributed to the fact that Carl is an academic; he has turned his back on the theatre and become a professor. And as his films suggest time and again, Bergman has never held academics or the academic life in very high esteem,

Enthroned on a platform stage in *Fanny and Alexander* (photo: Ingmar Bergman Foundation)

and to choose these over the theatre, as Carl has done, is tantamount in Bergman's worldview to committing emotional suicide.

The dramas enacted on three death beds (Oscar's literal death bed and the two *lits de parade* already mentioned) lead to a series of dramas staged on Vergérus beds, those affiliated with Edvard's grotesque aunt Elsa Bergius and with Edvard and Emilie's marriage both of which are massive and weighty and thereby contribute visually to the oppression this family and this house embody for the children. The people who occupy them stare vacantly into space as an indication of their emotional emptiness and sterility. Only when Isak, the nemesis of the Christian patriarchy, comes riding forth enthroned on his own platform stage can the benevolent order associated with the theatre be restored. In his house the children rest safely in beds whose red colouration links them visually to the décor in their grandmother's home. A final *lit de parade* of sorts appears when Emilie, back with the Ekdahls, lies on Helena's bed as the camera pans from a close-up of her pregnant body to her face with her eyes closed. This camerawork reinforces the assertion of the Bergman female that we find diegetically when Helena and Emilie take over the Ekdahl clan and its theatre. The *lit de parade* image here connoting pregnancy and maternality has replaced those of her dead husband. But because it is not filmed in long shot, Emilie's *lit de parade* is not theatricalised in the same way that Oscar's were. I would suggest that, because Bergman wants a 'happy ending' for his 'last' film, he is reluctant to 'stage' this image and to impart connotations of death or sexuality to it, that, in other words, he holds back from representing the congruence of issues that is so prominent elsewhere in his career. Indeed this ending is consistent with most of Bergman's later work where we see less and less the problematisation of spectatorship that so enriches works like *The Silence, Persona* and *Hour of the Wolf.*

Bergman's made-for-television film, *Larmar och gör sig till* (*In the Presence of a Clown,* 1997), not only grapples with many of the same issues as much of the rest of his productions, it also has the same 'look', as is evident in the fact that beds figure prominently in both the beginning and the end of the film. It opens of course in an asylum, in a room filled with beds, on one of which Carl Åkerblom struggles with madness, with childhood, with the experience of being an artist and with death itself.

After playing over and over again the first two bars of Schubert's *Der Leiermann,* Carl asks his doctor what Schubert must have felt upon discovering that he had syphilis, to which his physician responds 'ett nedsjunkande ... ett nedsjunkande i fasa' ('a sinking ... a sinking down into horror'; my translation). As the scene progresses, we learn that Carl identifies with Schubert, an identification so intense as to blur the boundaries between the two. Indeed the entire film centres on the transgression of boundaries, a frequent theme in Bergman's later career. But a few of the many boundaries that do not hold are those of time (Carl points out that Schubert and Mitzi Veith lived in different historical periods even though their performance posits them as contemporaries), of gender (Rigmor the clown is, like Ishmael, ambiguously gendered), of medium (film, theatre and music are conflated during the performance around which the film is structured), of individual works of art (characters from earlier Bergman films reappear here), of spectator and spectacle (the audience comes up on-stage and contributes to the evening's production), of sanity and madness, of theatre and life and, of course, of reality and illusion.

At the end of the performance, Schubert dies saying, 'Jag sjunker inte. Jag sjunker inte. Jag stiger' ('I'm not sinking. I'm not sinking ... I'm rising'; my translation), a statement that will contrast with Carl's last words. Once the audience has left, Carl cycles from violence into nostalgia as a confrontation with Pauline gives way to a dreamy description of what would have happened had they accepted his stepmother's invitation to stay the night – the good food, the playing with the boys and the memories of (and he emphasises this) *his* nursery. He then sees Rigmor, lies down on his bed and dies, sighing 'Man sjunker. Det gör man...' ('One sinks. Yes, one does...'; my translation). His deathbed statement suggests that art has romanticised the reality of death, that death is not a rising but a sinking, just as the doctor had claimed. Carl's death functions, then, as a reiteration but also a correction of the one he has just acted on-stage, a kind of ritual substitution. At the same time that the dialogue intimates that art has falsified reality, the connection between Schubert and Carl suggests a transhistorical connection between and among artists.

This transgression of boundaries, of both subjectivity and time is reinforced by the conclusion of the film. Carl's death takes place on-stage on his cot-like bed as

The icon of transcendence from *In the Presence of a Clown*

Pauline, both lover and mother, lies protectively and sexually on top of him. The tormented artist has found peace. The final image of the film, an upside-down close-up of Carl and Pauline's faces, zooms out to a long shot from a 'bird's eye' perspective. Some might suggest that this perspective could be read as the eye of God or of eternity but, however one puts it, it is, I think, clear that the image becomes a tableau, an icon of transcendence. We note too that this shot resembles the *pietà* from Peter Egermann's mental event sequence, but Peter and Katarina are surrounded by an indeterminate white space with no boundaries, a background that emphasises the distance and disconnection that characterises their relationship. The shot of Carl and Pauline is, however, clearly anchored on a stage, in a playing space. Their *pietà* composition is formed by two artists and takes place on a bed on a literal stage. Again the platform bed is a site of ritual. The ritual enacted on this bed/platform stage is not a repetition of what we see at the conclusion of *From the Life of the Marionettes*. For even though both images configure a return to childhood, Peter Egermann returns to that state alone in a prison-like cell while the camerawork of *In the Presence of a Clown* suggests that Carl Åkerblom is in the arms of the mother/lover. This image bears out Birgitta Steene's observation that 'Konstnärens ställning ... bottnar i samma slags osäkerhet som ... barnets: båda får utstå förödmjukelser och reagerar antingen med vrede och ett behov av att hämnas eller med att dra sig undan' ('The position of the artist ... is based on the same kind of insecurity as ... that of a child: both have to endure humiliations and react either with anger and a need for revenge or else by withdrawing') (1988: 126; my translation). Carl has suffered the former and now surrenders to the latter, as the otherworldly blue light from the Rigmor scene at the beginning of the film cantilevers dramatically in through the window. The extreme lighting, the bed, the platform stage and the ritualistic nature of Carl's death all resonate with impulses that figure prominently throughout the entirety of Bergman's theatre and film work. Ultimately fifty years of artistry culminate in this tableau – a convergence of childhood, sexuality, death and theatre. Stage and film merge in an image that for Bergman encompasses the span and the sum of human experience.

Notes

1   Bergman's use of proscenium stages both literal and figurative and their function within his aesthetic has been well-documented in Maaret Koskinen's *Allting föreställer, ingenting är* (2001). Koskinen furthermore in this and her earlier study *Spel och speglingar: En studie i Ingmar Bergmans filmiska estetik* (1993) examines other interartial aspects of Bergman's work: the use of direct address, of spectator surrogates and other meta-filmic/theatrical devices.

2   A partial list of his stage productions that feature platform stages includes *Sagan* (1945), *Macbeth* (1948), *La Sauvage* (1949), *A Streetcar Named Desire* (1949), *The Rose Tattoo* (1951), *Kronbruden* (1952), *The Merry Widow* (1954), *Don Juan* (1955), *Trämålningen* (1955), *Erik XIV* (1956), *Sagan* (1958), *Ur-Faust* (1958), *The Seagull* (1961), *Tre Kvinnor från Wei* (1964), *Don Juan* (1965), *Ett drömspel* (1970), *Spöksonaten* (1973), *The Misanthrope* (1973), *Till Damaskus* (1974), *Twelfth Night* (1975), *Tartuffe* (1979), *Nora* (1981), *Don Juan* (1983), *John Gabriel Borkman* (1985), *Hamlet* (1986), *Long Day's Journey into Night* (1989), *Peer Gynt* (1991), *The Goldberg Variations* (1994), *The Winter's Tale* (1994), *The Bacchae* (1996) and *Maria Stuart* (2000).

References

Bergman, I. (1987) *Laterna magica*. Stockholm: Norstedts.

Assayas, O. and S. Björkman (1993) *Tre dagar med Bergman*. Stockholm/Paris: Filmkonst/Cahiers du cinéma.

Koskinen, M. (1993) *Spel och speglingar: En studie i Ingmar Bergmans filmiska estetik*. Stockholm: Stockholm University Press.

_____ (2001) *Allting föreställer, ingenting är: Filmen och teatern. En tvärestetisk studie*. Stockholm: Nya Doxa.

Livingston, P. (1998) *Ingmar Bergman and the Rituals of Art*. Ithaca, NY: Cornell University Press.

Marker, F. and L.-L. Marker (1983) *A Project for the Theatre*. New York: Ungar.

_____ (1992) *Ingmar Bergman: A Life in the Theatre*. Cambridge: Cambridge University Press.

Sjögren, H. (1968) *Ingmar Bergman på teatern*. Stockholm: Almqvist och Wiksell.

_____ (2002) *Lek och raseri: Ingmar Bergman teater 1938–2002*. Stockholm: Carlssons.

Steene, B. (1988) 'Barnet som Bergmans persona', *Chaplin*, 215–16 (June), 122–8.

Törnqvist, E. (1993) *Filmdiktaren Ingmar Bergman*. Stockholm: Arena.

_____ (2003) *Bergman's Muses*. Jefferson, NC: McFarland.

Zern, L. (1993) *Se Bergman*. Stockholm: Norstedts.

PICTURING THE SELF – BETWEEN WORDS AND IMAGES

ANALYSING SELF-FASHIONING IN AUTHORING AND RECEPTION

Janet Staiger

A short-hand term for a more complex idea, 'self-fashioning' as a concept has come to be used widely recently. I take its meaning from the last publications of Michel Foucault where he is rephrasing his theories about how cultural discourses produce social and personal behaviours. In volume one of his *History of Sexuality*, Foucault argued, 'Where there is power, there is resistance, and yet, or rather consequently, this resistance is never in a position of exteriority in relation to power' (1976: 95). He continues, wondering how power relations create the discourses that govern us (see 1976: 97). As he works through these questions, he produces what I think is a much more sophisticated notion of power and the self. Shifting from a 'history of systems of morality based ... on interdictions' to a history of 'ethical problematisations based on practices of the self' (1984a: 13), Foucault claims, first, that morality is about how an individual obeys or resists a standard of conduct. Then, moralities may be either code- or ethic-oriented. In the case of 'code-oriented' morality, laws drive behaviour. In 'ethic-oriented' morality, self-regulation is the control (see 1984a: 25–30).

Thus, discourses speak what might function for an individual's 'art of existence' (Foucault 1984b: 43). These discourses are 'recipes, specific forms of [self] examination, and codified exercises' (1984b: 58) which habituate one's behaviour to achieve one's goals (1984b: 62). In other words, we monitor our own behaviours in relation to discourses; we 'self-fashion' in order to produce social effects. Our repetition creates our subjectivities in relation to others, positioning us within a social and discursive fabric. This is Foucault's famous 'technologies of the self' – his contemporary phrasing of how our own surveillance of our behaviour may be the most proximate governance system operating in producing our identities and how this surveillance relates to our subjectivity and our agency.[1]

Although Foucault is discussing sexuality, his concept of self-fashioning can be applied to subjectivities involved with both authorship and reception. In the case of authorship, 'By conceptualising authoring as a technique of the self, as a citational practice, an individual person "authors" by duplicating recipes and exercises of au-

Author at work: from the set of *The Silence* (photo: Ingmar Bergman Foundation)

thorship within a cultural and institutional context that understands such acts as agency and repetition of such acts as signs of individuality' (Staiger 2004: 2).[2]

This accords with Foucault's poststructural reformulation of the author. Although readers do not need authors to create meaning from a text (who bothers with the author of an encyclopedia entry or a news story on CNN – unless either turn out to be erroneous?), attributing causal sources to a human is a common way of interpreting some texts, especially those designed as art. Moreover,

> authorship is … useful for humanism and capitalism. … the concept [of author] has functions. [Foucault] describes four: (i) pointing by name to a person creates a designation; (ii) the designation permits categorising (a method by which to group texts and hence useful to criticism or to capitalist profit-making); (iii) the categorising may (and likely will) produce status in our culture; and (iv) the categorising infers meaning on the texts: 'revealing, or at least characterising, its mode of being.' This is what Foucault labels 'the author-function'. (Staiger 2003: 28)

Realising that attributing an authoring source to a text is a social construction does not deter even poststructuralists from having an urge to employ this concept in our routine, everyday lives. I go to the movies based on who the director is. 'Adrian Martin surveys reasons for still wanting to write about authors, suggesting the following: (i) to create "the richness of experience that may result" (quoting Tag Gallagher), (ii) to explain how films are made, (iii) to expand from an earlier shorter list the catalogue of directors whose "world visions" or "signatures" are discussed, and (iv) to examine, as [Thomas] Elsaesser writes, "the name of a pleasure"' (Staiger 2003: 29).

Thus, applying the self-fashioning approach to authorship allows a recognition that real people act as authors – they behave in ways that our culture recognises as acting the way that authors do – while still acknowledging the social, cultural and discursive restraints on an individual subject. Marcel Duchamp's placement of a urinal in a museum exhibit worked not because of the object's aesthetic value but because the act by Duchamp in 1917 could be perceived as an art act. Normally, in fact, to be an author requires producing texts our culture recognises as authored texts. Furthermore, one of the major requirements for authorship of art texts is repetition: repetition of form, motifs, discursive themes and so forth.

The case of Ingmar Bergman: autobiographical motifs and interview plots

Indeed, what does an author do to make him or herself into an author – especially an author as well known as Ingmar Bergman? Obviously, Bergman has produced a significant number of scripts, theatrical productions, films, television programmes, novels and even two autobiographies. These art texts alone might be sufficient to consider what recipes and exercises Bergman employs to create author as his subjectivity. However, Bergman has also produced many statements about himself acting as an author. In reviewing some of the accounts Bergman has produced, often stimulated by interview questions, I find that he provides comments about his working and creative practices, his intent for certain scenes, and media-specificity statements.[3] All of these should lead the scholar into what sorts of recipes, forms of self-examination and codified exercises of agency that Bergman understands as how he self-fashions his behaviour into his authorship, what he considers as able to make him into an author.[4]

For instance, Bergman indicates in 1961, 'A film ... for me begins with something very vague – a chance remark or a bit of conversation, a hazy but agreeable event unrelated to any particular situation. It can be a few bars of music, a shaft of light across the street. These split-second impressions that disappear as quickly as they come, yet leave behind a mood – like pleasant dreams' (in Alpert 1962: 63). It appears that for the first part of Bergman's career, these stimuli were transposed into rather detailed scripts with dialogue but that later in his filmmaking life, as he used the same actors and crew, the scripts become much less rigorous, and more improvisation occurs in terms of at least the words issuing forth from the actors.

Bergman also indicates that another working and creative practice is a focus on faces: 'There are many directors who forget that our work in films begins with the human face' (1995: 8, 10). And he often makes media-specific remarks such as 'Film is not like literature ... When we see film in a cinema we are conscious that an illusion has been prepared for us and we relax and accept it with our will and intellect. We prepare the way into our imagination. The sequence of images plays directly on our feelings without touching our mind' (1995: 8).

Another major thing Bergman does is that he works on his biographical legend, a set of discursive motifs about his life and persona by which he expects or hopes his work will be interpreted. This may be hardly intentional; explaining authorship via personality is a very normal act for authors to do since the romantic era, and readers use these biographies as background for interpreting. As Boris Tomashevsky, the creator of the concept of the biographical legend in 1923 explains, readers from the early eighteenth century on have sought biographical information about authors as a means by which to justify grouping together texts (see Tomashevsky 1978). In turn, some authors use autobiographical experiences to think about and create the artistic works they produce, indicating personal affinities with particular characters or transforming extra-textual events into fictional scenes.

Moreover, authors may create phony biographical details to promote themselves. For instance, Tomashevsky discusses how Pushkin spread less than totally factual biographical information about himself to generate a celebrity reputation and create frames for interpreting his work. Tomashevsky argues that while a cultural historian may be interested in the real biography of an author, a textual scholar needs only to consider the biography created by the author as one fact available for analysing the artwork. He summarises:

> Only this biographical legend should be important to the literary historian in his attempt to reconstruct the psychological milieu surrounding a literary work. Furthermore, the biographical legend is necessary only to the extent that the literary work includes references to 'biographical' facts (real or legendary) of the author's life. (1978: 52)

One of the best places to see this approach in film studies is David Bordwell's study of Carl Theodor Dreyer. Bordwell focuses on 'the persona created by the author in his public pronouncements, in his writings, and in his dealings with the film industry' because 'the biographical legend may justify production decisions and even create a spontaneous theory of the artist's practice. More important, the biographical legend is the way in which authorship significantly shapes our perception of the work' (1981: 9).

I want to underline here that for Tomashevsky and Bordwell the significance of the biographical legend is for adequately analysing a text. As Tomashevsky notes, some authors do not signal that their own biography is pertinent to the literary texts they author; others (such as Bergman) do. Instead, my interest in the biographical legend is a bit different. As I have suggested, the author's creation of a persona is one factor in the author's self-fashioning of his or her authorship. The author's persona may reflexively inflect the author's own interpretation of what he or she has produced and would thus become one of the forms of self-examination that becomes part of the material used by an author in creating. Thus, studying how Bergman articulates his biography can be one factor in understanding his authoring practices as well as being of value for the larger analysis of celebrity/author production and opportunities for taking pleasure in interpreting texts via authorship.

Motifs of biography are distributed through Bergman's statements, often in interviews or in autobiographical documents; such motifs seem to be generic formulae. One sort of motif is the *crystallised moment*, a biographical event that is supposed to explain something special about the author. For instance, in his 1960 statement, 'Why I Make Movies,' Bergman opens the essay with an anecdote describing working on *Jungfrukällan* (*The Virgin Spring*, 1960) when the crew suddenly sees a crane and then several cranes. All of the staff drop their tasks to watch. Bergman states, 'And suddenly I thought: this is what it means to make a movie in Sweden' (1969: 294). Such a discursive statement does several things: it reinforces the view that Bergman is a *Swedish* director (and his films ought to be interpreted as Swedish – whatever that means[5]); it also prepares the way for the image of the exile, when Bergman leaves Sweden for an extended period after the income tax debacle.

Another generic motif of biography is the *originary moment*. These stories are causal tales rather than epiphanies. So, for Bergman, a major originary moment is his first film projector. Bergman portrays this in 'Why I Make Movies' as well. He writes, 'My association with film goes back to the world of childhood', and he describes a magic lantern for slides that he had. He then continues, 'When I was ten years old I received my first, rattling film projector, with its chimney and lamp ... It showed a girl, lying asleep in a meadow, who woke up and stretched out her arms, then disappeared to the right' (1969: 295). If I were pursuing a psychoanalytical account of Bergman, this story is gold for its evocation of the elusive female object of desire.

Note, however, the much more extended and different account of this originary moment that Bergman provides in his autobiography, *The Magic Lantern*. In his opening chapter, Bergman recounts his strategies to secure his mother and father's love and attention and his experiences of terror and punishment in the strict household. By this point, he has also already conveyed a story of a plot with his brother to murder his younger sister, out of sibling jealousy. He then launches into the arrival of the cinematograph. This time, no prior magic lantern exists. However, 'more than anything else, I longed for a cinematograph' (1987: 14). He had seen a film, possibly *Black Beauty* (another story he likes to repeat), and had played with a toy film projector at a friend's. Then on Christmas Day, presents were opened. 'That was when the cinematograph affair occurred. My brother was the one who got it. At once I began to howl. I was ticked off and disappeared under the table, where I raged on and was told to be quiet immediately' (1987: 15). Later that night, Bergman awakes, to see his brother's gift on the table, 'with its crooked chimney, its beautifully shaped brass lens and its rack for the film loops' (1987: 15–16). Bergman trades his hundred tin soldiers to his brother, and 'the cinematograph was mine' (1987: 16).

This version of the originary moment emphasises a much more complicated family drama involving his infamous temper and self-absorption. The girl is still there:

> Asleep in the meadow was a young woman apparently wearing a national costume. *Then I turned the handle!* It is impossible to describe this. I can't find words to express my excitement. But at any time I can recall the smell of the hot metal, the scent of mothballs and dust in the wardrobe [where he was projecting the film], the feel of the crank against my hand. I can see the trembling rectangle on the wall. I turned the handle and the girl woke up, sat up, slowly got up, stretched her arms out, swung around and disappeared to the right. If I went on turning, she would again lie there, then make exactly the same movements all over again.
>
> *She was moving.* (1987: 16; emphasis in original)

The increase in details about this moment may simply be attributed to the extended length of the book form versus an essay. However, some of the details that might intrigue the biographer or critical analyst have changed. In 1960, Bergman emphasises his enchantment, describing it as 'my first conjuring set' (1969: 295) and opening the door to the famous associations of Bergman with magic and a pleasure in illusion-making. In 1987, Bergman underlines his control, initiating links to an also-familiar darker side to his directorial reputation. The point here is not that one story or the other of the arrival of the cinematograph is more authentic to Bergman's persona but to point out the ease with which he and we use such stories to create for him a persona to use to construct his author-function.

Another generic motif of biography besides the crystallised moment and the originary moment is the *essence motif*. The author provides statements of essential-ism to explain his authoring. For instance, Bergman writes, 'Ever since childhood, music has been my greatest source of recreation and stimulation, and I often expe-rience a film or play musically' (1969: 297). Note that Bergman does not have to attribute to his own nature a musical affinity. He might just as well indicate that he believes that film is better if treated as a musical piece – another move he often makes when proposing media-specificity statements. Instead, however, he offers up his per-sonal relationship to music as an autobiographical characteristic that might account for features in his artwork. And, indeed, they may do so, for treating a film as a piece of music is likely part of his recipe for crafting cinema.

I have noted three sorts of motifs to Bergman's autobiographical discourse that become part of his biographical legend. These three sorts of motifs are ordinary, and research on auto- and biographical narratives indicate that narratives about selves have common traits, likely because of cultural norms about telling such stories (see Barclay 1994; Bruner 1994; Gergen 1994; Neisser 1994). I want to turn now to an-other part of Bergman's self-fashioning, one that further indicates his investment in his public persona as well as to how self-fashioning also applies to audiences' recep-tion of authors for we are, indeed, equally invested in our authors.

One way audiences encounter authors is through the interview. Interviews come in at least three types: the essay of impressions and criticisms with a few quotations from the director tossed in;[6] the opposite extreme of a transcript of the questions and answers; and the fairly chronological account of the interview with the commentary but much more of the dialogue between the interviewer and the artist. These inter-views, like biographical statements, have norms. An obligatory scene-setting takes place, with a description of the interview's environment (often Bergman's small office and its furnishings), his body, and his legendary punctuality. The interview begins.

What is intriguing to me is that in the interviews with Bergman that I have read, three of them end up with the same 'plot'. The interviewers and Bergman discuss certain matters, disagreements occur and Bergman works to find common ground or understanding with the interviewers. For instance, in an interview with Charles Thomas Samuels in 1972 published in the transcription mode, Samuels clearly ar-

Placing yourself centre stage: from *A Ship to India*

rives with an agenda to test his interpretations of Bergman's films or to question Bergman about what he meant by X, Y and Z. Bergman does not want to affirm interpretations, and they tussle. Eventually, they find a resolution, and Bergman declares: 'Now I think we are in perfect communication' (in Samuels 1972: 192).

This same plot occurs in two other interviews, but because these interviews are of the third type much more can be said about how Bergman articulates himself as an author *and* how interviewers as author-seekers and also promoters of author-legends operate in a reciprocal fashioning of subjectivities.[7] The dialogical relationship created in these interviews reveals both sides of author-creation since the interviewers are also producing themselves as authors (they are honing their skills as interviewers and, one assumes, hope to secure additional work as authors of interviews), and the interviewers are producing themselves as audiences of the author (how do they see this author?). In both of these interviews, the individuals interviewing Bergman express ambivalence and hostility towards him during the interview, and both eventually negotiate their own responses to their perceptions of him as an individual, describing how Bergman seeks to create between them grounds for identification, for 'perfect communication'. The first interview is a 1959 essay by James Baldwin entitled 'The Northern Protestant'; the second is a 1977 interview by Mary Murphy, 'Face to Face with Ingmar Bergman'. As I recount and analyse these interviews,

Hamlet in Bergman garb (photo: Bengt Wanselius)

I want to underline that both Bergman and the interviewer-as-author-and-audience are creating each other relationally; they are also self-fashioning themselves as authors and audiences.

The case of Bergman vs Baldwin: fathers and sons

This relational self-fashioning is particularly true in the case of Baldwin, a gay African American who had already secured at the time of the interview a reputation in the United States as a major new writer and as an interpreter from the black perspective. Baldwin was born in 1924 in Harlem, the illegitimate son of a housekeeper. Early in his life, his mother married Baldwin's stepfather, a man he describes as rigid

Bergman in Bergman garb (photo: Ingmar Bergman Foundation)

and harsh. Baldwin was called to preach at the age of 14, which he did for three years, and then left home (and preaching) at the age of 17. He was able through his early writing to secure the patronage of Richard Wright, another famous African-American author. His first novel, *Go Tell It on the Mountain*, published in 1953, was thinly autobiographical; it was successful and is now considered an American classic. In 1955, he published *Notes of a Native Son*, a non-fictional work about the experiences of blacks in America. Baldwin's second novel, also thinly autobiographical, was *Giovanni's Room*, published in 1956, and deals with homosexuality, among continuing matters of racial inequality. During the 1950s, Baldwin participated in Southern civil rights activities. He gained the attention of the FBI, which during this period considered black agitators to be un-American (they made the US look bad during the Cold

War), and over the years the FBI produced a massive dossier on Baldwin. During his adult life, Baldwin lived large parts of the year outside of the United States, particularly in France. So when Baldwin visits Bergman in 1959, he is in the midst of his own self-fashioning as a major American writer.[8]

Baldwin was a movie buff, and he begins his essay with knowledgeable remarks about earlier alumni of Svensk Filmindustri: Victor Sjöström, Mauritz Stiller, Greta Garbo and Ingrid Bergman. After the dutiful depiction of the office and explanations for the delay of Bergman's arrival, Baldwin describes the director upon his entry:

> He came in, bareheaded, wearing a sweater, a tall man, economically, intimidatingly lean … something in his good-natured, self-possessed directness suggests that he would also have been among the most belligerently opinionated: by no means an easy man to deal with, in any sense, any relationship whatever, there being about him the evangelical distance of someone possessed by a vision. This extremely dangerous quality – authority – has never failed to incite the hostility of the many. And I got the impression that Bergman was in the habit of saying what he felt because he knew that scarcely anyone was listening. (1961: 166–7)

Now it is the case that Baldwin is writing this essay after the fact, in order to create a story of his encounter with this author, Bergman. So I do not take this as actuality so much as a useful setting of the scene. However, this beginning does two things. Firstly, it reaffirms the biographical legend already in play of Bergman as having a certain sort of temperament. Secondly, it also produces the image of a relation for Baldwin as subordinated, a position which I have already indicated via my biographical sketch of Baldwin would have particular resonance to him.

Bergman suggests tea, and also notices that Baldwin seems to be ill. 'I hadn't come there to talk about my health and I tried to change the subject. But I was shortly to learn that any subject changing to be done around Bergman is done by Bergman.' This is proof, to Baldwin, of Bergman's position of authority.

> 'Can I do anything for you?' he persisted; and when I did not answer, being both touched and irritated by his question, he smiled and said, 'You haven't to be shy. I know what it is like to be ill and alone in a strange city.'
> It was a hideously, an inevitably self-conscious gesture and yet it touched and disarmed me. I know that his concern, at bottom, had very little to do with me. It had to do with his memories of himself and it expressed his determination never to be guilty of the world's indifference. (1961: 167)

One does not have to be much of a psychologist to analyse what is going on here. Baldwin's ambivalence about his own father and authority figures – both black and white – pervades this text. Baldwin's recognition of the gesture of Bergman trying to signal identification with him is astutely seen through, and yet it 'touches' him. Baldwin then recounts Bergman as asking 'Well … are you for me or against me?' (1961: 168). Baldwin says that he is for him; in fact, he admits that might be why it will be difficult for him to write about Bergman. 'I felt identified, in some way, with what I felt he was trying to do. What he saw when he looked at the world did not seem very different from what *I* saw' (ibid.; emphasis in original).

A conversation about Bergman's films ensues between the two of them, and Baldwin reminisces to the reader his impressions and views of them. The talk turns to Stockholm and whether it is yet a city, described as a process of 'Americanisation'. Bergman's personality is covered: 'This [initial] lack [of confidence in Bergman] disguised by tantrums so violent that they are still talked about at the Filmstaden today. His exasperating allergies extended to such things as refusing to work with a carpenter, say, to whom he had never spoken but whose face he disliked' (1961: 173). Bergman's work in the theatre is covered as is his lack of desire to work outside of Sweden. Baldwin notes, 'I watched him. Something in me, inevitably, envied him for being able to love his home so directly and for being able to stay at home and work. And, in another way, rather to my surprise, I envied him not at all. Everything in life depends on how that life accepts its limits: it would have been like envying him his language' (1961: 176). Eventually, Bergman must return to his work, and he puts Baldwin into a cab. Baldwin observes, 'I thought how there was something in the weird, mad, Northern Protestantism which reminded me of the visions of the black preachers of my childhood' (1961: 177).

Identity theory has recently created a new concept: disidentification (see Muñoz 1996). Disidentification occurs when an individual sees another individual and assumes some commonality might exist but also simultaneously realises that the two people are not the same. These are 'incomplete, mediated, or crossed identifications' (Muñoz 1996: 145). An example that José Esteban Muñoz provides is when African- American theorist Michelle Wallace notes about film star Joan Crawford that 'she is so beautiful, she looks black' (1996: 150). The key point is that Wallace does not [think or] wish she were white; she retains her identity as black. What she sees is the potential for sameness but also the differences that matter. Muñoz underlines that perhaps in cross-identity identifications individuals do not abandon their own identity as they "step" into the other person's subjectivity' (Staiger 2005: 154).

In this scene Baldwin is disidentifying with Bergman on several identity terms: nationality, cultural heritage, race, religion.[9] Baldwin continues to ruminate on his trip back into Stockholm:

Since I had been so struck by what seemed to be our similarities, I amused myself, on the ride back into town, by projecting a movie, which, if I were a moviemaker, would occupy, among my own productions, the place *The Seventh Seal* holds among Bergman's. I did not have, to hold my films together, the Northern sagas; but I had the Southern music ... My film would begin with slaves, boarding the good ship *Jesus*: a white ship, on a dark sea, with masters as white as the sails of their ships, and slaves as black as the ocean. There would be one intransigent slave, an eternal figure, destined to appear, and to be put to death in every generation. (1961: 178)

Baldwin goes on:

It did not seem likely, after all, that I would ever be able to make of my past, on film, what Bergman had been able to make of his. In some ways, his past is easier to deal with: it was, at once, more remote and more present. Perhaps what divided the black Protestant from the white one was the nature of my still unwieldy, unaccepted bitterness. (1961: 179)

Baldwin concludes by recalling a snippet of conversation with Bergman in which the director admits to a much better relationship with his father now, something that once more separates Baldwin from Bergman. He hypothesises differences in relations with the past between white boys in Stockholm and black youngsters in America whom he sees 'searching desperately for the limits which would tell them who they were, and create for them a challenge to which they could rise. What would Bergman make of the American confusion? How would he handle a love story occurring in New York?' (1961: 180).

I really love this essay both for what Baldwin sees in Bergman, and how he writes Bergman's persona, *and* for how Baldwin fashions himself as a person and an author, and as an audience of Bergman the person and Bergman's films. Perhaps it is just a fortuitous encounter, but such lucky coincidences should be treasured. The self-consciousness of the engagement, the revelations about self-perceptions, the fantasies of authoring and the intelligent disidentifications between the two men are revealing of both.

The case of Bergman vs. Murphy: male power and female attraction

Ironically, the plot of encountering Bergman seems very similar when another American, this time a woman, interviews Bergman nearly twenty years later. I have been unable to find any biographical details about Mary Murphy, author of 'Face to Face with Ingmar Bergman'. However, this essay is published in 1977 after the US distribution of *Scener ur ett äktenskap* (*Scenes from a Marriage*) (in 1974) and a recent Academy Award nomination for *Ansikte mot ansikte* (*Face to Face*, 1976). It is also a decade of intense women's liberation, although where Murphy stands on those issues is not clear.

Murphy starts in a very different place than Baldwin; instead of intellectual homage to Swedish cinema, she begins with her own emotional response to first meeting Bergman: she says she cried at that time. 'A soothing confessor, Bergman says that my crying makes him feel good. He smiles warmly and sips a glass of red wine' (1977: 24). She continues, 'As Bergman speaks, there is no mistaking his power. When he stares, there is no avoiding his intensity … I begin to consider, as I have not before, the dimension that intimacy can add to one's life. Bergman tells me that he feels as if he is half man and half woman' (ibid.).

Obviously Murphy, as a very different individual, writes a different Bergman. She describes him physically: 'Bergman appears at precisely 3pm. With his thin body and stooped shoulders I would think him frail were it not for the ambience of majesty that fills the corridor.' The office is then described; 'he kneels to light a candle' (1977: 26). Murphy has asked to talk about his personal life rather than his films, and although he has consented to the interview, he declares, 'I do not like it' (ibid.). After discussing his marriages, Murphy writes, 'Bergman then talks about his mother. He learned the art of manipulation, he tells me, as a child' (1977: 27). As they conclude that session, Murphy notes that she feels as if she has been in a trance and although accustomed to interviewing celebrities only felt such a similar experience when in the presence of Marlon Brando, whose 'magnet, for me, was his sexual power' (ibid.).

Murphy pursues Bergman to Sweden, recounts his biographical details, his love of Sweden and then his self-imposed exile. She meets with some of his staff and friends. Then, while recounting her background interview from 1970 with Jonas Sima, co-author of *Bergman on Bergman* (1973), Murphy states, 'I think how smothering it can be to be sucked into Bergman's orbit. Already, he has drawn deep emotional responses from me – a range from tears to warmth to angry rebellion – and I have been with him only as a journalist. I decide I do not like him … It has all become a litany of man's abusive power' (1977: 28).

Again, one does not have to be much of a psychologist to analyse what is going on here. Where Baldwin's ambivalence about his own father and authority figures pervades his text, Murphy's ambivalence about male power and female attraction to that power saturates hers. In their next meeting, Murphy writes a drama of confrontation and crisis, laid out at first in the *mise-en-scène*. 'Like a professor on the first day of class, he assigns me to a seat ten feet from him. While we talk, the long, thin coffee table between us becomes a physical symbol of the emotional barrier he has erected. I am miserable, remembering Harriet Andersson's words. "When he cuts you off," she has said, "he can keep smiling, but you get absolutely nothing from him. The eyes can be so cold and he can make you feel so unhappy"' (1977: 28). They discuss his desire to control people, which he sees as actually caring for, protecting them.

Murphy remarks: 'The old siren song' (ibid.).

Finally, the crisis:

'I could tell you to go now', [Bergman] says softly, 'and I could keep smiling and say it was nice to see you again, and how lovely it is to talk to you. But that would not be the truth. You are angry, it is written all over your face, and so am I. We are not making contact?'...

... I pour out hurt and hostile feelings. He tells me that when I asked to go with him [on the flight back to Sweden], he felt 'raped'. He felt *what*? We shout at each other like lovers, and at different moments in the next few minutes we both pound our fists on the coffee table. (1977: 29)

Of course, reconciliation occurs, and Murphy intones, 'It is this combination – strength and softness, dark brilliance and humour, mystery, and vulnerability – that gives full dimension to Bergman's sexual power. Through this sudden intimacy, he touches in me things I am afraid to face in myself ... He looks into me and suggests that since I am emotional like he, I need protection' (ibid.). Finally, he says, '"We have come very far today ... and we are both now so tired. But because we have taken off our masks, it is an afternoon we will never forget"' (1977: 30). Murphy has a final cry and then receives a hug from Bergman – which is the end of the interview.

What are important about these two interview essays are several theoretical points. The first two are ones with which I previewed this section. First of all, Bergman and the interviewer-as-author-and-audience are creating each other relationally; they are also self-fashioning themselves as authors and audiences. Rules of the genre of interviewing control the material somewhat, but the interview genre also supports personal interpretation. When the interviewer is also famous, double work on biographical legends and self-fashioning occurs. This modern 'truth' is apparent in the magazine *Interview*, founded by Andy Warhol, in which celebrities interview each other.

The second point is the significance of the similarity of the plots. The interviewers and Bergman discuss certain matters, disagreements occur and Bergman works to find common ground or understanding with the interviewers. With Baldwin, the confrontation is less personally intense and direct, and Baldwin's disidentification remains in place for his further contemplation after the end of the interview. With Murphy, the confrontation is highly emotional and personal, and she seems to achieve a catharsis as well as a not-so-subtly desired sexual encounter.

I have phrased these interviews as plots. Indeed, a third point is that an interview that participates in producing and reproducing a biographical legend is a narrative, controlled by discourses about what constitutes its proper form. Interviews could be told via convoluted narrative structures, and often material from other temporal points in the interview is interspersed, but interviews seem to have a suspiciously familiar opening exposition, development, climax and dénouement. Moreover, both the interviewer and interviewee become 'characters'. And, because of norms of coherency, the raw material of the interview is worked on to achieve a theme and resolution. Intentionally or not, the motifs of the encounter that I have emphasised are very much on the surface, and I imagine both Baldwin and Murphy wanted their readers to see the racial politics in Baldwin's case and the sexual politics in Murphy's.

A final point is that the similarity in these interviews may well also have to do with Bergman having internalised his own biographical legend and method of creating his persona for that biography. He has a set way of self-examining his authorship and his production of his authorial persona which will be adjusted in relation to the subjectivities with which he is in contact but which also has a limited set of recipes or exercises by which he engages with other people, especially interviewers. This does not diminish the validity of the interview for producing features of the author's biographical legend. Rather it is simply a caution for the scholar of Bergman to watch not only for the motifs of his authorship but also for its self-fashioning via Bergman's own recipes, forms of self-examination and exercises, especially as he creates his persona and biographical legend. And it is a caution for the scholar to be aware of the scholar's own self-fashioning as author and producer of authors.

I appreciate the comments of the audience at the 2005 Ingmar Bergman Symposium, Stockholm, which responded to an earlier draft of this chapter.

Notes

1   Also see Alcoff (1988) on Teresa de Lauretis's version of this and Butler (1993: 12–15) on performative speech-act theory.

2   Also see Derrick (1997: 22–3).

3   I have been, unfortunately, limited to English-language texts. So this is by no means a full account of his authorship statements.

4   Early in his career Bergman often says he is not an author (at least in English translations) by which he means he does not write novels. I am obviously using the term here in the generic sense that 'author' has come to mean in English and film studies.

5   Birgitta Steene (1995 and 1998) and Miller (2003) discuss the 'Swedish' discourse within Bergman's reception.

6   See, for instance, Alpert (1962).

7   I am making no claim that these interviews are typical, merely that they are revealing. I have only read some of his US interviews.

8   Baldwin undertakes this interview for *Esquire*, a 'gentleman's magazine' and competitor of

Playboy. Bergman's reputation at this point as a Swedish director of films with brief nudity (*Summer with Monica* (1953) in particular) probably is not the reason for this interview. Rather both *Playboy* and *Esquire* published major fiction and non-fiction as part of their address to discerning men. The recent critical success of *Smultronstället* (*Wild Strawberries*, 1957) and *Det sjunde inseglet* (*The Seventh Seal*, 1957) is more pertinent.

9   Baldwin also does this in the famous example of his disidentification with Bette Davis. See Baldwin (1976: 6–8).

References

Alcoff, L. (1988) 'Cultural Feminism vs. Post-Structuralism: The Identity Crisis in Feminist Theory', *Signs*, 13, 3 (Spring), 405–36.

Alpert, H. (1962 [1961]) 'Ingmar Bergman', in *Dreams and the Dreamers*. New York: Macmillan, 62–77.

Baldwin, J. (1961 [1959]) 'The Northern Protestant', in *Nobody Knows My Name*. New York: Dial Press, 163–80.

____ (1976) *The Devil Finds Work: An Essay*. New York: Delta.

Barclay, C. R. (1994) 'Composing Protoselves through Improvisation', in U. Neisser and R. Fivush (eds) *The Remembering Self: Construction and Accuracy in the Self-Narrative*. New York: Cambridge University Press, 55–77.

Bergman, I. (1969 [1960]) 'Why I Make Movies', in L. Jacobs (ed.) *The Emergence of Film Art*. New York: Hopkinson & Blake, 294–302.

____ (1988) *The Magic Lantern: An Autobiography*, trans. J. Tate. New York: Viking.

____ (1995 [1966]) 'Each Film is My Last', trans. E. Munk, in R. W. Oliver (ed.) *Ingmar Bergman: An Artist's Journey, on Stage, on Screen, in Print*. New York: Arcade Publishing, 3–12.

Bordwell, D. (1981) *The Films of Carl Theodor Dreyer*. Berkeley: University of California Press.

Bruner, J. (1994) 'The "Remembered" Self', in U. Neisser and R. Fivush (eds) *The Remembering Self: Construction and Accuracy in the Self-Narrative*. New York: Cambridge University Press, 41–54.

Butler, J. (1993) *Bodies That Matter: On the Discursive Limits of 'Sex'*. New York: Routledge.

Derrick, S. S. (1997) *Monumental Anxieties: Homoerotic Desire and Feminine Influence in 19th-Century U.S. Literature*. New Brunswick, NJ: Rutgers University Press.

Foucault, M. (1976) *The History of Sexuality, Volume I: An Introduction*, trans. R. Hurley. New York: Vintage Books.

____ (1984a) *The History of Sexuality, Volume II: The Use of Pleasure*, trans. R. Hurley. New York: Vintage Books.

____ (1984b) *The History of Sexuality, Volume III: The Care of the Self*, trans. R. Hurley. New York: Vintage Books.

Gergen, K. J. (1994) 'Mind, Text, and Society: Self-Memory in Social Context', in U. Neisser and

R. Fivush (eds) *The Remembering Self: Construction and Accuracy in the Self-Narrative*. New York: Cambridge University Press, 78–104.

Miller, J. S. (2003) 'Scenes from a Marriage of Convenience: Ingmar Bergman and His American Audience', *Moderna Språk*, 97, 2, 122–31.

Muñoz, J. E. (1996) 'Famous and Dandy Like B. 'n' Andy: Race, Pop, and Basquiat', in J. Doyle, J. Flatley and J. E. Muñoz (eds) *Pop Out: Queer Warhol*. Durham: Duke University Press, 144–79.

Murphy, M. (1977) 'Face to Face with Ingmar Bergman', *New West*, 25 April, 24–30.

Neisser, U. (1994) 'Self-Narratives: True and False', in U. Neisser and R. Fivush (eds) *The Remembering Self: Construction and Accuracy in the Self-Narrative*. New York: Cambridge University Press, 1–18.

Neisser, U. and R. Fivush (eds) (1994) *The Remembering Self: Construction and Accuracy in the Self-Narrative*. New York: Cambridge University Press.

Samuels, C. T. (1972) 'Ingmar Bergman', in *Encountering Directors*. New York: G. P. Putnam's Sons, 179–207.

Staiger, J. (2003) 'Authorship Approaches', in D. A. Gerstner and J. Staiger (eds) *Authorship and Film*. New York: Routledge, 27–57.

____ (2004) 'Authorship Studies and Gus Van Sant', *Film Criticism*, 29, 1, 1–22.

____ (2005) *Media Reception Studies*. New York: New York University Press.

Steene, B. (1995) '"Manhattan Surrounded by Ingmar Bergman": The American Reception of a Swedish Filmmaker', in R. W. Oliver (ed.) *Ingmar Bergman: An Artist's Journey, on Stage, on Screen, in Print*. New York: Arcade Publishing, 137–54.

____ (1998) 'The Transpositions of a Filmmaker: Ingmar Bergman and Home and Abroad', *Tijdschrift voor Skandinavistiek*, 19, 1, 103–27.

Tomashevsky, B. (1978 [1923]) 'Literature and Biography', trans. H. Eagle, in L. Matejka and K. Pomorska (eds) *Readings in Russian Poetics*. Ann Arbor: University of Michigan Press, 47–55.

SELF-PROJECTION AND STILL PHOTOGRAPHY IN THE WORK OF INGMAR BERGMAN

Linda Haverty Rugg

Ingmar Bergman meditates with uncommon frequency in his films and writing on the relationship between the viewer of a photograph and the image, and also the relationship between still and so-called moving images. In these meditations, he uses the still photograph, which has a direct connection to other people, places and times, as a kind of portal to the past or a gateway to other minds, other worlds. He does this for instance with photographs of his parents and grandparents, which he uses as a gateway into their lives in his novel *Den goda viljan* (*Best Intentions*, 1991). He writes, 'Carefully I touched the faces of my parents', and this touching, to which I will return later, is something he also attempts to perform from the other side of the screen in his films. As Bergman touches photographs to enter them, the viewer of his films is invited to enter into his world, his self-projection, through the cinematic screen. It is not just that Bergman's films often involve obvious or veiled autobiographical allusions; they also offer new ways of imagining and representing selfhood, making use of the power and illusion of the cinematic medium.

In this chapter I am going to relate Bergman's self-projection to recent ideas put forward by scholars working at the intersection of philosophy and neuroscience, because some of the work they do finds eloquent expression in Bergman's work and vice versa. But before I go into this connection, I want to interject the following caveats: I do not mean to propose that Bergman studied neuroscience, nor am I interested in whether he ever had a neurological disorder, nor do I suggest that neuroscience should be taken as some kind of magic key for understanding Bergman's films; it is more that the kind of problems of selfhood that interest neurology and philosophy fascinate Bergman as well. I would like to propose that Bergman deploys representational media and strategies to interrogate commonly- and traditionally-held notions about what comprises a self. Ultimately I will link the neuro-philosophical understanding of selfhood to photography, and in particular to the way Bergman uses photography in his 1966 film, *Persona*.

The self: a transparent self-model

Recent interdisciplinary studies linking philosophy and neuroscience have suggested that the 'self' is itself a 'representational phenomenon'; according to neuro-philosopher Thomas Metzinger it is a 'two-way window that allows an organism to conceive of itself as a whole' (2003: 1). The philosophical argument is that the self, if it can be said to exist at all, must exist as a 'transparent self-model' in order for human beings to function. That is, the self is not an unassailable reality or a concrete thing, but a mental construction that tells me that my body and mind are integrated into something that I call 'myself', located in my body. Because it is necessary for me to apprehend myself as real, I cannot see the self as a construction or projection – that is why the model has to be 'transparent', invisible. But occasionally the fragility of the construction is revealed; the Swedish poet Tomas Tranströmer provides a vivid illustration of this in his poem 'Namnet' ('The Name', 1970):

> I get sleepy while driving and pull off under the trees at the side of the road. Curl up in the back seat and sleep. How long? Hours. Time enough for darkness to fall.

> Suddenly I'm awake and I don't recognise myself. Wide awake, but it doesn't help. Where am I? WHO am I? I am something waking up in a back seat, spinning around in panic like a cat in a sack. Who?

> Finally my life comes back. My name comes like an angel. Outside the walls a trumpet blasts (like in the Leonora Overture) and the rescuing feet come quickly quickly down the all-too-long staircase. It is I! It is I!

> But impossible to forget the fifteen-second battle in the hell of forgetfulness, a few metres from the highway where the traffic glides by with headlights on. (2001: 135; my translation)

From the perspective of neuro-philosophy, the crisis here is plain. The poet's self-model became unplugged and his unanchored mind took an interminable 15 seconds to fix it. It is the memory of his name that gives him his solution – the name attaches the mind to the body to the backseat of the car to the journey to the life. Here I am. It is I. But the trauma he experiences exposes the fragility of the self-model. It is not 'real' but constructed and destructible. We will see in looking at *Persona* how important the name's role as an anchor for the self-model really is. Tranströmer, a poet who is also a psychiatrist, has encountered the impact of speech loss in his work as well as in his own life. This forgetting of names, the disconnect between words and their meanings, is called aphasia.

During the period shortly before Bergman conceived *Persona*, he had a kind of episode brought on by illness that had aphasic qualities; he did not forget the meaning of words, precisely, but was dizzy, disoriented and unable to conceive of his creative ideas in words. When he is asked what the subject of his next film is to be, he answers that it will be 'about two young women sitting on a shore in large hats, absorbed in comparing hands' (in Björkman 1973: 206). This is not quite a story, but an image, and a highly enigmatic one at that. He extends it by saying 'it's about one person who talks and one who doesn't, and they compare hands and get all mingled up in one another' (ibid.). This is almost a story, and as succinct a summary of *Persona* as one is likely to hear. But I want to dwell on the silence and the comparison of hands for just a moment, in conjunction with the neurological self-model.

Bergman writes that, after a month or so of thinking about *Persona*'s screenplay,

> the two women were still comparing hands. One day I found that one of them was mute like me, the other voluble, officious and caring, also like me. I hadn't the energy to write in ordinary screenplay form ... I found it almost impossible to shape words and sentences. Contacts with the machinery of the imagination and cogwheels of invention had been broken off or severely damaged. I knew what I wanted to say but couldn't say it. (1988: 206)

He has no words, but the persistence of his initial image of hand comparison indicates its central importance to what he means to communicate through the film, the mingling of two physically independent beings. In Bergman's realisation of this mental image within the film, the silent patient Elisabet, an actress who has either lost her power of speech or refuses to speak, picks up the hand of her nurse, Alma, for comparison with her own. Alma chides her gently, 'It's bad luck to compare hands, don't you know that?' Elisabet gives Alma's hand back to her and returns to the book about mushrooms that she is reading. I have not been able to find reference to the superstition Alma cites as if it were a commonly-held folk belief. But there is a folk belief about the danger of doubles, the idea that if a person meets his or her double in this life, death is imminent. The comparison of hands offers a hint of the double's power; my self-model is threatened by my double because in doubling I no longer understand clearly where 'I' (my-self) am.

Hands are particularly important in this scene because, as the neurologist Harold Klawans writes, 'Anatomically, hands are the perfect example of mirror image structures' (2000: 45). Hands generally have to do with doubling and mirroring, so Bergman has hit upon something essential here. It might seem counterintuitive to imagine that a person could become confused about whether the hand of another person belongs to his or her own pair or not, but in fact this is what can happen when the self-model becomes disengaged, either by accident or intentionally, in scientific research. Recently results of a study were published based on the so-called 'rubber-hand experiment'. The scientists asked a volunteer to hide one hand below a table. On top of the table they placed a rubber hand directly above the location of the real hand. They then lightly touched the real hand and the rubber hand simultaneously with a brush, many times over. Eventually the volunteer believed that he received the sensation of the brush in the rubber hand. In fact, according to the scientists, 'eight of ten subjects spontaneously employed terms of ownership ... for example: "I found myself looking at the dummy hand thinking it was actually my own"' (Botvinick & Cohen 1998: 756). The research 'reflect[s] a three-way interaction between vision, touch, and proprioception' – that is, vision, touch and self-model (Tsakiris & Haggard 2005: 80). Another brief moment in *Persona* where Bergman seems to point towards a confusion of identity through a confusion of hands occurs, significantly, just after the scene in *Persona* when Elisabet's husband seems to confuse Alma with his wife and ends up having sex with Alma while his wife stands by.

From a cinematic perspective, the triangulation of sight, touch and self-model revealed in the rubber-hand experiment has fascinating implications. Film theorists have often discussed the ways in which the spectator identifies with the figures on the screen, for example. But they have most often applied psychoanalytic theory to these models of identification. What *Persona* seems to explore is something that more recent film scholarship has called the 'haptic' quality of film – that is, the way that film engages the sense of touch, which seems impossible, but not if we think about the photographic medium as a kind of 'rubber hand' (see for instance Marks 2000). Like the rubber hand, photographs of human beings are fake doubles, and we engage with the photographed images of people as if the images were the people themselves. The emotions and sensations represented on the screen are meant to have an impact, even a physical impact, on our bodies sitting in the theatre. If this sounds far-fetched, remember how *Persona* produces erotic reaction in many viewers through Alma recounting her sexual experiences on the beach. In that particular scene we do not see the so-called orgy; we only hear Alma's description of it. But we see Elisabet listening to Alma, occupying our space (the way in which the rubber hand occupies the real hand's space), and we can see her physical reaction. Or at least Bergman thinks so. He says: 'If you look at Liv's face, you'll see that all the time it's swelling. It's fascinating – her lips get bigger ... The story mustn't only have a suggestive effect on Elisabet – it must have a suggestive effect on you, enable you to experience it all deep down inside you, in your own cinematograph' (in Björkman 1973: 208–9). In the scene, Elisabet functions as our 'rubber hand' – the physical reactions we view in her are to be appropriated to our own bodies and self-models.

If we want to think further about the tactile qualities of Bergman's approach to photography and cinema, we can look at the opening of the film, when the unnamed boy who appears in a morgue-like setting seems to reach out and touch our space,

Touching the viewer (photo: © AB Svensk Filmindustri)

the viewer's space. It then transpires that he is running his hand over a large screen with a projected photographic image of first one woman's face, then another's. The need to touch this image and the apparent violation of the spectator's space, a moment in which the boy seems to want to touch us, suggest the confusion Bergman means to produce between photographed reality and reality, between the body and its photographic double, so to speak. The boy's desire to touch the image reflects his desire to touch the woman or women, and the viewer is involved in this through the reverse shot. Metzinger, the neuro-philosopher, finds it particularly fascinating that our concepts of grasping with the hand and grasping with the mind, through language, are located in the same area of the brain. In thinking about subjects who mentally attempt to grasp something with paralysed or non-existent hands, Metzinger writes, 'What is a mentally imagined hand grasping movement? It is an intended, phenomenal self-simulation. In particular, it is a self-simulation involving *making an external object your own*' (2003: 379; emphasis in original). The boy's attempt to touch the faces in the projected photograph seems like an attempt to grasp something essential about his relationship to the women pictured there; he tries to make this 'external object [his] own'. If, as many viewers assume, the boy is meant to represent the aborted or rejected child of one or both of the women on the screen, we could understand his gesture as a need to reintegrate with the maternal body. A pregnant woman's self-model includes not only her own person, but another human being, and the fact that both of the film's women negated their connection to the child leads perhaps to his attempt to grasp what is not there.

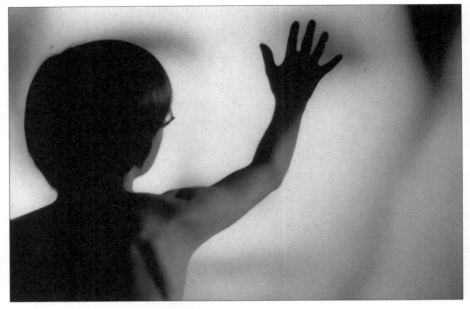

Touching the image (photo: © AB Svensk Filmindustri)

The self as disassociation

So far I have focused on the extension of the self-model to absorb another person's body. The other side of this is disassociation; we can lose the sensation of connection between ourselves and our bodies, as in Tranströmer's poem. A person who suffers damage to the left temporal lobe of the brain will most likely find both linguistic and hand function affected, sometimes to the extent that the person becomes disassociated from his or her own hand or arm, believing it to belong to someone else. Harold Klawans, in his collection of neurological case studies *Defending the Cavewoman*, describes the case of an intelligent, articulate five-year-old girl who suddenly lost all power of speech due to epileptic seizures affecting the left temporal lobe of her brain. Her seizures began with eye movements and ended with an odd hand pantomime: 'She put her two hands together and began to move them as if she were washing them. Over and over again ... [This is called] an automatism ... a complex movement or set of movements that would be considered normal done at the right time and in the right place but is instead performed at the wrong time or in the wrong place and serves no apparent function' (2000: 61–2). An uncanny moment in the opening montage sequence of *Persona* seems almost to represent such a pantomime.

Just before this is a brief sequence that asks us to imagine that we see an animated film as it moves through the projector, though we do not see the space between the frames – the cartoon appears to stall in the projector, revealing the fact that what we actually look at in films is separate still images and not 'moving' ones. Then we move to another view of the film running through the projector and listen to the sound it makes. Abruptly we cut to an image of a child's hands, moving as if the child were repeatedly washing them. The idea that the movement has to do with washing receives reinforcement from the preceding cartoon, in which the woman is washing herself. But there is no water in the child's hand-washing pantomime; the movement eerily resembles the automatism that Klawans describes in that it serves no apparent function.

I do not mean to conclude from this that Bergman necessarily knew anything about clinical automatism when making *Persona*, but obviously he understood a great deal about disassociation and its potential connection to both the work he did in film and theatre and to his own experience of reality. The description put forth by Klawans of automatism speaks of removing an action from its 'real' framework and making it into a kind of pantomime. Of pantomime, Bergman writes: 'When I was twelve, I was allowed to go backstage during Strindberg's *A Dream Play*. It was a searing experience. Night after night, I witnessed the marriage scene between the Lawyer and the Daughter. It was the first time I had experienced the magic of acting. The Lawyer held a hairpin between his thumb and forefinger, he twisted it, straightened it out, and broke it. There was no hairpin, but I saw it' (1988: 33). Perhaps readers will think it an unfair stretch to compare the 'magic of acting' with an epileptic seizure, but what I think Bergman is dealing with here is something we might call a disassociative poetics of representation. That is, the art of acting and the media of photography and thus film all involve a disengagement of the performance from the reality of its origin, a disengagement of the body from its experience as a self, a disengagement, in short, of the self-model.

The context of the odd hand-washing pantomime within the montage is a key to understanding how Bergman relates the medium of film to the problem of psychological disassociation. To emphasise how central this connection between medium and story is, we should keep in mind that the original working title of *Persona* was *Kinematography*. From the opening of the film, it is obvious that we are watching a film about film, with the projector warming up, the film strip flashing through the projector and across the screen, and the references to the history of film through quotation of cartoons and early silent cinema. The status of *Persona* as film rather than reality is emphasised both in the opening montage and the break that occurs in the middle of film. How is cinematography related to the concept of the persona? In a collection of interviews with Bergman, Torsten Manns (1973) points out that the word 'persona' referred originally to the masks worn by actors in classical drama, but wonders whether perhaps Bergman has a Jungian concept of persona in mind. Bergman, with his usual reluctance to appear well-read or intellectual, responds laconically, 'that sounds good'. But then he goes on to say, 'There's something extremely

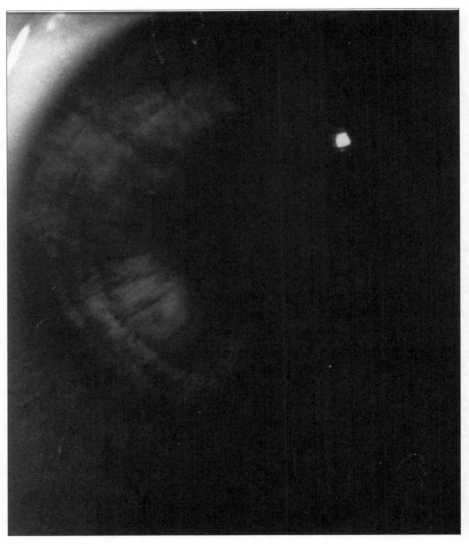

Entering the eye

fascinating to me about these people exchanging masks and suddenly sharing one between them' (in Björkman 1973: 202). It is not the case that the two women in *Persona* wear actual masks, as Bergman's statement would seem to suggest; rather, he means that they exchange faces or, more accurately, the photographic image of their faces as anchored to their names. Ultimately the two halves of their photographic images are merged into a single image, a 'mask' as he would have it, that they share between them. That Bergman identifies a photographic image with a mask is, to use his words, extremely fascinating.

It would seem at first glance that there is a significant difference between the animated cartoon strip of the woman splashing water on her breasts and the snippet of photographic film depicting the odd hand-washing pantomime. Although they are related in theme, one is based on drawings of a human and the other on photographs. Since we assume that there had to be an actual human present in order for the hand-washing scene to be photographed, we would accord that sequence more 'reality'. But one of the central projects of *Persona* is to throw the relationship between photography and 'reality' into question.

Film's power as a narrative medium depends in part on the connection between photographs and the real, that is, not only photography's resemblance to the reality it depicts, but its assurance to us that there were real people and objects present at the moment of filming. This is one thing that gives film its 'rubber hand' effect, allowing us to interpret the flat images of film as 'real people' analogous to ourselves, coextensive with ourselves. With the stalled animated sequence, Bergman the magician first shows us how the magic tricks of film are performed, through illusion, revealing that film is not comprised of moving images, but just a series of still images. Then he gives us something, the hand-washing, that looks real because photographed, but he has removed its reality by taking it out of narrative context. The quality of automatism discussed above serves Bergman well here; this is an action that is in the wrong place and the wrong time – as Klawans says, it 'serves no apparent function'. Because photographs are removed from the context in which they were made, they must be re-grounded in narrative in order for them to perform as reality. The hand-washing pantomime, like the various images of the montage sequence before the 'story' of *Persona* begins, has been so removed from its original reality that the viewer cannot integrate it into a story. It is not until the door opens and nurse Alma enters the room to receive her assignment from the doctor that the viewer can settle comfortably into a grounded narrative context that allows the photographs to represent the 'real' – for a while. In the middle of the story the film seems to break, and when we come back to the story space (after a tour of the capillaries of the human eye) the image is at first blurred. We see a woman in black crossing a room, and we can make out that the room and the woman belong to the story space of *Persona*. When the blurry photographic image suddenly clicks into focus it is like a photographic performance of the moment in Tranströmer's poem when the name, like an angel, suddenly returns. It is I! It is she!

Exchanging masks

A photograph of a person's face resembles a mask in that there is a space, both temporal and spatial, between the face as it was photographed and the photograph as we see it. The face is removed from its original context. Thus, when Bergman says that the two women exchange masks and eventually share one, he reminds us that the

The image is first blurred...

only anchor connecting a woman to her image is the narrative that attaches her to that image, particularly her name. Alma, slightly drunk after her orgy story, says she once saw a film in which Elisabet acted, and that she had been struck by the fact that they looked alike. Alma says: 'I thought, I could change into you if I tried. I mean on the inside. And you could change into me just like that!' It is striking that it is in viewing a film that Alma has this sense of interchangeability – she is ready to exchange masks with Elisabet after this experience. Later in the film when Elisabet's husband insists on calling her Elisabet, Alma at first resists – 'I'm not your wife, Mr Vogler', she protests. But then she enters into the performance, she speaks Elisabet's lines, she becomes Elisabet, her face is no longer anchored to her name, and her self-model is pulled into Elisabet's. This is performance as disassociation.

When Elisabet Vogler either loses or refuses her power of speech, she is in the midst of performing as Electra. A few things are striking about the sequence. We are located backstage, behind the actress, with the lights shining with full force into our eyes as they would into hers. She turns away from the stage and seems to look at us in despair. She explains later that she was overcome by an urge to laugh, which would be entirely out of keeping with the tragic nature of the role she has to play. She has become disconnected from the anchoring narrative of performance. In other words, she suddenly saw herself as if in a photograph; she was suddenly aware of the disas-

... but then clicks into focus

sociation she performs as an actress and she could then see herself exposed as an imposter, projecting a false self-model.

Elisabet's fall into silence and the way it is filmed tell us something about the loss of speech and self that Alma later experiences. Behind the lights in the theatre flashback is the invisible audience, watching as Elisabet breaks down. The viewer's space exists in one realm, the realm of the 'real', while the performer's space is the space of resemblance to the real. An engaged spectator must simultaneously accept what happens on the screen or stage as a reality related to the one he or she experiences and also understand that the spectacle is not part of our reality, that it is only a play or only a movie. The illusion of reality in both theatre and film depends on the presence of real human beings and material objects, either viewed in real time and theatre space or, in the case of film, at a temporal and spatial distance from the site of the original performance. But even when viewed in real time, actors are understood at some level to not be what they are representing. There is an act of disassociation that takes place for all concerned – viewers must mentally 'leave' their own physical time and space in order to accept the reality of the spectacle, and the actors must set aside their names and selves in order to become someone else for a brief period. In *Persona* the pathological implications of representation and spectatorship receive intense critical attention.

It has often been remarked how *Persona* violates the viewer's space and forces the audience into the realisation that what they are watching is not reality, but a representation. When we see what we imagine to be our film running through the projector (logically it cannot be our film), when the film appears to stall, break and burn in the midst of the story – these are instances in which our physical presence in the theatre seems to be apprehended by the film, when the film shows itself to us as film. This undermines the viewer's usual disembodied situation, in which the self-model (our awareness of ourselves as located in our own bodies) is held temporarily in abeyance. Sitting in the darkness, we disengage our self-models while engaging with the events on the screen as 'real'. When screen events flaunt their unreality, we can be plunged back into our body space quite abruptly. This happens when the film appears to break and burn and spectators turn their heads to the back of the theatre to try to see whether flames are emerging from the projection booth. Not only is Bergman interested in showing Alma's crisis of selfhood or the actress's experience of disassociation, he also wants to make the audience understand the disconnect in the self-model that usually occurs while watching a performance.

I would like to bring all of this back to Bergman himself, who says that he is both the mute woman and the speaking woman. In his autobiography, *Laterna magica*, he describes something he calls a 'professional disease', which he characterises as 'observing' himself or 'playing a role' (1987: 63; my translation). He says, '[for] more than forty years ... I existed on the memory of feelings. I knew perfectly well how emotions should be reproduced, but the spontaneous expression of them was never spontaneous. There was always a micro-second between my intuitive experience and its emotional expression. Today, when I fancy that I have more or less recovered, I wonder whether there are, or ever will be, instruments which can measure a neurosis that so effectively gave the appearance of reality' (1987: 118; my translation). Bergman, in other words, has experienced his own self-model in a state of disconnect. But he uses that disconnect to explore the possibilities of performance, he uses it professionally. And in *Persona*, he relates the disconnect explicitly to film.

My argument in this chapter stresses the pathology of disassociative selfhood in *Persona*. But Bergman also writes 'without a you there is no I' (1987: 63; my translation), stressing the positive necessity for openness in the self-model. And besides the terror of disassociation, there is an enormously creative moment in *Persona* as well, one in which Bergman demonstrates for us how our strategies of representation employ (have perhaps always employed) an awareness and manipulation of the transparent self-model only recently under investigation by neurologists. Metzinger proposes that human beings developed the self-model and its transparency through evolutionary adaptation. One question might be what will become of the self-model as adaptive device when it is made visible and its fragility is revealed in works of art like Bergman's *Persona*.

References

Bergman, I. (1987) *Laterna magica*. New York: Viking.

Björkman, S., T. Manns and J. Sima (1973) *Bergman on Bergman: Interviews with Ingmar Bergman*, trans. P. B. Austin. New York: Simon & Schuster.

Botvinick, M. and J. Cohen (1998) 'Rubber hands "feel" touch that eyes see', *Nature* 391, 19 February, 756.

Klawans, H. (2000) *Defending the Cavewoman and Other Tales of Evolutionary Neurology*. New York and London: W. W. Norton and Company.

Marks, L. U. (2000) *The Skin of the Film: Intercultural Cinema, Embodiment, and the Senses*. Durham and London: Duke University Press.

Metzinger, T. (2003) *Being No One: The Self-Model Theory of Subjectivity*. Cambridge, MA: MIT Press.

Tranströmer, T. (2001) *Samlade dikter, 1954–1996*. Stockholm: Bonniers Förlag.

Tsakiris, M. and P. Haggard (2005) 'The Rubber Hand Illusion Revisited: Visuotactile Integration and Self-Attribution', *Journal of Experimental Psychology: Human Perception and Performance*, 31, 1, 80–91.

ON INGMAR BERGMAN AND PHILOSOPHY: THE KAILA CONNECTION

Paisley Livingston

It may seem ill-advised to look for anything like a close connection between philosophy and the cinema, and indeed, some of the claims made about the philosophical nature of films are quite exaggerated (see Livingston 2006). Philosophers tend to write dense, abstract prose designed to convey general arguments and theses, while the filmmaker's primary medium is an entrancing audio-visual display, well-suited to stir up emotions and the imagination. We should not expect to find a fully articulated, rigorous argument on a philosophical topic in a film unless, of course, one has in mind an audio-visual recording of a philosophical lecture or interview.

Yet our recognition of the obvious and important differences between verbal and cinematic media should not blind us to important similarities. Both the verbal and the cinematic media can be used to express ideas and to get people to think about difficult, general issues, including philosophical ones. A film can resonate with and even comment upon philosophical notions and positions. Thus, while Ingmar Bergman is not a philosopher in any strict sense of the term, many of his films express and respond to philosophical ideas in interesting and valuable ways; or so I shall try to show in what follows, with reference to just a few of the many possible examples from Bergman's work.

One important similarity between film and philosophy should be mentioned at the outset. The significance of a philosophical treatise or essay emerges in relation to relevant, earlier moments in the philosophical tradition. For example, we understand René Descartes not only as the precursor to various modern figures, such as Immanuel Kant and Edmund Husserl, but also as a thinker who drew upon and responded to ideas and arguments that went all the way back to St Augustine, Michel de Montaigne, Plotinus and Plato. When we read a philosopher's works, one of our tasks is to decide which aspects of the intellectual background, such as possible sources and adversaries, are most pertinent and should be taken into account. A similar point holds with regard to our understanding of a film's philosophical significance, for here as well the meaning of a work arises in a context of prior questions and assumptions. In the case of Bergman, some interpreters have seen fit to opt for a background constituted by the works of Carl Jung (see Fredericksen 2005), while others have drawn upon Freudian psychoanalysis and existentialism (see Ketcham 1986). This raises the question of how to select the relevant background assumptions. Although I do not defend the untenable view that a film director's claims about his or her ideas and intentions somehow exhaust the meanings of the films themselves, I do believe that we can usefully draw upon the director's various statements, especially when they mesh well with what can be observed in the films. After all, the fact that a director has encountered and thought about a philosopher's work may help to explain why responses to certain philosophical claims, ranging from acceptance to rejection, find forceful expression in the films. Acknowledging the importance of an author's intentions and creative activities need not, however, amount to accepting any overly strong intentionalist doctrine (see Livingston 2005). I do not argue that 'retrieval' of the context of creation (as in Wollheim 1980) is the *only* valuable critical approach, but I do think that it is a very good and central one as long as our interest lies in the direction of aesthetic or artistic appreciation.

With regard to the problem of reconstructing Ingmar Bergman's context, I can think of no better place to begin than a fairly well-known remark, first published in 1957, in which Bergman commented on his philosophical sources: 'Philosophically, there is a book which was a tremendous experience for me: Eino Kaila's *Psychology of the Personality*. His thesis that man lives strictly according to his needs – negative and positive – was shattering to me, but terribly true. And I built on this ground' (1970: 12). Although this statement has been cited a number of times, I have the impression that few people have studied Kaila's book in relation to Bergman's work. (And here I include my own previous efforts at Bergman interpretation; see Livingston 1982.) Yet we may be more than a little bit curious about the nature of this 'ground' on which Bergman said he had built. What specific ideas expressed by Kaila could have resonated with Bergman's own intellectual and emotional inclinations? Did any of Kaila's specific philosophical propositions make their way into Bergman's films? If so, how were they transformed, adapted or revised in the process? In what sense could these notions have served as a 'ground' or intellectual foundation on which an artistic project could be based? And do Bergman's artistic explorations of Kaila's themes express any disagreement with the philosopher's positions?

There is a quick but misleading answer to these questions: Bergman got one specific philosophical thesis from Kaila, and that thesis is stated in *Smultronstället* (*Wild Strawberries*, 1957). In the midst of a quarrel with his wife, Professor Isak Borg's son Evald says: 'There is no right or wrong. One functions according to one's needs: you can read that in a school text.' At least one Bergman scholar identifies this fictional 'school text' with Kaila's book, partly because he thinks Bergman expresses his ambivalence towards his own father in Evald's conflicted relationship with Professor Borg (Gado 1986: 225). Yet I have some doubts about this simple equation. The line about functioning according to needs certainly echoes Kaila, yet as Bergman must have known, it is grossly inaccurate to characterise Kaila's difficult treatise as a 'school text' (in Swedish it is *Folkskolans läsebok*, a Primary School reader). Clearly Evald should not be taken as speaking literally, and is better understood as angrily using this rhetoric to browbeat his wife. More importantly, it is also far from clear that what Bergman found worthwhile in Kaila was the idea that there is no right and wrong, or in other words, a sweeping 'error theory' of moral discourse (see Mackie 1977; very briefly, Mackie's 'error theory' is the thesis that people never speak truly when they sincerely classify some actions as morally good, or others as wrong or evil, the reason being that the terms 'good' and 'evil' do not name anything real).

Clearly, if we are to address ourselves seriously to Bergman's relation to Kaila we need to know what Kaila has to say in his book. I shall not attempt here to provide a systematic and detailed recapitulation of Kaila's lengthy chapters, but will instead identify a few noteworthy features of his position. With this background in place, I will address myself to both the strengths and limitations of the Bergman-Kaila connection. It is not my goal to reduce Bergman's works to fictional illustrations of Kaila's theses. I do, however, maintain that the connection can reveal some important aspects of Bergman's accomplishments.

Kaila's philosophical psychology

Son of Archbishop Erkki Kaila, Eino Sakari Kaila (1890–1958) had a brief career as a dramaturge for the National Theatre of Finland but then devoted himself to science and philosophy. He became a docent in Psychology at the University of Helsinki, but moved to Turku in 1921 to take a position as Professor of Philosophy. He subsequently returned to Helsinki in 1930 to a professorship in Philosophy. He became associated with members of the Vienna Circle and conducted empirical work in Vienna on infants' reactions to the human face. Kaila's research interests in brain and behavioural sciences led to the publication of *Persoonallisus* (*The Psychology of the Personality*), the book which, many years after its initial publication in Finnish in 1934, had an impact on Ingmar Bergman. (The book appeared in Swedish translation in 1935, and was first translated into Danish in 1946. There are no non-Scandinavian translations (see Takala 1992: 126). Page numbers given below are to the first edition of the Swedish translation, subsequent editions of which differ slightly from this as Kaila chose to present some of the material in a different order and also reworked a few passages.)

At the time of its appearance in 1934, Kaila's treatise was a sophisticated general overview of key topics in theoretical psychology. Kaila begins by presenting his basic methodological assumptions, then devotes a chapter to a survey of neurophysiological research and contemporary experimental research, critiquing behaviourist and 'mechanistic' trends. His third chapter, ' The Biology of Character', draws heavily on Ernst Kretschmer's doctrine of personality types and includes digressions on graphology and corporeal expression. Kaila then turns to the 'emergence' of spiritual life and underscores the importance of the 'symbolic function'. Chapter Five is devoted to 'Psychic Forces', whereas Chapter Six takes up the individual's bond to the group. Chapter Seven, 'The Dynamics of Needs', discusses motivations, whereas Chapters Eight and Nine are devoted respectively to 'The Totality of the Personality' and 'Animal and High Spiritual Life'. In his discussion of this wide array of topics, Kaila creatively blended elements from Gestalt psychology, psychoanalysis, experimental psychology, theoretical biology and systems theory, as well as the insights of various literary and philosophical authors, including Hobbes, Renan and La Rochefoucauld.

Kaila offers programmatic statements about the nature of psychological explanation as well as related, substantive claims about both human and animal psychology. To begin with the former, he perceives himself as exploring a *via media* between the Scylla of 'mechanistic' psychology and the Charybdis of 'intellectualism', and he suggests that both of these erroneous approaches share a single, underlying fallacy, which is the 'analytic' error of assuming that the living organism can be understood and explained in terms of the structure and function of its individual parts (1935: 86). Kaila contrasts to this approach the idea of a 'non-additive holistic' unit or system, both the functioning and development of which take the form of a top-down, 'synthetic' mode of organisation. This 'non-additive' mode of organisation goes unrecognised in behaviourism and in reductionist explanatory programmes; yet the intellectualist tradition similarly underestimates the complexity of 'neuropsychic' life and therefore vainly seeks to find a place for 'reason' in the body. Consciousness and the higher reasoning capacities are instead to be understood as the emergent features of complex, living organisms. Kaila finds the beginnings of a viable, holistic psychology in the theoretical and experimental work of Kurt Lewin and other Gestalt psychologists, such as David Katz, yet he also acknowledges the value of the 'life wisdom' expressed by both classic and contemporary literary authors. He finds key insights in Freud, Janet, Nietzsche and Schopenhauer, but he also underscores what he takes to be the limitations of their perspectives.

Kaila's central substantive thesis in psychology is his recurrent claim that there is only one effective psychic force, which he refers to using the Finnish word 'tarve'. This term is, like the Swedish 'behov', ambiguous, falling between the English words 'need' and 'desire'. In what follows I shall translate it as either 'want', 'need', or 'desire'. Kaila explains that he conceives of a want as a 'driving inner force in an organism' (1935: 21). Living systems have a tendency to move, or at least to attempt to move, from a state of disequilibrium to a preferred state of equilibrium, and a want or desire is a 'state of tension' corresponding to such a disequilibrium. To a given want corresponds a 'direction' or behavioural tendency, which targets a return to equilibrium. Kaila contends that wants are the key to the explanation and understanding of behaviour: 'Spiritual [and] animal life are dominated by wants' (1935: 12); 'All psychic life, all life processes are subjected to their pressure and must be understood with them as our point of departure' (1935: 22).

It is crucial to understand that Kaila is definitely not talking about what people literally *need*, as opposed to what they happen to want, desire or long for. Kaila's perspective is a biological one, and though he certainly wants to emphasise the basic appetites or needs, he also thinks it important to stress a far greater diversity of human impulses and desires. In fact, he has something to say about what he calls the 'spiritual' and 'high spiritual' needs, which often conflict with lower or more basic biological urges. Yet one term, translated as 'need', is meant to cover everything from basic hunger and thirst to someone's longing for expensive jewellery or a luxurious summer house.

Kaila summarises some of his main points about needs at the beginning of his chapter on the 'dynamics' of need. A need 'functions as a psychic vector having a pressure to which the entire psychic and nervous life is subjected' (1935: 286). Kaila goes on in the same context to say that any need-dominated behaviour is 'immediately meaningful' (ibid.) and identifies the teleological or goal-directed force of 'need' as the very source of meaning: if anything is meaningful, Kaila proclaims, it is the teleological nature of all organic processes (1935: 19). 'What is meaningful is, within a given whole, everything that satisfies the needs of that whole' (1935: 10). To understand something is to identify the need that determines it, and as such there can be no understanding, in this sense, of inanimate nature (ibid.). Kaila tends to stress the continuity between the basic modes of organisation to be found in all living forms, yet he also distinguishes broadly between different levels of needs and corresponding orders of meaning. Thus, amongst the needs and forces of life he marks off three sub-categories: 'animal needs', such as hunger and thirst; 'psychic needs', such as the individual organism's need to assert itself in the group; and 'spiritual needs', such as the need to respect oneself. Kaila also discusses what he labels as 'high spiritual' needs, which explain various forms of religiosity. The example he gives is the need to revere something or someone as holy, and he comments that for most people, the only path to such high spirituality] is eroticism or romantic love.

Citing the work of his Finnish colleague, Erik Ahlman, Kaila identifies what he calls the most basic conflict within the human personality: while there is a strong need to realise various spiritual and high spiritual ideals, these needs tend to come in conflict with, and hinder the satisfaction of, basic animal needs. And while the latter, lower drives tend to have the greatest force and so generally dominate the psychic system, the higher needs often govern consciousness, making it impossible for individuals to recognise the central conflict between their lower and higher impulses. As a result 'inauthenticity belongs of natural necessity to the human personality' (1935: 372). He explains that while people have direct awareness of many of their own psychic states and needs, they do not necessarily have any recognition or awareness of the systematic relations between distinct stretches of experience, nor of the crucial 'dependency relations' between experiences and behaviour. In Kaila's example, someone may admire and identify with another person and be thereby motivated to imitate that person, yet not be aware that this admiration is the source of the imitative behaviour, and thus remain oblivious to its imitative nature. And if it is the person's need to perceive himself as an autonomous, self-directed agent that prevents any such recognition, there is no motivation to bring this factor into awareness either (1935: 356).

Kaila's main theme, then, is the interaction between our needs, or drives, and everything else in the human psyche, such as our beliefs, reasonings and decisions. Inverting the rationalist conception of the mind, he focuses on the decisive influence of motivational forces on cognition and belief. One of his main preoccupations in this regard can be introduced by referring to the fable of the fox and the grapes, which Kaila discusses at several key points in his book. As the fable goes, when the fox cannot reach the grapes he wants he deludes himself into thinking they are sour. Kaila comments that by denying the value of something valuable yet unattainable, the creature is spared the negative feelings of humiliation and low self-esteem (1935: 15). Such a response is, he says, a good example of a reactive compensation creating inauthentic value (1935: 311). Kaila maintains that this sort of thing is quite common, and he adds that this and similar stories demonstrate that people have long known that conscious needs and motives 'only make up a small part of the forces that determine human conduct' (1935: 15).

Kaila's combined emphasis on motivational forces and the decisive functions of the unconscious mind could lead some to think that what Ingmar Bergman and others were likely to have found in Kaila's book was a primer in psychoanalytic doctrine, but this would be a serious misrepresentation of the situation. Kaila's emphasis on unconscious drives does recall Freud's claim to have brought about a 'Copernican' revolution in psychology precisely along these lines. Yet Kaila uses the same rhetoric of a Copernican revolution (which Freud had no doubt taken over from Kant) to evoke a different set of breakthrough principles, namely the above-mentioned idea of a non-additive holistic approach to living systems, and the idea that the meaningful content of psychic states is derived from their relation to need and its satisfaction (1935: 152). Kaila explicitly rejects Freudian orthodoxy, especially with regard to the thesis that developmental episodes and structures are decisive in the formation of the personality. Kaila also refuses to acknowledge Freud as the discoverer of 'the unconscious', and adds that whether a psychological factor is conscious or unconscious is not the key issue (1935: 11). The real force of a mental item is not a function of whether it is conscious or unconscious, and there is a distinction between having knowledge of a need and 'feeling' it (1935: 353). Kaila also believes there is a distinction to be drawn between experience and 'conscious experience'. He rejects Freud's overarching emphasis on sexuality, just as he rejects Nietzsche's emphasis on the 'will to power'. Kaila also contests Freud's central contentions about the interpretation of dreams, allowing that dreams can have an 'escape valve' function, but denying that their effective content is always latent, repressed and wishful. He accuses psychoanalysis more generally of accepting the mechanistic idea that habit and the association of ideas constitute genuine psychic forces.

Yet Kaila does claim to have found something of value in Freud's work, namely the adoption of a dynamic or energetic model in which psychological events are to be explained in terms of psychic energies or forces. However, what Kaila grants to psychoanalysis with one hand gets taken back with the other:

> The service done by psychoanalysis is in no way the 'discovery' of the 'psychic unconscious', but the *discovery of the dynamics of the life of the mind*, or in other words, the 'discovery' of the fact that needs are the only psychic forces – which fact we have always been perfectly aware of in our practical knowledge of ourselves and in our accumulated wisdom about life. (1935: 237–8)

In light of such two-handed remarks, it is hard to see how anyone who was excited by Kaila's book could have come away from it with the idea that psychoanalytic doctrine has any great importance, since according to Kaila, what is genuinely original and most characteristic in psychoanalysis is incorrect, while what is correct is not original.

Kaila believed it to be the task of a truly scientific and naturalistic psychology to discover the laws that govern the inner dynamics of psychic life, which would at bottom amount to a plotting of the systemic patterns whereby motivational forces arise and find an outlet or discharge through various types of behaviour. These laws would not, he proposes, be simple, and they would certainly not permit a reduction of the variety of human desires or needs to one underlying impulse. Kaila makes no systematic presentation of the laws of human motivation, but he does identify a number of piecemeal theses which he presents as offering deep insight into the human personality, or the mental life, construed as a biological life form tied to the central nervous system. In this vein he espouses what he relates, with no great rigour, as David Katz's 'law of avidity' (cf. Katz 1932). This is presented as an experimentally confirmed finding to the effect that human desires become harder and harder to satisfy with each new success, as the organism's internal standard of satisfaction tends to vary in light of the results obtained. In other words, if the fox is fortunate and can jump high enough to get hold of the grapes, they may be sweet the first time around, but later, new desires will arise and the fox will no longer be content to satisfy his hunger with such ordinary grapes. Eventually the fox will discover some new, attractive fruit that is well out of reach, and it may turn out that this encounter with an unattainable object of desire will lead to a new instance of 'sour grapes' irrationality.

Kaila does not write explicitly of human 'irrationality', yet many of the observations he makes regarding 'inner inauthenticity' should be recognised as discussions of such forms of motivated irrationality as wishful thinking and self-deception (see Mele 2004 for a contemporary survey). And indeed the human tendency to display such behaviour is an overarching theme of Kaila's book, which finds its most hyperbolic expression in such pronouncements as the following: 'Human thought is generally a matter of *wishful thinking*' (*önskedrömmande* – emphasis in original, here and in what follows) (1935: 293); 'One can say that human beings, and especially cultured human beings, have a natural *inclination to see life incorrectly*' (1935: 153); 'In general, human thought and representational processes are dominated by non-theoretical desires – thought is in general a matter of a wishful dream' (1935: 293).

One might be inclined to object at this point that such broad conclusions do not follow from the claim that motivational forces play an overarching role in the determination of human behaviour. And indeed, it may be added that one of the best ways to satisfy one's desires is to have a clear-headed and reasonably accurate belief about the best means to one's ends, and to act intentionally or deliberately in keeping with such beliefs. Or more bluntly, garden-variety rationality serves, rather than hinders, the business of desire satisfaction to which Kaila grants such importance. None of these points is lost on Kaila, yet he thinks the picture is more complicated, in two interrelated ways: (i) the satisfaction of desire is not only, and perhaps not even most often, brought about through rational, intentional action; (ii) human desires are often conflicting and incompatible, and hence not susceptible to a rational ordering and deliberate control. Another way to put Kaila's point here would be to say that actual human motivational dynamics do not correspond to the philosophical ideal of the practical syllogism, according to which desires and beliefs about the means to their satisfaction, rationally conjoin to entail decisions and corresponding intentions. (In keeping with the 'anxiety of influence', such a rationalistic model was precisely the sort of account advocated by Kaila's most successful student, Georg Henrik von Wright.)

With regard to the first 'complicating' point, which concerns the modes whereby needs get satisfied, Kaila places a great deal of emphasis on the processes whereby motivational forces tend, under certain circumstances, to bring about varied forms of 'surrogate' satisfaction or 'discharge'. Thus, if the object of a desire cannot be obtained, the psychic energy associated with it can shift onto a 'sufficiently analogous' representation or symbol, which then serves as a source of surrogate satisfaction.

Anger and a desire for revenge, for example, readily displace themselves onto surrogate objects, giving rise to such symptoms as scapegoating and the sadistic punishment of children. More generally, Kaila holds that the authoritarian and moralistic personality is a delusional mask serving aggressive impulses. Kaila summarises as follows: 'When the tension of a need is blocked and cannot be discharged in a natural manner, the discharge will take place by means of a detour' (1935: 227). Kaila illustrates this point with reference to both animal and human behaviour: a chimpanzee vents its anger at being punished on an innocent bystander; a man who cannot strike back at his abusive boss takes it out on his son. Kaila's discussion of 'surrogate reactions' and irrational desire satisfaction includes a description of the lifelong impact on a child whose nanny punished him by locking him inside a closet (1935: 306).

According to Kaila, the detours taken by need-generated tensions or motivational forces may be quite twisted. To revert to the fable of the fox, the frustrated animal may come to believe he has already eaten the grapes; or he may find consolation in the conviction that even better grapes will be his reward in heaven. Kaila proclaims repeatedly that the great cathedral of wishful thinking is religion; religion is a weak and pathetic after-effect and mode of surrogate satisfaction. In another form of motivated irrationality stressed by Kaila, the fox starts out wanting the grapes, but when he cannot get them, ends up trying to satisfy himself with some prunes instead, and may become convinced that this is what any sensible animal should want. The fox may even end up being deluded enough to believe that the prunes are the grapes. Or if the fox is terribly frustrated by his failure to get the grapes, he may turn and blame some innocent bystander. He might viciously punish someone else for even thinking about wanting to eat grapes. Clearly, in Kaila's view, the 'analogy' supportive of energetic transfers and discharges can be quite tenuous, and one may wonder whether the condition this notion was meant to express serves as any kind of constraint at all.

So much for a brief, initial presentation of aspects of Kaila's book. I shall return to other issues and developments below as their significance for Bergman's work becomes more apparent.

The influence hypothesis

What is there in Kaila's philosophy that could have been 'shattering' to the young Bergman? And what 'ground' could Kaila have offered Bergman to build upon? To answer these questions, we must focus on the extent to which Kaila's psychological doctrine subordinates thought and action to the shifting configurations of desire. For shorthand, we may refer to this as the thesis of the primacy of motivational force. What Kaila challenges in promoting this thesis is the Aristotelian conception of the human being as 'the rational animal' as well as the Enlightenment ideal of the autonomous, reasoning, self-directed person. Kaila contends, on the contrary, that thought and action are determined by motivational forces that tend to produce various forms of irrationality.

It is not difficult to see how the young Ingmar Bergman could have found such theorising at once shattering and persuasive. These ideas about irrational behaviour must have seemed to correspond quite well to important aspects of his own experience, such as childhood humiliations and ritualised punishments, his own powerful ambitions and sexual desires, and the insights expressed by such literary masters as Strindberg and Shakespeare (both of whom Bergman had staged several times in the theatre by then). Nor is it hard to find correlatives in Bergman's cinematic characterisations. For example, the characterisation and story in *Ur marionetternas liv* (*From the Life of the Marionettes*, 1980) can be seen to rest rather firmly on Kaila's foundations. Egerman, the male protagonist, is privileged, well-educated and articulate. At work in his office he appears as a controlled master of strategic rationality; yet somehow his marriage has become a deeply frustrating source of maddening conflict. He looks for and finds a surrogate outlet, and through some mysterious, unconscious mechanism, years of pent-up forces are unleashed in the murder of the scapegoat-prostitute. In fact, Bergman's artistic oeuvre manifests a life-long interest in, and condemnation of, scapegoating in both its spontaneous and ritual, ceremonial and artistic forms (see Livingston 1982; Blackwell, this volume).

Consider the characters in *Tystnaden* (*The Silence*, 1963), who are driven and derided by individual constellations of impulse and desire. The film may be interpreted as an allegorical unfolding of the conflict between body and soul, or to revert to Kaila's idiom, the struggle between lower and intellectual impulses. At the end of the film, the young boy learns to find surrogate satisfaction of his needs in the world of words, as a more immediate gratification is denied him by his mother. Many of Bergman's most successful and attractive characters are clearly in the grip of what Kaila describes as the law of avidity. Just think of the aristocratic characters in *Sommarnattens leende* (*Smiles of a Summer Night*, 1955), who want most what they cannot have.

Other connections between Kaila's comments and Bergman's characterisations and stories support the hypothesis of an even more direct influence on the young writer's search for ideas for psychologically probing and dramatically engaging scripts. Kaila devotes evocative paragraphs to what could be called the phenomenology of schizophrenia, and more generally to the ways in which mental illness can strongly influence both the perceptual and affective states of the subject. The very landscape takes on a new appearance, he remarks, and the patient experiences a world full of secrets, a world on the verge of collapse. Could Bergman have found here some motivation for his cinematic adaptation of a story about a schizophrenic in *Såsom i en spegel* (*Through a Glass Darkly*, 1960)? In this film, Harriet Andersson portrays a young schizophrenic who succumbs to terrifying hallucinations. Kaila contends that one of the best ways to gain insight into the workings of normal human personalities is to study cases where the psychic system malfunctions and breaks down. He discusses various mental disorders at some length, including cases where the most general sense of 'reality' is weakened to such an extent that the patient perceives her surroundings as a kind of theatrical set. Kaila elaborates on how such basic distinctions as dream/reality, image/thing and name/object can collapse. Another of Kaila's themes is the magical thinking characteristic of children and members of early cultural formations, whereby symbols and their referents are confounded. One thinks immediately in this regard of Bergman's *Ansiktet* (*The Magician/The Face*, 1958), a film in which the crone played by Naima Wifstrand easily casts her magic spell over the servants and children who interact with her in the kitchen. Yet the actions and characterisation in this film also correspond to Kaila's insistence on the idea that even the most civilised and modern personality can easily revert to primitive thinking when in the grip of affect. Kaila claims that the animistic tendency to mistake purely natural events for the workings of spirits can manifest itself when the rational, educated person experiences a crisis of sufficient magnitude, which is precisely what happens when Bergman's magician uses his best tricks to upset the rationalist Egerman in *The Magician*. Kaila contrasts animal sexuality to the high spiritual needs manifested in romantic eroticism, a contrast played out rather vividly in Bergman's characterisations in *Smiles of a Summer Night*. Just as Kaila compares human courtship with the displays put on by competing birds, so does Bergman instruct the coachman to strut about like a rooster as he chases after the servant girl.

Another passage in Kaila's book may well have provided inspiration for a script. I have in mind the pages devoted to an analysis of the social and motivational dynamics at work in a character's shifting states of awareness. Kaila's example is the conceited and self-deceived pastor depicted in a story by the Finnish writer, Juhani Aho. Bergman of course had his own independent motivation and ideas for writing the script for *Nattvardsgästerna* (*Winter Light/The Communicants*, 1963), yet these may have found reinforcement in Kaila's comments on a pastor's highly problematic relation to his own faith and that of the others.

To mention another possible influence, Kaila devotes a number of paragraphs to discussions of the various senses of the word 'persona'. He begins his book by questioning the value of a single-minded focus on the persona, where this is understood as a being having self-awareness. Kaila also takes up Schopenhauer's discussion of the rift between the persona and the genuine personality, or in other words, between the socially presented mask and the real self. It is the clown who in festive and theatrical events is allowed to strip away the persona or mask to reveal human inauthenticity, a gesture Bergman, who often aligned himself with bedraggled clowns and circus people, never seemed to tire of performing (see Livingston 1999).

Grappling with the issues

One might wonder whether these themes found in both Kaila and Bergman have more to do with psychopathology than philosophy. And we may also wonder whether such notions have much to do with anything more than the most schematic aspects of Bergman's stories and characterisations. So I now want to show how themes from Kaila indeed resonate strongly with more philosophical aspects of Bergman's cinema. I also want to show how these ideas can be related to Bergman's skilful employment of devices specific to the medium. I shall also discuss some ways in which Bergman can be understood as actively exploring the problems Kaila and his sources raise.

I shall begin with a famous philosophical moment in Bergman's films. I have in mind an episode in the Knight's game of chess with Death in *Det sjunde inseglet* (*The Seventh Seal*, 1957). Here the medieval knight, Antonius Block, sounds rather anachronistically like an existential philosopher: Why is God silent? How can life have meaning if there is no God? How can we go on living once we have recognised the absurdity of existence? Is the individual's meaningful project something that emerges through a Being towards Death? Like Descartes, the Knight wants certainty, not surmise. If he cannot argue himself into believing in the immortality of the soul, he wants to find reason to believe in a more local victory, such as a sacrifice that can give his life meaning.

One could go on in this vein, interpreting or overinterpreting the Knight's lines. Yet consider now the context in which they are spoken. The Knight has entered a church and is standing in front of what he takes to be the grated window of a confessional chamber. Speaking to a hooded figure mistaken for a priest, he confides that he has a secret strategy to try to trick Death. But then the Knight learns his error and realises he was talking to Death all along. Instead of being outside the game of chess, his confession is part of the competition, and he has fallen for his opponent's ploy. The Knight's error has already been visually signalled by Bergman, since both the iron grid between the Knight and the figure of Death, and the shadows cast by this grid, strikingly resemble a chess board, and the grid literally has the same eight-by-eight configuration of squares. Thus Bergman visually makes the point that what the Knight mistakes as a truce is in fact a continuation of the deadly game.

Consider how this scene can be interpreted in light of the themes from Kaila sketched above. Religion, including Antonius Block's quest for salvation, is just wishful thinking, the irrational domination of belief by desire. The Knight's every attempt to forestall Death and defeat is more of the same, since his apparently strategic moves are dictated by what he wants to believe, rather than by what is actually the case. No one will really escape the reaper, nor find the kind of theological anchoring for which the Knight longs. Instead of offering absolution, the ritual of confession is

Chess: a deadly game (photo: Louis Huch. © AB Svensk Filmindustri)

only another moment in the hopelessly irrational thinking in which the Knight is caught. The chessboard imagery thus contributes to a more general, anti-liturgical critique of the vain and violent institutional forms of what Kierkegaard called 'Christendom' (epitomised by witch burnings, processions of flagellants, hysterical doomsday speeches and so on). It would seem to follow that the Knight cannot in any way outwit Death or win even a small victory: his strategising is all just wishful thinking, need-driven fantasy.

This sounds very much like Kaila, yet here we encounter a point on which Bergman's work cannot be reliably interpreted as an unequivocal illustration of ideas found in Kaila. *The Seventh Seal* certainly invites, even if it does not command, a reading in which the Knight does win a modest but meaningful victory by distracting Death just long enough to allow Jof, Maria and their child to escape for a while. Perhaps the Knight's act of love really does make a difference; the Knight, at least, seems to believe this is the case. This interpretation could be amplified with reference to the Pauline, 'God is love' theme that constitutes a positive leitmotif in Bergman's corpus (see Lauder 1987 and 1989). Interestingly enough, Kaila also mentions St Paul's remarks on *agape*, but he describes this kind of 'high spirituality' as a product of sublimation, and essentially as a kind of 'insurance agency' that is wrongly thought to offer compensation for all of life's woes (1935: 379). Bergman's implicit stance in *The Seventh*

Confession as part of the game (photo: © AB Svensk Filmindustri)

Seal is not so resolute on this point. Instead, a consistent critical perspective on religious violence and greed implies a rejection of cruelty based on the moral sentiment of sympathy. The Kaila-inspired thought that cruelty too arises from someone's needs or desires does not prevent Bergman from systematically aligning the viewer against the victimisers and alongside the victims, a perfect example being the scene in which Jof is cruelly scapegoated by a frightened mob. There is an implicit moral perspective here, quite at odds with Kaila's call for a scientific worldview in which values are recognised as purely subjective (1935: 186–7). If you doubt this, just look at how the witch-burning scene is edited to align the spectator with the squire's sympathetic perspective on the witch. 'We see what she sees', the squire tells us.

The relevance of the 'Kaila connection' can be further developed by considering the oft-cited speech in *Persona* (1966) in which the doctor offers her analysis of Elisabet Vogler's situation. The doctor employs the idiom of existential phenomenology to describe Vogler's willful silence as a kind of philosophical project – a fantastic search for authentic Being. Vogler is diagnosed as suffering from a kind of 'ontological sickness', and the prognosis is that reality will eventually subvert what is at bottom an admirable but vain philosophical quest. Vogler seems bothered by the doctor's remarks, perhaps because they strike home. Bergman, we know, sometimes endorsed at least one of the doctor's lines; he commented, for example, in an inter-

Bergman, cinematographer Gunnar Fischer and actor Gunnar Björnstrand: on location for
The Seventh Seal (photo: Ingmar Bergman Foundation)

view: 'It is as the doctor in the film says, "Silence too is a role"' (in Samuels 1975:
111). More generally, this fascinating crisis in the life of the actress does not appear
to be the symptom of any ordinary physiological breakdown, but seems instead to
be the product of an anguished self-reflection, or even an acute, singularly modern,
quasi-philosophical form of lucidity: Vogler has become aware of the limitations of
various social roles, conventions and constraints. She sees the horror of the sacrificial

violence that pervades the political as well as the domestic sphere. As she reacts in horror to the scenes on the television set, we can hardly fault her for having an incorrect perspective.

Yet there is more to the story, of course, and here the Kaila connection may help us probe a bit deeper. Remember the primacy of motivational forces. Kaila would have us observe that the doctor's speech is not just pure theory arising entirely from a scientific standpoint but is the product of her own situation, background and desires. She needs to impress her prestigious patient and wants to couch her remarks in terms that are at once flattering, imposing, tough-minded, sympathetic and helpful. The doctor may or may not be aware that her high-minded commentary on the actress's situation mentions none of Vogler's more decisive, interpersonal and emotional problems, some of which appear to surface in the encounters with nurse Alma. Just before we see the doctor's encounter with Vogler, we were shown Vogler's irrational gesture of tearing the photograph of her child in two. Now one might say this is a banal gesture, yet it is significant that this is a kind of behaviour that Kaila actually mentions as a paradigmatic sort of irrationality, namely the more or less temporary failure to distinguish between a symbol and what it stands for. Kaila comments further that under some circumstances, people fail to relate to an image as an image, and instead engage in 'magic' thoughts and feelings about what the image depicts – a remark that might fruitfully be brought to bear on the sequence in which Vogler is shown contemplating events depicted in a Stroop Report picture. Like Fredericksen (2005), and unlike Ohlin (2005), I believe Vogler's contemplative and mournful response to the acts of cruelty depicted in this picture is to be understood in terms of her own problematic relationship to the role of motherhood, as is subsequently suggested in nurse Alma's 'doubled' monologue.

More generally, the point here is that it is one-sided to set Vogler up as the source of great existential lucidity. Since the actress is not talking, the doctor has no way of knowing what really motivates Vogler to interrupt her career and take a break at the clinic. Perhaps the doctor is projecting her own conception of the romantic, beautiful soul onto Vogler. The cinematic presentation is significant here. Bergman begins the sequence with a shot of Vogler alone, then cuts to a medium close-up of the doctor beginning her speech; then he directs the viewer's attention back to Vogler to capture her reaction, and finally cuts to shots framing the two, which serves to emphasise the interactive, relational dimension of the sequence. The diagnosis is not just about Vogler, then; it is spoken to her and arises in a particular, motivated relation to her.

Yet there is just a bit more to be said about the putative existentialist motivation of Vogler's crisis. Perhaps the doctor is misleading in describing Vogler's quest in such philosophical terms, yet we are led back in the same direction subsequently in the film when Alma spontaneously reads a passage about the meaning of life from what sounds like a high school philosophy primer. (To my knowledge, no one identifies the source of these lines. My guess, which has been seconded by Birgitta Steene in conversation, is that Bergman wrote them himself.) The lines that Alma reads, and which make Vogler sit up and take notice, run: 'All the anxiety we bear within us, our thwarted dreams, the incomprehensible cruelty, our fear of extinction, the painful insight into our earthly condition, have slowly eroded our hope in an otherworldly salvation. The howl of our faith and doubt against the darkness and silence is one of the most awful proofs of our abandonment, of our terrified, unuttered knowledge.' Alma asks Vogler whether she believes this is correct, and the response is a very unambiguous affirmative nod – a significant gesture for someone who is supposed to be trying not to communicate.

Here as well the cinematic rhetoric is quite significant. As Alma reads, we are shown a series of static, 'landscape' shots of the rocks on this stony beach; then there is a cut to Alma and then to Vogler's acknowledgement. These images seem to have been chosen so as to illustrate and thereby 'confirm' the propositions being read aloud by Alma (see the image above). Surely there is no humanly recognisable 'meaning' or 'comfort' to be found here in these mute rocks; no sympathy for our concerns, no promise of salvation, just the indifferent forces of nature. Are we to conclude that Vogler is right about this? Does she here implicitly and *correctly* endorse Kaila's statement that a 'scientific conception of the world is only possible to the extent that we are aware of the "subjectivity" of all values'(1935: 186–7)?

This question leads us directly to a central problem raised by Kaila's book. Whenever someone defends a theory saying that all thinking is distorted or irrational, one question should quickly come to mind. What are the implications for the theorist's own claims? If thought is just wishful thinking, fantasy or a form of substitute satisfaction for frustrated desires, what about philosophical thought? What about Kaila's own philosophy? Does consistency require him to allow that his own theorising is just wishful thinking too? And if that is so, why should anyone believe it? A thoroughgoing cynicism in philosophy is patently self-defeating, since it has to dethrone philosophy along with the ego and everything else (for repeated use of this venerable '*tu quoque*' argument, see Lewis 1969). Kaila does say that much of philosophy, such as Platonic metaphysics and Christian theology, is indeed an elaborate kind of fantasy. Yet Kaila wants to add that this does not mean that all philosophising has to be false. Objective, rational thought is possible, but such moments of lucidity only emerge in the relatively few cases where there is some drive compelling us in this direction, a drive that prevails over the non-theoretical desires that normally turn thinking into wishful thinking or some other form of motivated irrationality. Kaila remarks, then, that people engage in 'objective, factual, rational thinking only in the relatively few cases where they have a need to do so, for example, a genuine researcher doing scientific work' (1935: 293). And he comments that 'scientific knowledge of humanity only begins to make essential progress when the compulsion to paint a pretty picture of humanity gives way to a striving to achieve the naked truth', and here he credits the 'revelatory psychology' to be found in Schopenhauer and Nietzsche (1935: 23). Kaila adds some comments about the particular motives that allowed such figures to gain psychological insight – in Schopenhauer's case, a particularly bitter and powerful desire for recognition.

To couch Kaila's more general point here in terms of the fable of the fox, normally the fox does not observe the springs of irrationality operating in himself, though he may be quite lucid about their operation in others, provided that such lucidity sufficiently repays one of the fox's various desires, such as the desire to feel superior by contemplating the foibles of others. Another way in which people can become lucid, Kaila says, is by falling so short of social norms and ideals that they are forced to engage in painful reflection (1935: 371–2). Full lucidity is never acquired, Kaila adds, but life is in some cases a series of 'awakenings' in which light is shed on more and more aspects of one's life and situation (1935: 368). Such remarks make possible a better perspective on the story in *Persona*, as both nurse Alma and Elisabet Vogler are subject to painful moments of awareness motivated by the other's observation. Alma gains insight into both herself and the actress when she reads the letter in which the actress relates her thoughts about Alma; and at least some of Alma's subsequent statements about Vogler seem to strike home.

In short, the thesis of the primacy of motivational forces is not contradicted by the idea of an at least partial lucidity into the mainsprings of the human personality. Instead, different kinds of motivation are identified, including some that advance, rather than hinder, a cognitive exploration of the world. And this is a point that Bergman also explores in his own way. Consider in this regard some of Bergman's remarks about his own artistic activities. I have in mind, in particular, his 1965 Erasmus Prize reception essay, 'The Snakeskin'. The negative and critical thrust of the essay consists of a sweeping rejection of various traditional justifications for art. The only positive contention is the purely personal claim that Bergman's own artistic work finds its sole source in an innate curiosity: 'The reason is curiosity. An unbounded, never satisfied, continuously renewed, unbearable curiosity, which drives me forward, never leaves me in peace, and completely replaces my past hunger for fellowship.' A few lines later, Bergman adds: 'As a basis for artistic activity, during the next few years it is entirely adequate, at least for me' (1972: 14–15).

Bergman's manner of describing his curiosity squares neatly with Kaila's points by identifying a spontaneous drive or need as the sole basis for complex cognitive and artistic processes; at the same time, the specific nature of this 'drive' holds out some promise, since curiosity is an inclination that can lead one to try to find out how things really are, which could in turn give rise to some insightful or cognitively valuable work. Thus we have a kind of 'escape' clause that allows us to see how a cynical philosophy can avoid being self-defeating. Yes, all thinking is wishful thinking, as Kaila proclaims, but not all wishes are the same, and the quality of thoughts can vary with that of the wishes, or better, needs and desires, that determine them. Someone who is basically driven by curiosity may enjoy a kind of local lucidity that is not shared by someone whose ruling passion is vanity or sensual lust. Curiosity makes you observant, and coupled with the desire to record or capture what has been observed, leads to art-making impulses. And so we return to the issue with which we began, the connection between cinema and philosophy. If the philosopher's defining virtue is a love of wisdom, a sense of wonder and curiosity, in this respect he resembles the artist as Bergman describes himself, driven by a curiosity to seek to represent and express at least some fragments of our experience of the world.

To sum up, Bergman often follows Kaila in emphasising the primacy of motivational forces over reason, yet he is also motivated to affirm a basic cognitive value, namely the idea that it is better to recognise unpleasant facts or 'terrible truths' than to indulge in fantasy and wishful thinking. Bergman carries forward Kaila's affirmation of the epistemic value of fictions, creating works that help us explore the multiple tangles of human thought and passion, the underlying assumption being that this is a good, though often distressing, thing to do. Even the scientific perspective that Kaila wants to promote depends on this evaluative stance, and in Bergman's case, this first affirmation of the sway of value extends to a moral antipathy for violence and victimisation. Bergman certainly does not give us anything resembling a naïve return to Enlightenment myths, but nor does he present nihilism as the only alternative. He may or may not have been theoretically persuaded by Kaila's restatement of a positivist anti-realism about values, but it is clear that in his artistic practice, value and its various qualities are an immanent and ineliminable feature of experience, including the carefully valenced experience the director prepares for the spectator in the design of a film.

Author's note

The work described in this project was partially supported by a grant from the Research Grants Council of the Hong Kong Special Administrative Region, China. I am very grateful for this support. Many thanks also to Professor Bo Pettersson for help with Kaila's Finnish, and to Maaret Koskinen for helpful editorial comments.

References

Bergman, I. (1970 [1957]) *Wild Strawberries: a film by Ingmar Bergman*, trans. L. Malmström and D. Kushner. London: Lorrimer.

_____ (1972 [1965]) 'The Snakeskin', in *Persona and Shame*. New York: Grossman, 11–15.

Blackwell, M. J. (2008) 'Platforms and Beds: The Sexualisation of Space in Ingmar Bergman's Theatre and Film', in Maaret Koskinen (ed.) *Ingmar Bergman Revisited*. London and New York: Wallflower Press.

Fredericksen, D. (2005) *Bergman's Persona*. Poznan: Adam Mickiewicz University.

Gado, F. (1986) *The Passion of Ingmar Bergman*. Durham, NC: Duke University Press.

Kaila, E. (1935 [1934]) *Persoonallisuus*. Helsinki: Otava, trans. J. Gästrin. Personlighetens psykologi. Stockholm: Natur och Kultur.

Katz, D. (1932) *Hunger und Appetit: Untersuchung zur medizinischen Psychologie*. Leipzig: J. A. Barth.

Ketcham, C. B. (1986) *The Influence of Existentialism on Ingmar Bergman: An Analysis of the Theological Ideas Shaping a Filmmaker's Art*. Lewiston, NY: Edwin Mellen Press.

Lauder, R. E. (1987) 'Ingmar Bergman: The Filmmaker as Philosopher', *Philosophy and Theology*, 2, 44–56.

_____ (1989) *God, Death, Art, and Love: The Philosophical Vision of Ingmar Bergman*. New York: Paulist Press.

Lewis, C. I. (1969) *Values and Imperatives: Studies in Ethics*. Stanford: Stanford University Press.

Livingston, P. (1982) *Ingmar Bergman and the Rituals of Art*. Ithaca: Cornell University Press.

_____ (1999) 'Self-Reflexivity in Strindberg and Bergman', *TijdSchrift voor Skandinavistiek*, 20, 1, 35–43.

_____ (2005) *Art and Intention: A Philosophical Study*. Oxford: Oxford University Press.

_____ (2006) 'Theses on Cinema as Philosophy', *The Journal of Aesthetics and Art Criticism*, 64, 1, 1–8.

Mackie, J. L. (1977) *Ethics: Inventing Right and Wrong*. New York: Penguin.

Mele, A. R. (2004) 'Motivated Irrationality', in A. R. Mele and P. Rawling (eds) *The Oxford Handbook of Rationality*. Oxford: Oxford University Press, 240–56.

Michaels, Lloyd (ed.) (2000)* *Ingmar Bergman's Persona*. Cambridge: Cambridge University Press.

Ohlin, P. (2005) 'The Holocaust in Ingmar Bergman's *Persona*: The Instability of Imagery', *Scandinavian Studies*, 77, 2, 241–74.

Samuels, C. T. (1975) 'Ingmar Bergman: An Interview', in S. M. Kaminsky (ed.) *Ingmar Bergman: Essays in Criticism*. Oxford: Oxford University Press, 98–132.

Takala, M. (1992) 'Eino Kaila and the Psychology of Personality', *Acta Philosophica Fennica*, 52, 117–27.

Wollheim, R. (1980) 'Criticism as Retrieval', in *Art and its Objects*, second edition. Cambridge: Cambridge University Press, 185–204.

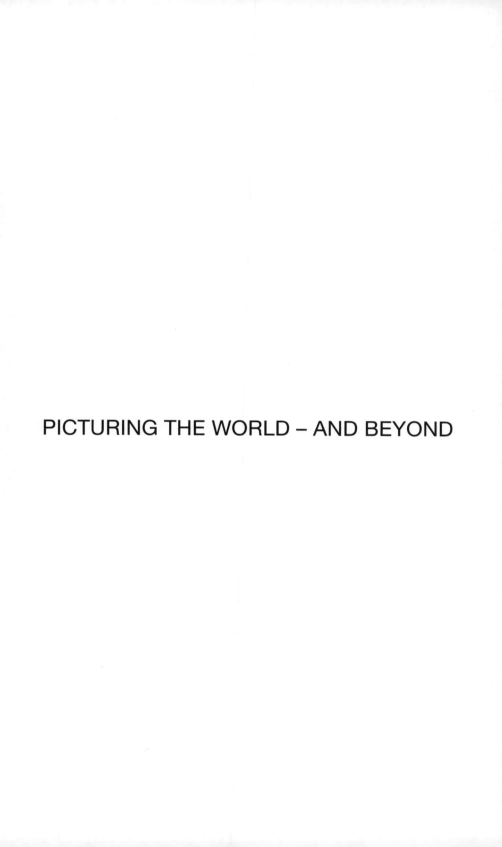

PICTURING THE WORLD – AND BEYOND

BERGMAN, NIETZSCHE AND HOLLYWOOD

John Orr

In his film memoir *Images: My Life in Film* (1995) Ingmar Bergman notes that Lorens Marmstedt, the independent producer whose company Terrafilm made many of his post-war pictures, told him during the shoot of *It Rains on our Love* (1946): 'Bear in mind that Birger Malmsten is no Jean Gabin and *most of all* that you're no Marcel Carné' (1995: 132; emphasis in original). It was advice shrewdly given and, in the long run, well taken. In the 1950s Bergman dispensed with Malmsten, his bohemian alter ego, as lead role and stopped making films like Carné altogether. It was not enough to go from one seedy room or bar to another or meditate glumly on one anguished tryst after another. Something more was needed to create pace and levity. To start with, many key characters became feisty, resilient women played by talented young actresses like Maj-Britt Nilsson in *Sommarlek* (*Illicit Interlude/Summer Interlude*, 1951) or Harriet Andersson in *Sommaren med Monika* (*Monika: The Story of a Bad Girl/Summer with Monika*, 1953). Likewise, the leaden interiors of drab studio sets gave way, bit by bit, to the summer light of the Stockholm archipelago. It was part of Bergman's new formula for dividing his directing talents according to the seasons: autumn and winter for the stage, late spring and early summer for shooting movies. The gloom of Nordic existentialism – a contradiction in terms since Bergman's films are nothing like Albert Camus, the French writer of the time he admired most – began to yield to a new lightness of touch, a new lyricism in the image. Partly inspired by neo-realism, its deeper aesthetic root, as Egil Törnqvist has noted, came when Bergman began to adapt Strindberg's stage concepts to the cinema. The playwright's modernist motif of a 'dream journey' shifting elliptically across space and time as it did in *To Damascus* and *A Dream Play* was transferred to Bergman's self-styled 'road movies' with a difference *Det sjunde inseglet* (*The Seventh Seal*, 1957) and *Smultronstället* (*Wild Strawberries*, 1957) (Törnqvist 1995: 123–4). Bergman then added in the 1960s a filmic version of the late Strindberg *Kammerspiel* – chamber play – to his new paradigm. The lightness of touch aligned to the radical shifting of space and time ushered in a bolder, deeper exploration of human existence. From *Såsom i en spegel* (*Through a Glass Darkly*, 1960) to *Höstsonaten* (*Autumn Sonata*, 1978) 18 years later,

Bergman's films for international audiences were now to be viewed as either dream journeys or intimate chronicles, or both.

At the same time Bergman admitted to popular American sources of inspiration that included Buster Keaton, film noir, Alfred Hitchcock and Michael Curtiz (see Bergman 1973: 29, 156; Cowie 1992: 92, 99, 111). The American connection makes it tempting to suggest that as well as the exit-routes offered by the summer archipelago and the challenge of Strindberg's dream journey two other avenues opened up, but not as self-consciously. They were antithetical sources that Bergman somehow absorbed into his artistic bloodstream. The first is the demonic, aristocratic Friedrich Nietzsche and the second, you could say, his complete antithesis in popular culture – classical Hollywood comedy. Through the latter we can also explore the uncanny connection between Bergman's reflexive glossing of the acting profession, or performing troupe, as plot-object in his middle period and two Hollywood classics that had earlier done the same – Ernst Lubitsch's *To Be or Not to Be* (1941) and Joseph Mankiewicz's *All About Eve* (1950).

Nietzsche and Hollywood are unlikely bedfellows, so let us start with Nietzsche first. The links between Nietzsche and Strindberg had been strong and, through their letter-writing, personal. As a deep admirer of one, it was clearly a challenge for Bergman to explore the other. His memoir *The Magic Lantern* mentions Nietzsche in passing with a list of other writers the teenage Bergman admired next to Strindberg (1988: 112). It may well have tied in with the inarticulate attractions of National Socialism discovered on his teenage exchange to Germany in 1934 – especially its open belligerence and its staged delirium. For both wayward philosopher and mass movement proclaimed a delirious and pagan aggressiveness, a lure, perhaps, for the young Bergman to escape the Lutheran straightjacket of childhood and adolescence. By the 1940s the young bohemian who now had left home to direct in the theatre led a double life in a different way. Enthralled by Strindberg and Nietzsche he also, as we have seen, had a love of Hollywood genre, thus of two opposite sources of attraction: an insane European genius (in fact, two of them) and a glitzy American culture industry. The puzzle now is how to piece together this odd synergy, where Bergman sources a particular kind of Nietzsche and a special form of Hollywood. Both feed into Bergman's emergent persona as a new kind of auteur, a driven, ruthless writer-director of original screenplays he brings alive through the collective art of filmmaking. In his landmark films like *The Seventh Seal* and *Persona* (1966), there results a strange and uncanny blending.

Bergman and Hollywood 1: role rotation and the comedy of remarriage

Bergman's 'shift' towards the feminine in the early 1950s may well have its theatrical roots in the dramas of Ibsen. Certainly the ending of *Summer with Monika* where

Monika abandons her young husband and infant child, has strong echoes of *A Doll's House*. In general, Bergman's cinema veered in the direction of Ibsen's vision of modern women and away from the sporadic misogyny of Strindberg and Nietzsche. Yet he did not produce Ibsen on-stage until 1957. Immediate inspiration for his 'women's pictures' of that decade lie elsewhere in key motifs Bergman translated into his own film language. The first is in what Stanley Cavell calls the 'comedy of remarriage', seen at its best in Frank Capra's *It Happened One Night* (1934) and Howard Hawks' *Bringing up Baby* (1939) or *His Girl Friday* (1941) (1981: 8–15); the second is its role rotation of 'performing' also to be found in *To Be or Not to Be* and *All About Eve*. At the same time Bergman used complex flashback in the style of *Citizen Kane* (1941), film noir and Mankiewicz's social dramas, much liked for their time-structure by the critics of *Cahiers du cinéma*, who also admired Bergman's 1950s cinema. *Kvinnors väntan* (*Secrets of Women/Waiting Women*, 1952) seems to have been inspired, three years later, by Mankiewicz's *A Letter to Three Wives* (1949). Beyond film there is a more harrowing role-reversal in the power conflicts of Strindberg's *Miss Julie*, one of Bergman's favourite plays. Yet for laughter on the same theme he turned to the remarriage comedy. Rotation is a source of farce and laughter in his films *before* it becomes emblematic of the dark side of modernity in the 1960s.

Cavell deemed remarriage comedy the key romance element in 1930s sound cinema, seeing it as a variant both of Shakespeare and of what Northrop Frye called 'Old Comedy', both forms highlighting a central heroine who undergoes rebirth by restoring a foundering intimacy against the odds (1981: 1–2). Cavell notes the creation of the New Woman persona of Katharine Hepburn or Rosalind Russell – feisty, determined, independent and above all equal protagonists to their male counterparts. Of course there are biographical add-ons. The tough-talking women of Hawks' films were said to be based on his stormy relationship with his wife Slim. Likewise Bergman's 1950s cinema is inflected by his tumultuous, short-lived relationships with a number of women, but especially that with third wife and top journalist Gun Grut (his 'Girl Friday'?) who worked with him on the screenplay of *Secrets of Women* and was in part the model for Marianne Erneman (Eva Dahlbeck) in *En lektion i kärlek* (*A Lesson in Love*, 1954) (see Cowie 1992: 93, 109, 120). The irony of the parting ways of life and art are clearly exposed. Unlike the endings of *A Lesson in Love* and *Sommarnattens leende* (*Smiles of a Summer Night*, 1955) Bergman's own intimacies involved, on his part at least, many betrayals and *no* 'remarriage'.

While these two films *are* bona fide comedies of 'remarriage', literal and metaphorical, that prompt the renaissance of intimacy long on the rocks, they remain so under duress. In *It Happened One Night, Bringing up Baby* and *His Girl Friday* impending marriages to a third party are called off at the last minute as our fractious couple sort themselves out. Yet the original marriage promise lingers as a threat (and a form of dramatic suspense) should the path of 'remarriage' prove too rough. Berg-

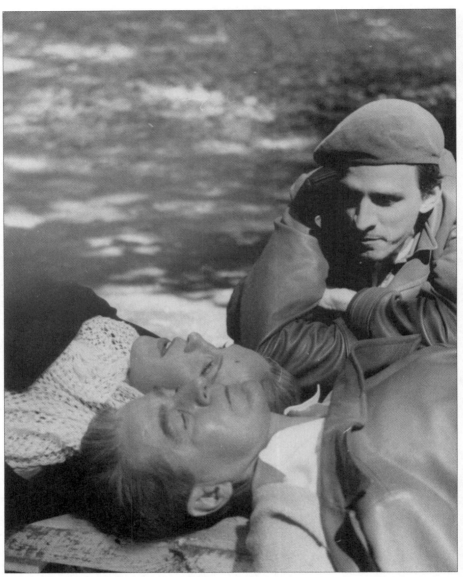

Bergman with Eva Dahlbeck and Gunnar Björnstrand: on location for *A Lesson in Love* (photo: Olle Björk)

man of course has his own variations on the theme. While Cary Grant was paired with Hepburn, Russell and with Irene Dunne in Leo McCarey's *The Awful Truth* (1937), Bergman relies on the trusty pairing of Gunnar Björnstrand with Eva Dahlbeck for *Secrets of Women*, *A Lesson in Love* and *Smiles of a Summer Night*. Not bound by the early Hollywood no-adultery clause, infidelity is close at hand in a variety of combinations. *A Lesson in Love* starts with gynaecologist David Erneman

Pratfalls and humiliations: Björnstrand in *Smiles of a Summer Night* (photo: © AB Svensk Filmindustri)

(Björnstrand) dumping client-mistress Susanne Verin (Yvonne Lombard), who had 'ruined' his marriage, with a view to seducing new clients only to encounter estranged spouse Marianne (Dahlbeck) unexpectedly on a train to Copenhagen. After much banter and recrimination, and a meeting with their teenage daughter Nix (Harriet Andersson), he resolves to snatch Marianne from the arms of her sculptor ex-fiancé Carl-Adam (Åke Grönberg) in a Copenhagen night club and start all over.

Bergman's turn-of-the-century drama *Smiles of a Summer Night* varies the options. It has a middle-aged Björnstrand, as Fredrick Egerman, snared into returning to his actress mistress Desiree (Dahlbeck), a metaphorical 'remarriage' while in a surprise trade-off his young second wife, Anne (Ulla Jacobsson) is entranced by his tortured Lutheran stepson Henrik (Björn Bjelvenstam) and runs off with him. Reconciliation of a married lover and his long-term mistress involves the unlikely loss of a virgin spouse to his unworldly stepson. Hollywood, you might argue, had allowed Bergman to step out of the shadow of Carl Theodor Dreyer by treating the dark family transgression of *Day of Wrath* (1943) as a comic *l'amour fou*. Yet Bergman is responding to near neighbour Dreyer in a way no Hollywood comedy would ever need to. His reshuffling of the Eros cards is sweetly provocative with its juxtaposition of libertine father and Lutheran son, sensual mistress and virgin second wife. Anne falls for her egocentric stepson while Egerman is ever humiliated in his jousts with Desiree's other slicker lover, the dandified Count played so brilliantly by Jarl Kulle. Like Cary Grant, Björnstrand takes his fair share of pratfalls with great aplomb but his character Egerman is genuinely debased by his loser's experience. Maybe Berg-man is updating Molière and Marivaux to the start of the twentieth century in his deft symmetrical shifting of intimacies: he also endows his sense of comedy with a spiritual abjectness that is more pronounced than in Hawks or Lubitsch, or for that matter in the films of Woody Allen for whom this was a key comedy of manners on which to base his Manhattan (and East Coast) cinema. In Bergman, humiliation is for real and lingers through the elegant acting-out of a perfect burlesque. It is a hu-miliation that never wavers or diminishes.

Infused with the abject, Bergman's comic spirit is allied more to resignation than romance in the remarriage scenario of his Björnstrand/Dahlbeck twosome. They are mature, worldly-wise beings and have lived long and fruitfully without the daily presence of the other before they reunite. Here, the second time around, there is none of the loving uncertainty of first encounters, but a knowing sense of human frailty and bemusement, perhaps, at the residual power of their (supressed) mutual dependency. It was a formula that gained audiences too. The contemporary flavour of *A Lesson in Love* made it a big hit in Sweden while Cannes recognition for *Smiles of a Summer Night* sent Bergman's name racing around the international film world. Comedy was thus the indispensable link in the financing chain which prompted Carl Anders Dymling to bankroll at long last an unlikely project called *The Seventh Seal* (see Bergman 1995: 234). In Bergman's case comedy was not only the *artistic* but also the *financial* source of tragedy. And while many would say the medieval epic is scarcely a bundle of laughs, humour does act as a vital counterpoint to his dark vi-sion of plague and death. It does so through the durability of the travelling players, the performing trio who act out entertainments from the back of their wagon in the midst of pandemic and chaos. This brings us to another kind of role rotation that Bergman would know not only from Hollywood pictures but also practically, from his growing experience in Swedish theatre: the very culture of performing becomes an indispensable plot-line for his film narratives.

Hollywood and role rotation 2: Bergman, Lubitsch and 'Nazi' theatricality

Lubtisch's comedy *To Be or Not to Be* is one of the most controversial of twentieth-century cinema; or if it is not, it ought to be. On the eve of the German invasion of Poland a group of Warsaw actors, fronted by Jack Benny and Carole Lombard, are performing a satire on Nazi militarism. Dressed in SS uniforms, they look at first to the spectator as if they are meant to be the real thing. Yet a sudden pullback to reveal the play's director and the proscenium arch of the stage upon which they are acting reveals it to be a *trompe l'oeil*. They are actors after all, mocking the enemy. But when the Germans invade Poland and the actors are pushed to help the Resistance, they put their skills of imitation and authentic stage costumes to more practical use. They 'become' Nazis to aid the escape of a special agent, so that in the confusion of the moment we no longer know when they are acting and when they are not, or at times who is who, the 'real' Nazis or their impersonators. In his study of Lubitsch, William Paul has put the result succinctly. Because their impersonation is successful and they pull off a dramatic rescue attempt for the Resistance, the tables are turned. The Nazi leadership of the occupation regard themselves as superior beings while as individuals the Polish actors often come across as laughable fools. On the other hand, when the acting troupe pulls together in its mimicking strategies the roles are reversed. It assumes the superior position as a group by making complete fools of the Nazi elite (1983: 241). Without the clear politics of Lubitsch this is exactly the dramatic strategy that Bergman uses to chart the perilous fate of his travelling performers in *Ansiktet* (*The Magician/The Face*, 1958), set in 1846. The Lubitsch film was controversial because although directed with unerring touch by a German émigré keen to rouse American support for the anti-Nazi cause, it ends as a feel-good Hollywood comedy praising Resistance sabotage: its sharp mockery seems credible *only before* the tragedy of the Warsaw Rising and the ineffable horror of the Final Solution. Its tone would appear flippant in retrospect, as the world came to know of such horrors. Yet its tone of effective mockery of evil has much in common with Brecht's satirical portrait of Hitler as a Chicago gangster in *The Resistible Rise of Arturo Ui* (1957): its sophisticated brand of casual derision remains daring and controversial to this day.

If he had seen this film in the post-war period – the odds are that he did – it could well have helped Bergman exorcise his Nazi demons. We shall never know, but there are strong traces of its composition and sensibility in *The Magician*. It translates into nineteenth-century Sweden the Lubitsch ploy of the 'under-group' (the performers) upstaging their 'super-group' protagonists (the political officials) who interrogate their methods and motives, even though as individuals the troupe's flaws and in-fighting are mercilessly exposed. In 1846 Stockholm Bergman's pompous officials are the fall-guys in a Flaubertian parody of the origins of the Swedish 'age of reason' with also, one suspects, a sly dig at the welfare state of his own time. The travelling players are the irrational Mesmerists offering displays of animal magnetism, their hypnotist-leader a bearded and (unusually) dark-haired Max von Sydow – Albert Emmanuel Vogler – about to be investigated for their possible 'offence' to enlightened reason by Dr Vergérus (Gunnar Björnstrand), a medical officer aided by Consul and Police Commissioner. Like *To Be or Not to Be* this is a comedy of errors and illusions; but there is a troubling darkness not to be found in the Lubitsch farce, a demonic edge in Bergman's match of the *ludic* with the *agonistic* – a sharp usage of Nietzschean aesthetics in itself – and in its eerie sense of menace as Vogler and Vergérus play out their mutual hostility. Perhaps we can see it as superior Lubitsch farce endowed with Nietzschean overlay in its play upon masks, which for Nietzsche were not the medium of idle masquerade but a necessary means of protection against elemental

Unusually dark haired: Max von Sydow (left) in *The Magician* (photo: © AB Svensk Filmindustri)

forces that threaten the fabric of civilisation. This is a theme to which Bergman re-turns with such devastating effect in *Persona* and Vogler's 'mask', his disguise of black wig and beard, looks forward to that film.

Emmanuel we might say is the distant ancestor of Elisabet, the thoroughly mod-ern actress of the later film, similarly mute and also a Vogler, a 'bird' or in Bergman's lexicon 'bird of prey'. The face of the magician when we first see it is uncanny. Von Sydow, the tall, gorgeous blond of *The Seventh Seal* is transformed by masking: now dark, mute and menacing. At first Bergman films his face partially, from different angles – first from the side, now obscured by his hand, now in extreme close-up that cuts his face off just below the lips. He is a figure of evasion. Critics have seen in his face, wig and beard a nineteenth-century effigy of Christ and in Bergman's story a version of the Passion with the jaded magician as a personification of the 'crucified one' persecuted by officialdom and yet rescued or 'resurrected' by the summons from the king to perform at the royal palace. Yet the uncanny artifice of the face and the piercing deadness of the eyes suggest something deeply different from the iconog-raphy of the Passion. Here we can fast forward to the opening montage of *Persona* where in his play on masks, Bergman alternates on the screen before the young boy close-up images of Bibi Andersson and Liv Ullmann to the point where it is impos-sible to identify the difference between them. Staring too closely at the mask of von

Sydow as Vogler can have a similar vertiginous effect, but here the doubling structure seems utterly outrageous. The trimness of the beard, the ultra-darkness of the hair flopping forward at the side of the forehead, the waxed delineation of the moustache all suggest a disturbing composite – Vogler's mask as an elision of absolute opposites, the features of Jesus and Hitler.

There may be a literary precedent for the spectre of the latter in Thomas Mann's story *Mario and the Magician* (1929). Set in a northern resort in fascist Italy, Mann's magician-hypnotist, Cipolla, who also specialises in humiliating members of his gullible audience, is a clear embodiment of the demonic spirit of fascism, Italian style, but his physical description is close to that of the emerging Hitler. The story's ending is tragic. Mario, a handsome local boy, is tricked by Cipolla into believing the hypnotist is his fiancée and kisses him passionately on the corner of the lips: awakening to his mistake, he becomes deranged, pulls out a pistol and shoots dead his tormentor. Like Vogler – but of course without the Christ-like beard – Cipolla also has top hat, waxen moustache and hair flopping forward at one side of his forehead. In Bergman's comedy there is likewise tragic subtext. Vogler hypnotises the muscular coachman Antonsson into believing he is bound by invisible chains. When eventually set free, Antonsson springs on his hated enemy and 'strangles' him. Afterwards distraught at committing 'murder', he hangs himself. Yet while the coachman's suicide is not faked, Vogler's death is, by the substitution of the corpse of his double Spegel, the actor, who has just expired. Here Mann and Bergman seem to converge – courtesy also of Doctors Caligari and Mabuse from the highpoints of Weimar cinema. But Bergman inhabits another world and another decade. His devaluation of values is more appropriate to a world he considers bereft of any true belief, even in the powers of magic and illusion. Vogler is a fake, like his face. Beneath it, he is a burnt-out case who believes in nothing, a nonentity, a hustler desperate for a handful of kronor. Bereft of performance, he gives his own answer to Hamlet's (and Lubitsch's) fateful question. He ceases to be. And that is his modern predicament.

Bergman and Nietzsche 1: The Knight with Death and Devil

In *The Birth of Tragedy* (1872) Nietzsche used a specific image to invoke Schopenhauer's heroic pessimism that was taken from Dürer's famous drawing 'the knight with devil and death ... the armoured knight with the stern cold gaze who can pursue his dreadful path undaunted by his ghastly companion, yet hopeless, alone with horse and hound...' (Safranski 2003: 332). In the conservative writing of Thomas Mann just after Germany's defeat in 1918, the knight would become a doomed romantic emblem of a pure German culture facing the predations of Western reason and 'civilisation'. Later in the Third Reich he would become someone more ominous, an emblem of racially pure Aryanism and then grotesque, given the face of Hitler in both Germanic drawings that extolled him and anti-fascist cartoons that mocked him. In the post-Nazi period Bergman gives us his own post-Nietzschean version of Dürer's knight facing death and devil in *The Seventh Seal*, an icon fully embodied on-screen by the tall, blond, Aryan-like figure of the 27-year-old Max von Sydow. This character Antonius Block, however, is no Dionysian figure we see before us. It is the solitary Knight returned from futile Crusade, the double defeat of body and soul etched into his melancholy face. Although Bergman's film credits the hooded Bengt Ekerot as Death the double description of the twin adversaries confronting Nietzsche's Knight seems more apt. Ruefully, Block philosophises about defying Death but in the confession sequence, where Ekerot, his chess opponent, masquerades as a priest to listen in on his tactics and thus destroy him, the hooded figure is clearly marked out as someone or some thing of demonic tendency. Yet the taboo on naming holds: the D---l does not appear in the credits.

The film has two remarkable coincidences with the chronology of Bergman's own life. The period of the Knight's absence at the Crusades, ten years, corresponds roughly to the period of Bergman's flirtation with National Socialism in 1934 and the end of the war when it all evaporated. Von Sydow's age when he played the part was also Bergman's age in 1945. Bergman's film, many years in its forming before shooting began in 1956, is not only a medieval anti-epic about Christianity in crisis made at a time when Hollywood started churning out biblical epics like *The Robe* (1953) in a new Cinemascope format; it could also be seen, as many audiences did in the late 1950s, as a veiled allegory of the Cold War and its deadly nuclear threat. But if this double reading was not enough, a triple one intrudes, superimposing on duality a third term. The homecoming of Block after ten long years, the defeated one now stripped of ideals, to a plague-afflicted Sweden obliquely mirrors Bergman's own predicament at the war's end: his former idealism in tatters as news of the Final Solution filters through, his clear sense that the war's legacy of destruction across Europe – though not neutral Sweden – had all been in vain, that all Politics was a Great Lie. In the post-war period his films made scant reference to this, a glancing exception the train journey through Germany in *Törst* (*Three Strange Loves/Thirst*, 1949) where the couple inside feed the remains of their picnic to the starving beggars with upraised hands gathered on the station platform outside. Only with *Skammen* (*Shame/The Shame*) in 1968 does he envision a controversial past, screening a passage of virtual history in which Sweden has been unexpectedly invaded, its distinctive 'neutrality complex', to use a term adopted by Jörn Donner (1972: 10), put severely to the test, its inhabitants forced to choose between fleeing, resisting or collaborating.

The Seventh Seal is hence enigmatic, certainly no fable of manly courage in the Hollywood idiom. Yet it is post-Nietzschean too since the Knight is no longer an emblem of *metaphysical* courage against the odds but a haunted loser who has made a big, big mistake. The medieval *Übermensch* undergoes burn-out and images of the crucified take over. Yet in his continuing quest to break open the seventh seal and discover the secret of life, there is a residual fanaticism, a fanaticism without substance. The Knight's journey is a life precarious amidst death and ruin which he barely notices, a theme Hollywood could never touch: at best his damaged life is a last recovery of faith's bare remnants amidst the debris of shattered belief. The terms of disenchantment are severe. As Jöns, his cynical squire remarks: 'Our crusade was so stupid, only an idealist could invent it.' Embedded here in this double reading is Western Christianity's double nadir, the primary one that of medieval Catholicism promoting murderous invasion of the Holy Land, the secondary one that of a pious Lutheranism hitching its wagon to the Nazi juggernaut that was even more destructive, out-of-control and catastrophic. And yet Bergman counterbalances Christian nemesis, its desperate flagellants, dead souls and effigies of an ever-suffering Christ with the humour and resilience of his travelling players Jof (Nils Poppe) and Mia (Bibi Andersson) – a ludic riposte to all deathly metaphysics. At first their modest song and dance performance is upstaged by the flagellant procession, their audience quickly diverted to a more forbidding spectacle, the mortification of the flesh designed to exorcise the perils of the plague. But in the end they are the survivors while Raval, the flagellant's villainous leader, dies a horrible death from the disease.

Here Bergman's ingenious use of *mise-en-scène* is both Hollywood and not-Hollywood at the same time. The 'upstaging' of the players by the flagellants starts off as a superb piece of melodramatic suspense in which the spectator's gaze is guided to the reverse-angle cut revealing the source of the new commotion by the sudden apprehension on Mia's face. Thereafter, however, Bergman denies us the comfort of such mediation. There are no more point-of-view shots from the players as the procession assumed a momentum of its own and *mise-en-scène* moves into objective mode with its fragmented montage. Similarly the comeuppance of Raval seems at first like a smart Hollywood device to punish the wicked, yet Bergman's *mise-en-scène* deliberately frames the separation of Raval from the Knight's entourage by a fallen tree trunk spread horizontally across the screen. In his agony the dying man retreats even further away and his deathly convulsions are encompassed by a single long shot of his distant body in the forest, his figure framed by a beam of sunlight. The technique is pitiless. There are no close shots to encourage spectator satisfaction with his agony, or alternately, pity. And yet beyond this comeuppance there is something else too...

Early in the picture, Jof's waking vision of the Virgin and Child in the nearby field is an angelic vision that Mia mocks on Jof's telling, just as Block's seashore vision of Death in monk's robes is dark and diabolic but one his sceptical squire would loudly deride. Yet vision and mockery go hand in glove, and play off each other in contrapuntal form, twice over. For this is a film in which Bergman's angels and devils *do* contest each another to the end. Both win – and lose. At twilight, the grim reaper leads the Knight's entourage in silhouette across the brow of the distant hill.

Yet watching, Jof and Mia (Joseph and Mary?) and baby Mikael (the Saviour?) survive. Is this the nexus of the Second Coming? Earthbound – human and not divine? For Jof's vision could indeed have been a dawn hallucination of his own wife and son as icons of salvation, a rebirth amidst the humble and the dispossessed, an eternally recurrent beacon of hope.

As Jacques Aumont points out, Jof is the one who abounds in Grace yet has no sense of its meaning. By contrast, Block consciously and compulsively seeks it out yet never finds it (2003: 100). If anything *The Seventh Seal* shows up Bergman's affinity with Nietzsche but also the latter's limitations. Both were prodigal sons of Protestant pastors disavowing their devout past, both psychosomatic and morbidly sensitive. For Nietzsche, writing and the play of language was a deep physical act that impacted directly on the body and its fragile constitution (see Safranski 2003: 180). For Bergman the strenuous act of filming and thus translating language into moving image was equally visceral. Both had their breakdowns, and relentlessly both persisted. Yet Bergman also avoided Nietzsche's final insanity, perhaps by refusing the atheistic certainty of the Death of God and replacing it with something he first cues in here, the agonising uncertainty of God's silence, his withdrawal from the world and its catastrophes, which then become a force-field left to angels and devils, with the latter, it seems, at a clear advantage. Nietzsche's Dionysus, by comparison, seems skin-deep by being made devoid of demons, as if the philosopher, pitching for recurrent affirmation, was agonisingly in denial. We can note a further departure from Nietzsche. Bergman was no pure Dionysian for the simple reason that in *Twilight of the Idols* Apollonian was the mode of the visual artist, Dionysus the muse and medium of language and music (Nietzsche 1990: 84). A multi-talented Bergman combines the Apollonian and Dionysian, sabotaging the dichotomy, an intermedial artist with powerful eye and strong musical ear; in short, a visionary open to the suggestiveness of all emotions.

The austerity of Bergman's film does, however, suggest something of convergence, an Old Testament iconophobia he shares with Nietzsche – the hatred of idols and of representation of the divine. In Bergman's cinema visual forms of God are subjective and grotesque, like the spider Karin sees in *Through a Glass Darkly*. At the same time the figure of Christ is reduced to the suffering figure of the Passion, no longer a source of redemption or of compassion. This explains the particular hue of *The Antichrist* (1895) where Nietzsche preserves the word-image of 'the crucified' yet demolishes the preaching of the Gospels – pity, mercy, compassion, sacrifice and divine resurrection – in short everything associated with the lives of the Nazarene prophet and his disciples. It is a demolition that may well have rebounded upon him and taken his own sanity. Bergman, by comparison, seems more complex. The Nietzschean renunciation of pity as a mask that conceals cruel and naked conflict is seductive to his demonic, aggressive nature. Yet in his cinema it rebounds upon itself *in a fruitful way*: and in this film it is finally defeated. Many of Bergman's later films also start off with Nietzschean premises but they end up salvaging compassion out of the mechanics of cruelty. Krzysztov Kieślowski has said of the scene in *Tystnaden* (*The Silence*, 1963) for example, where Anna humiliates her sister Ester by sleeping openly with the waiter she has picked up from a bar in the foreign city, that she laughs because she hates her but then, suddenly and unexpectedly, cries because deep down she loves her (2000: 423). In Bergman's greatest films, love and hate are finally inseparable, and locked in stalemate.

Thankfully, as philosopher, Nietzsche has more to offer us than the flayed despair of *The Antichrist*. His attraction for many twentieth-century artists lay in his vision of artistic energy, its constantly innovating powers, of the artwork as a thing so utterly personal and yet so utterly impersonal its vitality is almost out of control: having no rational goals it encounters no civilisational limits. This is a different Nietzsche but one that to Bergman is equally important. If anything, therefore, Bergman was a practical Nietzschean charged with a special kind of impulsion – the will-to-art, an impulsion based around the transformation of energy into cinematic signs. This is, and never was, a humanist enterprise. Artists are often lonely, driven figures, their lives an artistic production in which they exploit power over others without scruple. Working through the medium of film, which is not strictly 'Dionysian' of course, Bergman would never attempt to match the musical homage to Nietzsche of Strauss or Mahler, and it is significant that the Nietzschean anti-hero of Mann's *Doktor Faustus* (1947) is the modernist composer, Adrian Leverkuhn. But as a film director Bergman took Nietzschean aesthetics out of the isolation of Sils Maria, Nietzsche's cul-de-sac in the clouds, and transformed into an eternally repeating but *collective* moment in the world below. In producing film, you work collectively and insofar as you work for yourself you work for the other members of the collective. Bergman was aggressive, authoritarian and democratic at the same time. The realisation of his own vision, the maximisation of his own talent depended on maximising the talent of others around him. He produced insofar as they did: the act of collaboration was central and decisive. A true sign of auteurship is this flair for deadly collaboration, of producing the best out of oneself by drawing out the best in others.

The Nietzschean 'impulsion', to use Pierre Klossowski's term, that is at the core of all human energies including the will-to-power in all its forms, is highly personal and impersonal at the same time (see Klossowski 2005: 36–7). It is a vision of the will-to-art that surfaces critically during the height of Bergman's demonic modernism in *Persona* and *Vargtimmen* (*Hour of the Wolf*, 1968). At that time Godard, impressed by the powers of invention in *Persona*, remarked in *Cahiers du cinéma* that the Swedish director had reached the stage 'where the film is created by the camera, suppressing anything that's not the image' (1986: 298). After interviewing Bergman about *Hour of the Wolf* in the same journal Jean-Louis Comolli went further in

The artist … (photo: © AB Svensk Filmindustri)

claiming the film had run away with itself, 'as if from the very first shot [it] has a life and force of its own' (1986: 315). This anthropomorphic position prompted him to state that in *Persona* the film shows it is in pain by cracking up halfway through the story and that in *Hour of the Wolf* the film, set in motion reflexively by the word 'roll' to kick-start Elisabet's 'confession to camera goes back to the credits two thirds of the way through not to jolt the viewer awake but to demonstrate its secret logic of auto-projection' (ibid.). Comolli perches perilously here on the edge of a metaphysics that pronounces the death of the auteur and the birth of the cinematic machine. The irony here might be that Bergman, the supreme auteur of his generation, inadvertently set up the delusion of auteur-extinction that drove 15 years of film criticism up a blind alley. And yet the kernel of what Godard and Comolli say *is true*. Both of these films have a life-force that seems to propel them of their own volition, independently of their director.

Bergman's pragmatic response to Stig Björkman at the time offers a fascinating gloss on the Nietzschean question. He claims that Johan Borg's view of the artist in *Hour of the Wolf* as one of the elect is not romantic but is inseparable from his own torment, a spiritual torment that finds its material analogue in his excruciating toothache, since both are inescapable (Bergman 1973: 219)! Borg and toothache: Nietzsche and syphilis? As played by von Sydow, Borg the painter may well be a Bergman-Nietzsche composite who succumbs to his own demons, not because he

... and his demons: Max von Sydow in *Hour of the Wolf* (photo: © AB Svensk Filmindustri)

knows he is specially gifted but because the gift runs through and beyond his control. At its best it takes possession of him and uses him as its material instrument: at its worst, it deserts him. The film then is about Borg's manic fear of loss of control, of his mind and work reduced to a pure force-field for demons that prey upon him. It is no wonder that Bergman, admitting his aggressive nature as auteur, sees in film a medium by which that aggression is transmuted into object, a medium perfect for the ritualisation of violence (1973: 227). That, after all, is embodied in the title of his lacerating television drama of ritual humiliation *Riten* (*The Ritual/The Rite*, 1969), shot in the following year. Here Judge Abrahamsson (Erik Hell), pseudo-beacon of Social Democratic enlightenment, is a shifting signifier of rational domination interrogating an evasive squabbling performance troupe about their on-stage pornography, tax evasion and skeletons in the cupboard. When the 'servant' of enlightenment suddenly turns monster and rapes actress Thea Winkelmann (Ingrid Thulin), the troupe pulls together and plans its deadly performance of revenge, a pagan rite that kills off their pseudo-rational enemy.

Unlikely merger: *Persona*, Nietzsche and *All About Eve*

The commanding performances of von Sydow in *The Seventh Seal*, *The Magician* and *Hour of the Wolf* are subtle variations within an *aristo* triptych – Knight, Magician,

Artist – stages of disintegration in the myth of a Nietzschean nobility. To Nietzsche's question 'What is noble?' posed in *Beyond Good and Evil* (1885) Bergman gives a post-Nietzschean answer: paranoia, subterfuge and silence. Meanwhile the other Vogler, Elisabet, offers a very different kind of variation in *Persona*. As star actress mentally afflicted, she ritually embodies aristocratic revenge upon the humble nurse appointed to care for her during her breakdown. Her first appearance on-stage as Electra, heavily made up, her face for the world a painted mask, is a clear signifier. Her father is dead, her dynasty in ruins, but the noble grieving Electra must plan revenge on its destroyers. The enormity of the role seems to psych out the actress: Elisabet's face creases into an enigmatic smile and she becomes mute. Instead of acting out the nobility of revenge in Greek tragedy, she tries for something on a different scale, a whimsical revenge on an unknown, humble servant of the welfare state, a hospital sister dubious about caring for her celebrity patient on a remote island. The doctor who dispatches nurse Alma with her patient to her distant summer house, is a higher servant of the welfare state, expert on psychic malaise, maestro of the cause-'n'-cure syndrome that tries to bring back the spiritually dead from the poisons of unreason. Yet she exudes in the brief scenes where she separately briefs the two women, a menacing, satanic air. Officially promoting care and cure she is unleashing beneath the mask of pity, unequal combat between actress and nurse, a disguised cameo of Nietzschean class struggle from above into which at her veiled suggestion Elisabet enters with devious relish as a mute, performing vampire.

Intentionally or not the film's *fabula* reverses the narrative progression Mankiewicz's earlier film of theatrical usurpation, *All About Eve* (which won six Academy Awards in 1950). Here story-line is conventional and clear-cut. Bette Davis plays a celebrity idol Margot Channing whose Broadway stardom is undermined by her upstart admirer Eve Harrington (Anne Baxter). Eve is mousy, silent, self-effacing and seemingly reverential. She is often photographed at the edges of the frame, stressing the contrast with the garrulous theatre circles that Margot dominates. As opposed to Margot's fashion glamour, she wears a tight-fitting coat and tiny hat, dowdy in the extreme. Yet her progression from servant to understudy and finally to leading player who usurps Margot's star role reveals her modesty to be a subtle, studied performance. Of course we never see her 'acting' in rehearsal or in performance, because she is 'acting' in her daily life. Yet Mankiewicz performs a chilling *volte-face* when we see her near the end for the one and only time, in her dressing-room after a star performance: she is now heavily made up, ostentatiously glamorous, exotically dressed in the costume that was once Margot's own. She has appropriated the role of the theatre aristocrat, a ruthless upstart who has risen without trace. Mankiewicz's film thus deconstructs the rags-to-riches story that often lies at the heart of the musical romance in Hollywood genre, for this has a genuine sting in its tale.

Bergman's film could well be a sequel that transforms the style utterly. It reverses and fractures the earlier narrative while retaining the motif of usurpation, and physical resemblance in the two films is uncanny. The single shot of Eve in stage costume is echoed in the single shot of Elisabet as Electra. The dowdy outfit of the devoted servant is echoed in the austere uniform of nurse Alma. Yet instead of the upstart usurping the celebrity we have the opposite, the aristocratic actress devouring her career, the revenge of the strong (through faking weakness and silence) upon the weak, talkative servant. While the American melodrama has a clear-cut resolution, Bergman's fractured narrative gives us anything but and its enigma still reverberates through the history of cinema. But finally when the two women who had seemed to merge their persona go their separate ways, the ending is a stalemate in which nobody 'wins'. The strong no longer overcome the weak, because the weak fight back and cruelty cannot overcome compassion. Both women are bruised and bloody, at times literally. And so is Bergman's audience, torn apart, their hearts ripped out by the harrowing spectacle of a damaged relationship involving two solitary women, as if this single pinpoint exchange encompassed a whole world.

References

Aumont, J. (2003) *Ingmar Bergman*. Paris: Cahiers du cinéma.

Bergman, I. (1988) *The Magic Lantern: An Autobiography*, trans. J. Tate. London: Penguin

_____ (1995) *Images: My Life in Film*. London: Faber & Faber.

Björkman, S, T. Manns and J. Sima (1973) *Bergman on Bergman: Interviews with Ingmar Bergman*, trans. P. B. Austin. London: Secker & Warburg.

Cavell, S. (1981) *Pursuits of Happiness: the Hollywood Comedy of Remarriage*. Cambridge, Mass: Harvard University Press.

Comolli, J.-L. (1986 [1968]) 'Postscript: *Hour of the Wolf*, in J. Hillier (ed.) *Cahiers du cinéma Volume 2: 1960–1968*. London: Routledge, 313–18.

Cowie, P. (1992) *Ingmar Bergman: A Critical Biography*. London: Andre Deutsch.

Donner, J. (1972) *The Films of Ingmar Bergman*, trans. H. Lundbergh. New York: Dover Publications.

Godard, J.-L. (1986 [1967]) 'Struggling on Two Fronts: Godard in Interview', in J. Hiller (ed.) *Cahiers du cinéma Volume 2: 1960–1968*. London: Routledge, 294–8.

Kieślowski, K. (2000) 'Bergman's Silence', trans. P. Coates, in J. Orr and O. Taxidou (eds) *Post-war Cinema and Modernity: A Film Reader*. Edinburgh: Edinburgh University Press, 422–5.

Klossowski, P. (2005) *Nietzsche and the Vicious Circle*, trans. D. W. Smith. London: Continuum.

Mann, T. (1975 [1929]) *Mario and the Magician and Other Stories*. London: Penguin.

Nietzsche, F. (1990) *Twilight of the Idols/The Anti-Christ*, trans. R. J. Hollingdale. London: Penguin Classics.

_____ (1999) *The Birth of Tragedy and Other Writings*. Cambridge: Cambridge University Press.

_____ (2002) *Beyond Good and Evil: Prelude to a Philosophy of the Future*. Cambridge: Cambridge University Press.

Paul, W. (1983) *Ernst Lubitsch's American Comedy*. New York: Columbia University Press.

Safranski, R. (2003) *Nietzsche: A Philosophical Biography*, trans. S. Frisch. London: Granta.

Törnqvist, E. (1995) *Between Stage and Screen: Ingmar Bergman Directs*. Amsterdam: Amsterdam University Press.

INGMAR BERGMAN'S *THE SERPENT'S EGG*: REFLECTIONS OF REFLECTIONS ON RETRO-FASHION

Thomas Elsaesser

This chapter locates Ingmar Bergman's contribution and response to the so-called 'retro-fashion' of historical films made during the 1970s by many notable directors all over Europe (among them Luchino Visconti, Bernardo Bertolucci, Pier Paolo Pasolini, François Truffaut, Louis Malle, Joseph Losey, Rainer Werner Fassbinder and Volker Schlöndorff). They invariably deal with the phenomenon of fascism and Nazism, but unlike the first post-war 'rubble films' of Italian Neo-realism and its national variants in France or Germany, these films of the 1970s approach Europe's troubled past across showbusiness, the mode of spectacle and excess, or of sexual perversion. In Bergman's case, this resulted in one of his most expensive but least loved films, either by the critics or apparently by himself.

I will thus take a doubly reflected look at a number of complexes in the representation of history in film, in order to indicate how one might extend, displace or simply re-affirm some of the dominant auteurist and aesthetic approaches to the work of Ingmar Bergman. In particular, I hope to use Bergman's *Ormens ägg* (*The Serpent's Egg*, 1977) as a lens across which to discuss several issues in European cinema. In the process, I also try to test a more theoretical proposition, which has to do with the cinema's relation to memory, both collective and individual, as well as suggest a kind of epistemic break also occurring in the 1970s, and refiguring the 'value relation' between Europe and America, itself such a crucial aspect of the auteurist cinema's self-definition and thus central also to Bergman's work.

Texts, sub-texts, intertexts

The Serpent's Egg, made in Munich in 1976 during Bergman's five-year exile outside Sweden, was one of several films the director had contracted with the Italian producer Dino De Laurentiis, who wanted to use Bergman's extraordinary international reputation in order to break into the American market, with a number of films made in English and featuring at least one international star or American actor. After a few false starts, Bergman eventually hired David Carradine to play Abel Rosenberg, an American trapeze artist stranded in Berlin in November 1923 together with his brother Max and Max's estranged wife, Manuela, played by Liv Ullmann. After the suicide of Max, Abel drifts through the city, which is in the grip of hunger, cold, rain and hyper-inflation, recklessly spending the hard-currency dollars his brother had stashed away. Suspected of involvement in a series of murders and suicides, Abel is summoned several times by the police commissar Bauer, but also meets a former acquaintance, now having a sexual relation with Manuela. This acquaintance, a Dr Hans Vergérus, runs a clinic, and is also in charge of a series of experiments for which he recruits unemployed and destitute men and women of Berlin, several of whom die as a consequence. When Manuela, too, seems to have been killed or has committed suicide, Abel challenges Vergérus, who, sensing his game to be up, explains his vision of the future and commits suicide in front of Abel. Bauer returns Abel's papers to him and tells him that he has to leave for Switzerland, where his former circus employer is willing to give him work. But Abel escapes into the Berlin night.

As noted *The Serpent's Egg* became Bergman's most costly failure, and was universally condemned by the critics for its melodramatic and improbable story, its bad acting, poor dialogue and superficial characterisation of the central protagonist. Bergman, too, did not seem to appreciate the film – although, as I shall try and argue, the director was in fact more ambivalent about *The Serpent's Egg* than the wholly negative evaluation that he gives in *The Magic Lantern* (1988) would suggest. Be this as it may, I think it is time to give *The Serpent's Egg* another look, and this from a number of possible vantage-points. I shall mention a few that have struck me, but will then concentrate on one in particular. First of all, *The Serpent's Egg* clearly has a rich cinematic intertext, with allusions to a host of films, but also commenting more subtly on the conditions of production in Munich's Bavaria Studios, where Bergman made the film. For instance, one is tempted to read the film allegorically, coming as it does at a point of personal crisis for Bergman, so that the obsessive mention in the film of worthless money, plus the fetish importance given in the story to the dollar, nicely symbolises Bergman's own position between the threat of huge tax repayment and the well-stuffed wallet of Dino De Laurentiis, who in the film would be Hollinger, the circus owner anxious to hire Abel, and who gives him all the German money he, Hollinger, no longer needs, since he is leaving for Switzerland, the country at the root of Bergman's tax troubles.

Also, even without tracing the film's three main character constellation of dependency, jealousy and sexual humiliation back to Bergman's own cinematic universe (*Gycklarnas afton* (*The Naked Night/Sawdust and Tinsel*, 1953); *Ansiktet* (*The Magician/The Face*, 1958); *Riten* (*The Ritual/The Rite*, 1969) and many others), there are a number of motifs that seem worth reconsidering. The elaborate apparatus of

Bergmannstrasse at Bavaria Studios (photo: Rialto Film Gmbh, Berlin)

surveillance, installed by Vergérus to spy on his patients and subsequently on Abel and Manuela evoke Fritz Lang's *The Testament of Dr Mabuse* (1933), while the manner of his death is adapted from Michael Powell's *Peeping Tom* (1960). The Piranesi-like corridors in the clinic and the prison cell at the police station cite Lang's *Spione* (*Spies*, 1928), but surveillance also makes allusion to the situation in West Germany at the time Bergman had exiled himself there, in 1976–77, the years at the height of the Red Army Faction's acts of terrorism, and the state's response in the form of state-of-emergency measures (briefly) imposed by the Bonn Government. There are thus several topical interests in play.

The pervasive sense of surveillance and paranoia puts in stark relief another key theme of the film – that of (monetary) inflation as a metaphor for the suspension of all other values, ushering in a black market of humanist principles, as well as the nihilist reversibility of moral stances and choices. The black market theme was very much also among Fassbinder's abiding preoccupations, in both *Berlin Alexanderplatz* (1980) and *Lili Marleen* (1980) – the former, covering almost the same period and shot on Bergman's Munich set three years later. *The Serpent's Egg* thus opens up an interesting basis of comparison between the two directors, in other ways so different from each other.

Finally, the notion of society as a laboratory, where everything seems possible and permissible, offers Bergman the opportunity to identify different ethical positions, where notably any absolute contrast between victim and perpetrator is replaced by a quite different scale of possible agencies. Bergman questions the roles of active and passive, participant and bystander, insider and outsider, in order to explore the more difficult moral laws of unintended consequences that may require one to redistribute blame and virtue, while not releasing anyone from accountability. This, too, is a Fassbinder theme, but as I will indicate, not only his.

Thus, even if the box-office failure of *The Serpent's Egg* is a fact, the subsequent and still persistently negative evaluation of the film – with a few exceptions that I shall mention – is still surprising, or should I say symptomatic? On the face of it, *The Serpent's Egg* may be a difficult, but totally fascinating film, and this within quite a few discourses, familiar from film studies as well as wider afield, such as the debates about Europe's historical identity. It also has some very remarkable scenes that no one who has seen the film is likely to forget. I am not so much thinking of the spectacular set – the famous Bergmannstrasse erected at Bavaria Studios in Munich-Geiselgasteig, kept there and put to good use for years to come – but also of scenes of barely supportable physical intensity, rarely encountered in Bergman's other work. Here the violence is visceral and graphic in a way Bergman did not often permit himself either before or after *The Serpent's Egg*. Unusually frank is the scene of humiliation of the black homosexual Monroe in the brothel, and quite unbearably shocking is the brutal treatment meted out by a group of anti-Semites to the Jewish owner of *Der blaue Esel* ('the Blue Ass'), the night club where Liv Ullmann performs.

The Serpent's Egg: an auteurist reading

Conventional wisdom has it that *The Serpent's Egg* was a failure because it did not engage with the political reality of the period in a realistic or psychologically credible way: the skills that forged his unique intimate cinema are entirely opposite to those required for this historical drama, and Bergman's lack of overt political analysis for once does make the work superficial. Like *Beröringen* (*The Touch*, 1971), *The Serpent's Egg* was a commercial and critical disaster (see Ford 2002).

However, one could also argue – still in the auteurist vein – that *The Serpent's Egg* is a typical Bergman film, in that it reworks the Master's familiar constellation of an Oedipal triangle. It makes Dr Vergérus the paternal authority, against whom the son has to prove himself over the possession of the mother, that is, the nurturer/whore (also the basic configuration of film noir, if one follows Slavoj Žižek (2001: 245–6), with Vergérus the 'enjoying' superego father: beyond the law, as the master of life and death). The son – unable to meet/defeat the father head on – seeks out substitutes, or tries to stage scenes of the father's humiliation and defeat: the humiliation of the cabaret owner by the gang of virile young men who smash his face into a piece of meat; the priest who has lost his faith, on whom Abel spies; the proxy fight with the Jewish grocery shop owner; the demonstration of impotence by the black musician Monroe, whom Abel pays in order to observe him, thereby assuming the role of Vergérus in relation to himself and Manuela. Abel is 'trying out', as it were, what it means to be the superego. Then, by practically raping one of the prostitutes, he compensates for his inability to make love to Manuela, the mother figure and mistress of Dr Vergérus. Another substitute parricide would be the scene where he kills the man who attacks him in the clinic's stairwell. Vergérus's suicide, in the face of the imminent arrival of Bauer, the police commissar (another, benevolent father), finally would be Abel's wish-fulfilling fantasy, ridding him of the oppressive father figure, without him having had to carry through and execute the Oedipal revolt. Abel's brother's suicide, which opens the film, provides the negative version of this fantasy, the alternative road not taken by Abel, namely constructing a scenario, where the son punishes the father by killing himself.

Another reading of the same symbolic matrix, but with an added inversion, is proposed by one of the few positive assessments of the film. Frank Gado, in his study *The Passion of Ingmar Bergman*, also argues that the scene in the brothel is crucial, in that it makes explicit the homosexual subtext sustaining Abel's dilemma (framed by the two suicides), suggesting that *The Serpent's Egg* shows Bergman 'working through' a latent homosexuality that is not free of homophobia, which might explain the torn, tormented and darkly despairing personality portrayed by David Carradine (1986: 471–81).

A third notable reading is that proposed by David Aquilon *et al.* (2005), a former graduate student from Lund, whose work on Bergman and *The Serpent's Egg* has recently been posthumously published. Aquilon sees the central male protagonists Abel, the Commissar and Vergérus as forming three obliquely communicating and intersecting circles. These circles describe complementary movements that together make up the necessary constellation for genocide and the totalitarian state: the apathetic, compliant or cynical citizen (Abel), the bureaucrat who just follows orders (or as Bauer says, needs to create a little corner of order on his desk as a defence against the chaos around him), and the visionary or ideologue, the man seemingly above the law, who can see through the thin membrane of reality, identifying the fully-formed reptile, while knowing exactly what is his historic task. This analysis of the Nazi mentality, taken from Zygmunt Bauman's study *Modernity and the Holocaust*, allows Aquilon to read *The Serpent's Egg* as a kind of allegory of how Bergman thinks responsibility for the Holocaust ought to be apportioned across these three social fields which, of course, are neither confined to the Weimar years nor to Hitler's Germany. Aquilon also contrasts the circular movements that the characters execute around each other with the vertical axis in the film, introduced most dramatically through the stairwells and elevator shafts in the clinic and the prison, associated with the attempt to gain perspective and vision, and indicative of Abel's attempt to wrest panoptic control from the figures of authority. The two – the circle and vertical – are resolved or compressed in the homophony (in Swedish) between the word for 'egg' and 'eye', thus effectively combining or uniting the instances of the genocidal social field around the ubiquity of surveillance and the proliferating mechanisms of social control.

I think this is a very challenging argument, and certainly the only essay I have come across that actually engages with the specific architecture of Bergman's very sophisticated *mise-en-scène* in the film. My own – at this point very general – approach would, as indicated, first focus on the period and circumstances when the film was made, and thereby comment on the significance of Bergman's engagement with the dominant genre of European art cinema of the 1970s, responding both to the demand of 'mastering the past', but also to the challenge (manifested in films like *Cabaret* (1972), and subsequently by television series like *Holocaust* (1979)) that Hollywood was 'taking over' typically European subjects, by, as Edgar Reitz was to call it, 'taking away our history' (1979: 21). Europe, in its retro-fashion films was beginning to tell 'its' own stories – and to tell them also to America. For it was precisely with these films that took the Third Reich and its aftermath as their subject that European auteurs were able to enter the international market, notably America. Fascism, ironically, became continental Europe's own version of the (British) heritage industry. Or as one might prefer to see it: it became that moment when the European cinema – but not only the cinema, the European Union, too – began to be haunted by history and Empire. And luckily (one is almost tempted to say), Bergman failed in this endeavour to 'sell' European history to the Americans, on the Americans' own terms. Let me explain.

The Hitler Welle

When describing the origins of *The Serpent's Egg*, the context that Bergman specifically evoked and referred to is that the idea of a film about Berlin in the 1920s came to him after reading Joachim Fest's biography of Hitler, first published in German in 1973 and translated into Swedish the following year (Bergman 1994: 191). Fest's book, which was an international bestseller, sparked off in Germany what became known as the 'Hitler Welle', a wave of publications, television programmes and coffee-table books, as well as feature films that 'discovered' Hitler and the Nazi regime as a topic for popular culture. Denounced as nostalgia or retro-fashion, and critiqued for giving legitimacy to the growing surge of right-wing politics, the Hitler Welle, at least in Germany, became also connected with a left-wing demand, voiced mainly by the radical student movement, that West Germany finally face up to the legacy of Nazism. Much of the violence of the RAF, for instance, was justified by this argument. The need for Germany to 'master its past' – or *Vergangenheitsbewältigung* as it came to be known – led in more academic circles to the internationally known Historians' debate, in which the sociologist and philosopher Jürgen Habermas openly attacked what he saw as the revisionist historical theses of historians such as Ernst Nolte, Andreas Hillgruber and Joachim Fest – a debate notably about the nature of fascism and National Socialism, and its supposedly historical function in 'providing a buffer against' Soviet Communism.

Bergman himself was most directly inspired by Fest's description of the inflation period, and in particular the sense of the loss of all values – moral, personal, political – that seemed to go hand in hand with the hyper-inflation experienced by the German post-war currency. Hence Bergman's choice of the period and date: the week from 3–11 November 1923, at the height of inflation (the mark was 'reformed' on 16 November 1923) and during the week when Hitler launched his unsuccessful Munich beer-hall putsch (on 8 November), which should have put him behind bars for five years, but only cost him nine months, during which he wrote *Mein Kampf.* Bergman's choice of a very precise set of dates is thus over-determined by at least these two events – the peak of hyper-inflation and the foiled beer-hall putsch, as well as particularly early and severe winter weather.

As far as film history was concerned, the Hitler Welle must be referenced also to the extraordinary worldwide success of *Cabaret*, directed by Bob Fosse, which, based on Christopher Isherwood's novel *Goodbye to Berlin* (1939), depicted the life of a group of American and British expatriate thrill-seekers in the nightclub, showbusiness and homosexual milieux of Berlin in the early 1930s, just prior to Hitler's accession to power. *Cabaret* consolidated many of the thematic motifs as well as defining a whole iconography of decadence, showbusiness and ambiguous Nazi glamour that was already present in Visconti's La *Caduta degli dei* (*The Damned*, 1969) and Bertolucci's *Il Conformista* (*The Conformist*, 1970), but which return in force in subsequent films. We only have to recall Louis Malle's *Lacombe Lucien* (1974), Joseph Losey's *Monsieur Klein* (*Mr Klein*, 1976) and Truffaut's *Le Dernier métro* (*The Last Metro*, 1980), to realise that this was a European phenomenon, and not limited to Germany. In Germany, the group of films to which *The Serpent's Egg* belongs extend from Fassbinder's *Despair* (1976), with which it has many similarities, to Syberberg's *Hitler – ein Film aus Deutschland* (*Our Hitler*, 1976–77), Fassbinder's *Lili Marleen* (1980) and Schlöndorff's *Die Blechtrommel* (*The Tin Drum*, 1980), after the novel by Günter Grass. What can be said about the films within a European context is that they broke many of the previously-held taboos about the representation of the Nazi period, not least by acknowledging the ambiguous fascination of fascism. Yet by doing so in terms of spectacle, glamour and erotic perversion, they also 'took back' neo-realism as the dominant filmic language of the post-war period. None of the films, however, is as bleak and pervaded with squalour as is *The Serpent's Egg*.

What the 'retro-fashion' often bracketed off was the fate of the Jews under Nazism and, in particular, the genesis and history of their persecution, deportation and destruction in Germany, as well as Western and Eastern Europe. It was another US production, this time the television series directed by Marvin Chomsky, called *Holocaust* that in 1979 gave rise not only to a vivid controversy in Germany about telling the story of the extermination of the Jews as a family melodrama and soap opera, but also contributed to a shift in the dominant discourse: from now on, the history of Jewish persecution became generally known as 'the Holocaust', and with it the subject left the specialist historians' domain and has entered popular culture, where it has remained ever since, not least thanks to other controversial and successful Hollywood blockbusters, such as *Schindler's List* (1993).

Bergman's film thus situates itself on the one hand within the Hitler Welle and at the beginning of the refocusing on the fate of the Jews rather than the Nazi elites or the sexual danger and social decadence of the dying Weimar Republic.

The 'retro-fashion' of the 1970s has sometimes been called 'the return of history as film' (see Kaes 1989), indicating two distinctly new moments in modern cinema's relation to and depiction of the past. One speaks about the specific role of the moving image in the representation of extreme historical events such as genocide, civil war and other man-made disasters, involving large numbers of victims, and often concerning political regimes that either deny the occurrence of these atrocities, or are actively engaged in obliterating their traces, notably any photographic evidence.

The other aspect of the return of history as film names the fact that much of our collective or cultural memory of the twentieth century is now constituted by precisely the filmic and photographic record that has been preserved or passed on, where the generic distinction between fiction and documentary, between 'the truth' and 'the staged', between 'record' and 'propaganda' seems to become more and more indistinct and even irrelevant, as the distance in time increases and the popular media, notably television, use these images over and over again, often out of context and in order to 'authenticate' often very different arguments and positions.

The two aspects – the limits of representation on one side, and on the other the constructed or staged nature of what we now understand as the past – are of course intimately intertwined. They are the two sides of the same dilemma of what to trust: media memory (also called prosthetic memory) combined eyewitness accounts, or painstakingly researched, multi-faceted factual history, which presents its arguments on the basis of written documents. For those who distrust the first kind of memory, it seems as if only that which has survived in the dominant media of the twentieth century, namely film, radio and photography, may soon be said to have 'existed' at all, at least in the popular imagination.

The Bergman turn and return to (film-)history

It is easy to see how Bergman's *The Serpent's Egg* situates itself very precisely and totally lucidly within this problematic. It does so in a number of ways that I just

Decadence and cabarets: Liv Ullmann as Manuela (photo: Ingmar Bergman Foundation)

briefly want to sketch or indicate, firstly by Bergman's own invocation of just such a popular media memory, by what used to be called postmodern citation and pastiche, but which – as indicated – I prefer to see in a broader, epistemological or even onto-logical context. *The Serpent's Egg* is full of references to other films, beginning with *Cabaret* itself, insofar as one of its major locations is the nightclub where Manuela performs; but of course, Liza Minnelli's Sally Bowles in *Cabaret* already trades on and invokes Marlene Dietrich in *Der Blaue Engel* (*The Blue Angel*, 1930), clearly alluded to in Bergman's cabaret *Der Blaue Esel*. But this is only the most obvious reference: as already mentioned, Fritz Lang's *Dr Mabuse*, both the original 1921 film (which ex-plicitly deals with inflation and black-marketeering), and the sequels *Das Testament des Dr Mabuse* (*The Testament of Dr Mabuse*, 1933), and *Die 1000 Augen des Dr Ma-buse* (*The 1000 Eyes of Dr Mabuse*, 1960)) are cited, not least through Gert Fröbe, the actor playing the commissar Bauer (who also plays the commissar in *Die 1000 Augen des Dr Mabuse*). At one point Bauer refers to one of his predecessors, a Commissar Lohmann, who was indeed the policeman who tracked the child-murderer in Fritz Lang's *M* (1931) – the inverted temporalities of this reference being surely deliber-ate. We find references to G. W. Pabst's *Die freudlose Gasse* (*The Joyless Street*, 1935), where Greta Garbo played a kind of Liv Ullmann character; there are allusions to several of the chamber play films of classic Expressionism, such as Karl Grune's *Die Strasse* (*The Street*, 1923), as well as to Lang's *Metropolis* (1927), which critics thought they recognised in the pre-credit scene of the silent crowd shuffling in the cold, not unlike the underground workers in that film's opening. The list of citations could go on, especially since we know that Bergman showed the cast two famous Berlin films from the late 1920s – Ruttmann's *Berlin: Die Symphonie der Großstadt* (*Berlin: Symphony of a Big City*, 1927) and Piel Jutzi's *Mutter Krausens Fahrt ins Glück* (*Mother Krause's Trip to Happiness*, 1929), as well as newsreels and other documentary material. He also put on record that the set was inspired not by a real location (he scoured Berlin and could not find anything that struck him as suitable), but by the charcoal drawing of a Berlin street he discovered in a contemporary magazine (sometimes it is *Simplizissimus*, at other times it is from *Berliner Illustrierte*). Another intertextual reference was provided by Bavaria's and Bergman's set designer, Rolf Zehetbauer, who had received an Academy Award for his sets for *Cabaret*, which, as indicated, became (and still is) the template for what 'Berlin' had to look like in a film about it in the last years of the 1920s and 1930s.

What interests me, however, about these references to a shared cinematic cultural memory is not so much the intertextuality or postmodern mania for allusion and pastiche; instead, it is what one might call a constitutive anachronism: meaning in the first instance that a set of signifiers – props, colour schemes, hairstyles, fashions (which may or may not be 'authentic') – have come to stand for the era, providing a kind of autonomous reality, cut off from period, class, circumstance or motive. Furthermore, *The Serpent's Egg* shows a certain tension between the very exact time frame and historical referentiality that the voice-over provides (maybe a late addition by De Laurentiis, seeing how difficult the film was for a general public) and the essentially a-chronological quality of the film, and of the suspended lives of its characters. This astutely uses the drawbacks of the film – clearly a studio-made Berlin, with always the same cars, the same tram, the same section of street visible – in order to emphasise the claustrophobia, the timelessness but also the allegorical aspect of the story. Given that time is floating, space becomes very important, in that each of the interiors has a clear symbolic value: the tavern where Abel lives with his brother, the apartment of the rich widow with the expensive chairs and furnishings, and then the flat they rent from Dr Vergérus. Each space abuts on some other quite different space, creating its own kind of incongruous contiguity. Or the characters have to traverse spaces, wasteland, cemeteries, the bas-fonds, past rubbish, rats or near-dead people. It is a film full of thresholds, liminal spaces and hyper-expressive spaces – imprisonment being the key metaphor, but also the contrast of squalor and hospital whiteness in the St Anna Clinic, the long endless corridors of the medical archive, backstage at *Der Blaue Esel*, the transitional space in the widow's house, the frosted

Anachronisms: David Carradine as Abel faces an anti-Semitic gang (photo: Ingmar Bergman Foundation)

glass partitions at both the widow's house and the brothel, together making up the many spatial rhymes achieved through repetition of location and setting.

Bergman (1994) himself alluded to several specific anachronisms by saying that he realised the anti-Semitic attacks by gangs of thugs and SA men did not belong to 1923, but to the mid-1930s, that is, well after Hitler had come to power. Similarly, in the scene at the end of the film, when the commissar says that Hitler's march on the Munich city hall had failed miserably because he had underestimated Germany's democracy, we are tempted to put the apparently tragic irony of this remark down to hollow wisdom gained with hindsight. But other readings are possible, not least one that points out that with the stabilisation of the mark, Germany experienced a veritable recovery, in fact five golden years of prosperity and reconstruction, dashed not by Hitler, but by the Wall Street Crash of 1927 whose catastrophic consequences for Germany resulted in widespread unemployment, the radicalisation of the working class on both the left and the right, and thus the conditions that eventually led the National Socialists to their electoral victory in 1933.

Bergman was chided for these and other 'mistakes' in his portrayal of November 1923, so much so that he was advised to return to his chamber settings and leave history alone. He tended to agree with this verdict, as he generally did in considering the film a failure. Interestingly enough, however, the reasons he gave for the failure varied from period to period. At first he put it down to having opted for a realistic, historically-located cityscape, that is, Berlin in November 1923, rather than his imaginary city of war and imminent dread, as in *Tystnaden* (*The Silence*, 1963) or *Skammen* (*Shame/The Shame*, 1968). But, as indicated, both the date and place are crucial to the cultural memory the film works on and contributes to. Then, he argued that the reason he demanded such a big set was that during the period he was shooting, coming so directly after his nervous breakdown and the tax *imbroglio*, he was on beta-blockers, which made him have a permanent fever and terrible mood swings, including periods of megalomaniac self-delusion. Then again, it was Dino De Laurentiis's \$4 million budget that seduced him into having Zehetbauer construct the set that consumed most of the money, then it was the fact that the charcoal drawing referred to the Bergmannstrasse, a real street in Berlin at the time, which the director evidently saw as a good omen, and even later, in *Images: My Life in Film* (1994), the failure was due to the fact that the Vergérus story of what he called voyeurism had nothing to do, according to him, with the story of inflation. In other words, reading this, one begins to wonder whether in these all too many explanations of failure we do not have a case of rationalisation, and even more so, a case of disavowal: the disavowal being that Bergman himself, deep down, may not have considered the film a failure at all, but thought of it as rather crucial, in fact one of his masterpieces. Only the dismal reception it received persuaded him to disown it, siding as he so often claimed he did on other occasions in his life, with those who were out to punish him, or thought him to have failed or done wrong. Bergman's own self-advertised guilt complex would thus seem to be involved in these many negative and half-exculpatory justifications he has offered for the failure of *The Serpent's Egg*.

However, I would want to de-personalise this whole aspect of failure for a moment, and come back to what I called the film's – but also the wider genre's, that is, the return of history as film genre – constitutive anachronism. I am not convinced by what critics at the time complained about, namely the shameless nostalgia, the retro-fashion or the revival of the Nazis own kitsch and death fantasies, in Saul Friedlander's graphic phrase (see Friedlander 1993) as being a satisfactory explanation for the phenomenon. After all, it has persisted since, all the way to today, with yet another Hitler wave, if one thinks of *Der Untergang* (*Downfall*, 2004), about Hitler's last days, or the television series *Speer und Er* (2005), about Albert Speer and Hitler. What keeps returning, I would argue, is a crucial aspect of media memory or prosthetic memory: what I would call history's new temporalities. To put it perhaps a little too briefly, once media memory has become our cultural memory, our *lieux de mémoire* to cite Pierre Nora (1984–92) then the whole notion of a linear chronology, or of time's arrow only pointing in one direction, becomes difficult if not impossible to sustain. After all, these moving images from the past are so alive, they exude so much presence, that to call them 'passed' in the traditional sense would not do justice to either their power or their fascination, especially when we see them associated with so much evil or such troubling actuality, as happens to be the case with the most violent periods of the last century. These images, I would say, whether in the form of historical period material or as restagings and uncanny recreations, have become the undead of history. Which makes our film and media-saturated history not so much a new ontology but a new in-between state, or a kind of hauntology, to evoke a term used by Jacques Derrida to allude to the spectral quality of our contemporary world (1994: 25–6), in its relation to both the unfulfilled pasts of socialist utopias and the no longer even imaginable future of our paralysed societies.

This sense of being haunted by history, so typical of Europe since the end of World War Two, is of course intimately linked to a more general sense of historical failure, notably the failure of the European Enlightenment, but also our Christian traditions, to have prevented Nazism, and more crucially, to have prevented the discrimination, deportation and eventual destruction of European Jewry in the death camps of Auschwitz. Again, two kinds of failure seem to converge and never quite confront each other in these films from the 1970s: the failure of keeping to a strict but no longer credible linear or causal chronology (the anachronisms) already mentioned, and the failure of not having foreseen and thus not done something to forestall Auschwitz and the Holocaust. There is a link between the two, if you like: namely the breakdown of the belief in progress – the end of the grand narratives of European civilisation – and the unresolved Christian legacy of anti-Semitism. For when we look at these films of the 'retro-fashion' today, after more than twenty years of the media seemingly talking about nothing but the Holocaust, we realise that the Jews are indeed missing from the films, or rather their presence, such as in *The Serpent's Egg*, presents a particular burden of representation, where they are either the signifier of a radical and irrecoverable 'otherness', at once 'sacred' and 'inhuman', or their Jewish-ness is no more than a psychological attribute in an individual's fate, and thus not capable of bearing the burden of the knowledge of what was to be their collective fate. Bergman's male protagonist Abel Rosenberg is just such a figure: not 'other' enough to be 'the Jew', and not 'ordinary' enough to be one of those who will eventually make up the six million German, French, Polish, Czech, Dutch, Hungarian or Romanian citizens who, deprived of their most basic rights as human beings, perished in the camps.

Important, however, about these skewed temporalities of the constitutive anachronism of media memory and the equally constitutive feelings of guilt and regret about not having foreseen the dangers of Nazism, are other noteworthy aspects within European post-war consciousness: one is that we know such a different temporality in the realm of psychic pathology, notably in the case of trauma. There too, the traumatised subject lives in a different temporality, one where the traumatic event or experience from the past can come upon him or her, all of a sudden, without warning, triggered by whatever incident, and then manifest itself in the full force of the present. A traumatised subject lives almost by definition in a permanent potential presence of the past, never quite able to relegate the traumatic moment to the temporality of an ordered, that is to say, chronological or causal narrative. Haunted by history, through the ever-present presence of media images of the past on television, in books and in the cinema, is thus to be quite literally 'traumatised' by history, as if 'the cinema' and 'history' stand in an epistemologically impossible relation to each other. How often have we heard that a film does not reproduce a given historical reality 'accurately', and how often have we heard this complaint voiced especially against films dealing with the Holocaust. Yet the accusation, if based on realism, misses its goal, it seems to me, because in the case of traumatic events what would be an accurate rendition if not one that took account of the hauntological, traumatic dimension; this is to say, which did not somehow include the failure of narrative emplotment, of causal chronology and objective depiction. If the cinema and history thus relate to each other as each other's representational failure, then we can also see Bergman's own discourse on the 'failure' of *The Serpent's Egg* in another light.

For instance, we could also note that ever since the 1970s, and even more intensively in the last 15 years, that is since the fall of the Wall, we have seen in European cinema the emergence of protagonists who are not so much unable to act – paralysed or aimless – but who are abject, who seek to divest themselves or allow themselves to be divested of all the symbolic supports of selfhood and identity. I am thinking of the line that goes from Fassbinder's victim figures in *Der Händler der vier Jahreszeiten* (*The Merchant of Four Seasons*, 1972), *Faustrecht der Freiheit* (*Fox and his Friends*, 1975), *In einem Jahr von 13 Monden* (*In a Year of 13 Moons*, 1978), to Agnès Varda's heroine in *Sans Toit ni Loi* (*Vagabond*, 1985), from the hero of Mike Leigh's *Naked* (1993) and the protagonists of the films of the Dardenne Brothers (such as *Rosetta*, 1999), to the characters in Gaspar Noé's *Seul contre tous* (*I Stand Alone*, 1998) or Fatih Akin's *Gegen die Wand* (*Head On*, 2004). In the light of this genealogy of abject heroes, Bergman's protagonist in *The Serpent's Egg* has all the potential for being not just an outsider or victim, but in truth fulfils a more ambiguous but also for that very reason, more interesting role, where the general script we have learnt to apply to the Holocaust and Nazism, with its clear divisions between victims and perpetrators, between by-standers and outsiders, between collaborators, tolerators and traitors, no longer seems to hold.

Personal failure as the parapraxes of historical agency

Important in this reading is what I have called the constitutive anachronisms, not as wisdom through hindsight or nostalgic retro-fashion, but drawing the consequences of a new kind of media memory in which the cinema and history are confronted in such a way that each is the other's 'failure' of representation.

By this, I mean to draw attention to another feature of Bergman's film, what one might call the film's parapraxes, its bungled actions or apparent role-reversals: the wrong man at the right place, the inversion of the meanings of an act or gesture (the smashing of the shop window, the kiss on the old woman's mouth, the Vergérus role that Abel assumes in the brothel). In one sense, as we saw, these scenes provide the motifs for an auteurist psychoanalytic reading. But I would argue that they make equal sense in the historical context, manifesting something like a political unconscious, an unconscious turned inside out, to document the law of unintended consequences – for instance, the causal chain that leads from throwing the stone through the shop window to Manuela's death and the smashing of windows to reveal the hidden cameras of Dr Vergérus.

It gives a different meaning to the all too familiar literal mirrors in Bergman's films, as well as to the metaphoric mirrors, echoes and repetitions that thread themselves through his work over the years and decades, where characters' names repeat themselves (such as Rosenberg and Vergérus), as do the situations and character constellations, and the emotional climaxes of humiliation and moments of shame. All of these phenomena, I would argue, permit one to put the explicitly historical and political references in a slightly different context.

What makes Bergman's film remarkable in light of this argument is the combination of a very precise historical moment – a turning point or crisis moment in Germany's but also Europe's history – and the a-temporal, science fiction or time-travel quality of the film, once more indicating why the idiom of realism no longer sustains the new media temporalities of prosthetic memory, after scholarly history or eyewitness testimony.

Thus Abel's permanent bouts of drunkenness, his mood-swings between catatonic apathy and violent aggression, his alternation between self-pity and self-aggrandisement, between being a sheepish victim and a sadistic aggressor, could also be read as ways of trying to unfix and unhinge himself on the way to that status of abjection, across which the hero seeks to attain a cleansing redemption in a world without either stable values (the inflation) or religious transcendence (here signalled by the scene of the priest, unable to give comfort and solace to his parishioner, because of his own spiritual doubt or lack of faith). In reaction to the dance on the volcano (in the bars and nightclubs), the biting poverty, hunger and cold of the Berlin masses, and the failure of Christianity, the abject state of Abel Rosenbaum and the amoral medical experiments of Hans Vergérus confront and complement each other across the abyss of lawlessness and nihilism of the epoch, each escaping the non-functioning of Weimar society by inventing another one, so to speak, above and below the bankrupt symbolic order.

Bergman's failure, or Europe's failure?

Here, I think, we need to come back to Bergman's own discourse of failure, and what I suggested is a more complex matrix of defensiveness and disavowal regarding the place of *The Serpent's Egg* in his own trajectory and oeuvre. I think it is clear that he was genuinely shocked if not traumatised by the public's and critics' reaction, asking himself how he could have been so self-deceived. Now, this very posture is, of course, one that Bergman assumed many times in his career and in his comments on his own work, being part of his lifelong, ongoing self-examination and auto-analysis. It applies, however, with special force to his relationship to Germany, and notably Nazi-Germany.

He was always most candid about the time he spent there as a 16-year-old boy in the mid-1930s while an exchange student, and how he returned to Sweden an enthusiastic and fervent National Socialist, inspired not so much by the ideology (for which he was both too young and too apolitical), but by the combination of youthful idealism, the general air of excitement and anticipation, as well as the tenderness and affection lavished on him by the young people and especially a girl whom he met through his aunt, who initiated these German connections. In fact, the chapter in *The Magic Lantern* describing the stay, as well as his interview with Swedish television in 1977 (originally aired in three parts in 1975 and 1976), on the occasion of the opening of *The Serpent's Egg*, gives one the sense that this may have been one of the very few periods of his life where he felt completely happy. When asked during the same interview in 1977 whether he had ever fully come to terms with the Nazi within him, he replied: 'No – learning about the camps after 1945 was above all a profound emotional shock. As if I had discovered that God and the Devil are two sides of the same coin. It was a horrible experience.' He was asked if this experience gave rise to a film like *The Serpent's Egg*? He replied, 'I am not sure. I cannot give a definite answer to this question. The week of November 1923 is a metaphoric frame; it's also about what could happen to all of us, here and today, or even tomorrow. That is the real subject of the film: almost science fiction.' So, what Bergman highlights is his profound shock at having been so deeply mistaken about his own emotions and convictions (but, as he points out, not that different from many Swedes of his and his parents' generations, who remained Germanophile and anti-Semitic well into the 1940s). Yet he also sees this very specific historical moment caught or suspended in several temporalities: the past, the present, the future – history as time-travel and science fiction, and melodrama as the genre of bad timing par excellence or, rather, the combination of the temporality of regret: 'if only' (if only I could turn back the clock/ if only I had known) alongside the temporality of the hypothetical 'what if' (what if the end of the Weimar Republic and the Nazi regime had been a kind of historical fast-forward, which the second part of the twentieth century was doomed to re-run and repeat, in slow motion, just like the grey masses we see at the beginning and the end of the film?).

This emphasis on a certain notion of failure as programmed into the genre of 'the return of history as film' allows me to re-read Bergman's own explanations of the film's failure symptomatically: as in itself contradictory, and thus requiring a more parapractical reading, namely in relation to his own sense of the importance of the film, and secondly in relation to his shock at not being able to trust his own political instincts. This in turn leads me to the historical implications of this shock, namely his own seduction by Nazism in the mid-1930s. Again, however, we should guard against interpreting this solely in the light of Bergman's own moral dilemma and individual psyche, but recognise it in the context of all the other, more open accounts of culpability on the part of European societies, and notably the bourgeoisie, in the acknowledgement of their common responsibility for not having opposed fascism. In this respect, Bergman was not only in the European mainstream, but in a sense ahead of others.

This brings me back to the broader context of the film, and Bergman's assertion that the Vergérus theme of voyeurism, experiment and auto-analysis did not fit with the inflation theme, that is, the emphasis on the black market and on the complete meltdown of civilised values as hunger, unemployment and lawlessness grip post-war Berlin society. But the fact that Bergman actually connects Vergérus's experiments with something he had read about the CIA gives one pause for further thought. For the 1970s were not only the moment of postmodernism and the end of the grand narratives of progress. It was also the period when the narratives of progress based on what one might call political-cultural values, give way to a narrative of progress based on science, and in particular on the neuro-biological and genetic sciences. What Bergman saw and recognised in Vergérus may have been something like an epistemic break, where the self-examinatory, self-observational and self-analysing impulses of Protestant religion and Freudian psychoanalysis – the twin poles of Bergman's own moral world – began to give way to the self-experimenting, species-enhancing scientific tendencies of the US-dominated behavioural sciences. These would catapult – as many feared and still fear – the human species out of its traditional self-definitions and towards its own self-obliteration; as if the end of psychoanalysis and the beginning of the dominance of the neuro-sciences and bio-genetics amounted to a paradigm shift in the relation between culture and nature. Those who fear this turn are also likely to be those who consider such 'advances' a belated victory of fascism, although – as Bergman makes clear – the figure who stands for this self-transcending vision of mankind's future, namely Dr Vergérus, is not a Nazi (how could he have been one in 1923?), or more precisely perhaps, is not necessarily a Nazi.

In the face of this alternative to bourgeois humanism, we see Bergman contrasting the vision of the new man embodied in Vergérus, with the most creaturely aspects of humanity, embodied in his unsuspecting victims: the vulnerability of, literally, flesh and blood, reduced or purified to the state of 'abjection' in Julia Kristeva's terms (1982), or to 'bare life' as Giorgio Agamben (1998) calls it. Flesh, meat, spurting blood, the palpitating heart of a cat, under the gaze of the cinematic apparatus turned into the clinical apparatus of surveillance, science and medicine, are among the images Bergman chose to give a sense of the extremes he saw emerging from the break-up of bourgeois humanism, and thus, it would seem, the Vergérus story and the inflation/abjection story do indeed belong together, in fact implicate and necessitate each other: another parapraxis or disavowal at the heart of European (fascist) history.

What *The Serpent's Egg*, I think, allows one to reassess is that the 1970s really was a key decade, and not only that, but a genuine fork-in-the-road where the cultural-humanist way of understanding the world had definitely begun to hand over to another narrative of progress, that of genetic evolutionism. What inflation was to Germany in the 1920s, postmodernism may turn out to have been for the 1970s: the period of everything goes, before the 'currency' had once more become stabilised, but on the basis of a quite different ontological 'gold standard'.

In this narrative, the Holocaust marked a watershed, insofar as it did indeed give the world a glimpse of what it means to look at human beings without looking at their humanity, and instead simply regard them under the aspect of their species identity, upon which judgement can be passed, selection can be made and science can intervene. Bergman's vision, bleaker than most of us would wish to countenance perhaps, because infused by his own sense of guilt and failure, nonetheless reminds us that this particular look has found in the cinema one of its instruments, but also its anti-bodies or *pharmakon*, its counter-poisons – provided it can remain sufficiently Bergmanesque, that is, not afraid of being hysterical and melodramatic, or as I would now call it, not afraid of being anachronistic and parapractic.

References

Agamben, G. (1998) *Homo Sacer: Sovereign Power and Bare Life*. Stanford: Stanford University Press.

Aquilon, D., L. G. Andersson and E. Heddling (2005) *Magisk cirkel*. Lund: Film International förlag.

Bauman, Z. (1989) *Modernity and the Holocaust*. Ithaca, N.Y.: Cornell University Press.

Bergman, I. (1988) *The Magic Lantern: An Autobiography*, trans. J. Tate. New York: Viking.

_____ (1994) *Images: My Life in Film*. New York: Arcade.

Derrida, J. (1994) *Spectres of Marx*. London: Routledge.

Fest, J. (1977) *Hitler – Eine Karriere*. Berlin: Ullstein.

Ford, H. (2002) 'The Radical Intimacy of Bergman', *Senses of Cinema*, http://www.sensesofcinema. com/contents/directors/02/bergman.html (last accessed 24 October 2006).

Friedlander, S. (1993) *Reflections of Nazism: An Essay on Kitsch and Death*. Bloomington: Indiana University Press.

Gado, F. (1986) *The Passion of Ingmar Bergman*. Durham: Duke University Press.

Kaes, A. (1989) *From Hitler to Heimat: The Return of History as Film*. Cambridge, MA.: Harvard University Press.

Kristeva, J. (1982) *Powers of Horror: An Essay on Abjection*. New York: Columbia University Press.

Nora, P. (1984–92), *Les Lieux de Memoire*. Paris: Gallimard.

Žižek, S. (2001) *Enjoy Your Symptom: Jacques Lacan in Hollywood and Out*. London: Routledge.

Reitz, E. (1979), 'Statt *Holocaust*, Erinnerungen aufarbeiten', *Medium*, 5, 21–2.

THE WELFARE STATE DEPICTED: POST-UTOPIAN LANDSCAPES IN INGMAR BERGMAN'S FILMS

Erik Hedling

A neglected approach to the art of Ingmar Bergman is the study of the relationship between his films and the affluent Swedish welfare society in which they were conceived and received over a period spanning almost exactly sixty years. Film has always enjoyed a most ambiguous social status in Sweden, a country where the predominantly literary establishment has tended to aggressively defend its cultural borders against any potential intruders. Yet, it was here that most of Bergman's films received finance and initial distribution, even before the introduction of a governmentally-sponsored art cinema in 1963, when the *film d'auteur* became a sort of established mainstream.

While hundreds of scholars have studied Bergman from religious, philosophical, existentialist, psychological, literary, theatrical, cinematic and even postmodernist perspectives (regarding the latter see, for instance, Gervais 1999), no one has really chosen to regard the director's films as a social critique of Swedish society, in the sense of, say, Godard of France, Bertolucci of Italy or Fassbinder of Germany, to mention a few examples among Bergman's great contemporaries within the European art cinema of primarily the 1960s and 1970s. If regarded at all in overtly political terms, Swedish criticism has labelled Bergman as the archetypal bourgeois, the reactionary individualist, or the naïve and sexually frustrated teenager, who portrays hopelessly dated characters from an unsecularised era already vanished. In the 1960s he was also claimed as a spokesman for the Pentagon by the influential Swedish author Sara Lidman (see Lidman 1968).

In such an enormous corpus of criticism there are, of course, a few exceptions to the general rule. Here, I would like to mention Maria Bergom-Larsson's monograph *Ingmar Bergman and Bourgeois Ideology* (1977) published in Swedish at the very peak of Marxist influence on the baby-boom generation and young Swedish intellectual culture. Even if Bergom-Larsson's conclusions often adhere to the criticism of Bergman's political naivety – her general idea is that the director does not understand that he is really describing collective bourgeois anxiety over the inevitable advent of collectivist and proletarian modernity – I still want to stress her role as a source of methodological inspiration for this chapter. At least she tries to take into account the relationship between Bergman's films and the Swedish welfare phenomenon of the post-war era, and how the films might be described as melting pots representing in different ways contemporary social, cultural, political and philosophical Swedish discourse.

In this chapter, consequently, I intend to address precisely this important issue: Bergman and the development of the Swedish welfare state. 'Bergman' is here encoded to implicate individualism, anxiety, religion and tragedy, while the welfare state connotes collectivism, social engineering, agnosticism and material prosperity. Also, I will pursue my study somewhat paradoxically by drawing attention to two sequences of landscape depiction in the films *Nattvardsgästerna* (*Winter Light/The Communicants*, 1963) and *Persona* (1966) respectively. But in order to analyse these examples more in detail, I will first have to outline very briefly a tradition of landscape depiction in Swedish film.

Utopian landscapes

Swedish cinema became famous in the late 1910s for its highly expressive use of landscape, as in the epics by Victor Sjöström (also known as Seastrom) and Mauritz Stiller. In the first more or less serious attempt to write a systematic history of early Swedish cinema, film critic Bengt Idestam-Almquist's *The Drama of Swedish Film: Seastrom – Stiller* from 1939, the author writes enthusiastically about Sjöström's *Berg Ejvind och hans hustru* (*You and I*, 1917).

> The new thing was landscape. Not in the sense of just beautiful pictures of landscape. That had been seen earlier. But here landscape interacts. Sometimes hospitable, sometimes inhospitable, the mountains carry one of the major roles. They bring atmosphere and feeling. Had this been in the traditional theatre, this would have occurred through the use of theatrical thunder and roaring wind machines behind the scene. But here the real living landscape has entered the theatre. (Idestam-Almquist 1939: 145; my translation)

The intimate relationship between landscape and narrative in Swedish cinema was also encoded by international film history, as is shown by Louis Delluc's famous claim that Sjöström's *You and I* was the most beautiful film ever made. Besides its leading stars, Sjöström and his wife Edith Erastoff, the film also contained a third megastar: '*le paysage*', the magnificent Swedish landscape (Sadoul 1952: 200).[1]

Under all circumstances, a cinematic tradition was gradually established, both by the aesthetics of the films and by the critical discourse. In this tradition, which came to be popularised in the 1930s, the Swedish landscape eventually became an integrated part of a decisively chauvinist cinematic rhetoric, celebrating modernity, social change, heritage and tradition while politically preparing audiences for the emergence of the modern and very urban social democratic welfare state. What was usually unequivocally praised in these films was the aesthetic 'beauty' of the homeland.

Landscape, in fact, became a firmly encoded metaphor for the high values of Swedish-ness, while other discourses in the films could be more critically charged. In his study of Swedish cinema in the 1930s, native film scholar Per Olov Qvist (1995) underlines the ethnic strategies in the typical opening sequences with their landscape imagery. Qvist's argument is illustrated by the beginning of, for example, *Pensionat Paradiset* (*Guesthouse Paradise*, 1937), a popular classic, where we see a group of singing men and women going by steamer out into the Stockholm archipelago with its beautifully sunlit cliffs, billowy sea and verdant island landscapes. These images, Qvist claims, 'all have a decisive meaning: this is us and our culture and our home in the world. [The images] constitute a code system of the utmost importance, more richly varied than in any other medium' (1995: 288; my translation).

In another book, this time devoted entirely to landscape and heritage, Qvist emphasises the celebration of the Swedish landscape as an integral part of more than a third of all films made between 1940 and 1959 (1986: 7). Indeed, Qvist maintains, this tradition was even more strongly encoded in Swedish cinema than in most other national cinemas; and that this realm of beauty – or, as it were, demi-paradise – should remain untouched by alien elements is made clear by American film scholar Rochelle Wright's (1998) seminal study of ethnic outsiders in Swedish cinema. There, she analyses some of the films of the 1940s and 1950s studied earlier by Qvist. With a post-colonial rhetoric, Wright tackles, for example, some films about the Sami, the indigenous minority in northern Sweden. Among all the beautiful landscape imagery in the films, she discerns an unrealistic and blatant ethnic stereotyping, verging on racism (1998: 157–63), a discourse that Swedish critics otherwise normally attribute to American cinema. Anyway, the point is that through the idyllic representation of an exotic part of the Swedish landscape and the stereotyping of its alien inhabitants, the Sami – non-ethnic Swedes – become defined as intruders on the holy Swedish soil.

The creation of extremely popular cinematic odes to the Swedish landscape consequently was one of the ways through which Sweden gradually could adapt itself to the rapid development into industrial urban modernity and the creation of a modern welfare state, in which the actual presence of a real or imagined Swedish landscape became lesser and lesser. In 1960, in the wake of Swedish neutrality in World War Two, rapid industrialisation, political consensus on the labour market and highly effective social engineering, the former farming country in the northern outskirts of Europe had, beside Switzerland and the United States, become one of the world's richest countries. The welfare Utopia, in its undulating cinematic landscape, thus seemed to have been achieved.

And post-utopian

Even if no one has really investigated the issue, I would claim that post-1960s Swedish art cinema does contain a tradition of anti-chauvinist social criticism, sometimes even articulated through a creative use of landscape that I would label as being post-utopian. This tradition has remained largely unnoticed, however. I think that this refers to the supposition that would not often occur to indigenous Swedes, the ethnic group from which I myself as well as most other film scholars and film critics are recruited, that Swedish landscape – the inherited earth – could even be depicted as drab, barren or sordid in modern film, and thus subtly and implicitly suggesting the presence of something rotten in the state of Sweden.

In this context it is, however, useful to mention yet another revisionist study of Swedish cinema history, where the notion of cinematic landscape and the expression of potential social criticism comes into focus: journalist Leif Zern's highly interesting book on Ingmar Bergman, published in Sweden in 1993. Even if this is not a scholarly work of film history or film analysis in the strict sense, Zern – a well-known theatre critic in Sweden – often manages to create a surprisingly fresh understanding of Bergman's films in a series of readings that prove highly relevant for the neglected approach advocated in this chapter.

In Zern's work, the aspects of Bergman as the bourgeois individualist mentioned earlier are turned into a powerful social critique of 1960s, social-democratic Sweden, an ultra-modern society gone somewhat existentially astray. The social success story of Sweden was accompanied by a suitable modernisation of the Swedish self-image. Zern argues that when we Swedes watched ourselves in the mirror in the 1960s we saw ourselves as successful, healthy, rational and just. The notion of tragedy did not exist in this country. He continues:

> In the films of Bergman this mirror is cracked. And what he shows us is not even a consciously created image mocking the dominant ideology, but a warped image of all that we thought we had left, all that we had repressed, all that we thought ancient and, at worst, incapable of life. Bergman's characters live on as if nothing has happened. They suffer, have bad consciences, they have complexes, and refuse to be like all others: that is, grown up, cooperative, integrated. It is questionable whether they have noticed that the country by now is secularised and that all troubles of the mind have long since been cured by material rewards. (1993: 25; my translation)

To add an ironic touch to Zern's argument, it occurs to me that an obvious lack in the education of Bergman's characters is that they do not seem to be at all familiar with the written work of Uppsalian philosophy professor Ingemar Hedenius. At the time – the 1950s and early 1960s – Hedenius exerted an extremely strong influence on Swedish intellectual life primarily through his articles in the major Stockholm daily newspaper *Dagens Nyheter*. According to his recent biographer Svante Nordin, Hedenius incorporated the ideals of 'the secularised welfare state, utilitarianism, and social engineering' (2004: 507; my translation). He also became the official rationalist prophet of Swedish modernity at the time, having delivered a devastating blow against the intellectual power of the Church and the university theologians in his atheist classic collection of essays from 1949, titled *Faith and Knowledge*. According to Nordin:

> Hedenius's book caused one of the most important cultural controversies ever in Sweden. The book handled the question of Christianity and truth but also dealt with the public position of the Church and the role of theology. 'There is no God and Ingemar Hedenius is his prophet' as some wit summarised the situation. (2004: cover; my translation)

As a critic and scholar, Hedenius was well received by the social-democratic Swedish intellectual establishment. It might be added here that Zern in rather comical terms emphasises the intellectual abyss between Hedenius and Bergman. In an autobiographical note in his book, he writes: 'After *Through a Glass Darkly* the barrier between my world and Ingmar Bergman's widened. In 1960, I went to Uppsala in order to study philosophy with Ingemar Hedenius, a distance which could in these terms be described as an expedition from the equator to the Northern polar circle' (1993: 158; my translation).

From the point of view of Bergman's films, however, the Hedenius type was most aptly represented by rationalist martinets like Professor Isak Borg and his son Evald in *Smultronstället* (*Wild Strawberries*, 1957), the health official Dr Vergérus in *Ansiktet* (*The Magician/The Face*, 1958), or, one might add, Death himself in *Det sjunde inseglet* (*The Seventh Seal*, 1957). Actually, Dr Vergérus's blunt question to Vogler in *The Magician* – 'Can you call forth visions, Mr Vogler? Yes, or no?' – is highly reminiscent of Hedenius's brutal objections to Ragnar Bring, professor of dogmatics at Lund University, and at the time a distinguished defender of the Faith: 'But how is it really: did God create everything or did he not? A Christian ought to be able to answer yes or no to this' (in Nordin 2004: 161; my translation). Bergom-Larsson's description of Vergérus amplifies this connection: 'Vergérus is possessed by his longing for supreme knowledge, his whole existence is devoted to proving the non-existence of the inexplicable and consequently no God' (1977: 111; my translation). In an essay

Cold, greyish and deconstructed Swedish landscape in *Winter Light*

specially devoted to the juxtaposition of the Anglo-Saxon analytical philosophy of Hedenius and the metaphysics of Bergman, Bergom-Larsson mentions the existential quarrel in *Wild Strawberries* on precisely the question of faith and knowledge between the two students – one of theology, the other of medicine – as a parody of the Hedenius debate (1992: 12). It could here be noted that the rationalist Hedenius's stance was also parodied in contemporary Swedish literature, as exemplified by authors like Willy Kyrklund and Lars Gyllensten.

Warped vegetation in graphite

Sometimes a Bergman film displays the Swedish welfare mirror cracked through drab images of earlier canonised Swedish landscapes, as is proven in Zern's own analysis of *Winter Light*, Bergman's bitter tale of a priest who believes neither in his vocation, nor in God, nor in life itself. Regarding the metamorphosis of Sweden from the tentative establishment of the welfare state in the 1930s to modern affluence in the 1960s, Zern writes:

> When this epoch is at an end Bergman will go his way and Sweden another, and the most fascinating aspect of *Winter Light* is something Bergman hardly intended when the film was shot in the autumn of 1962. We sit in the darkness of the cinema and watch a vanishing Sweden. The benches of the church are as empty as the countryside, where the distance between farms and humans increases. The horse led over the hill is Death. On the roads, the last cars drive and the fog freezes to ice at twilight. In Bergman's imagery a society is exposed which no one will want

to be identified with during these pioneering years: that is, the impoverishment of the rural districts and the rootlessness of the individuals. We are here miles off official ideology, which instead focused on the future and the creation of a new suburbia. But we have nevertheless not left reality. (1993: 159–60; my translation)

Zern's shrewd and poetically delivered analysis can be illustrated by the beginning of the film, where we see the priest, played by Bergman's favourite actor Gunnar Björnstrand, preach to the practically empty benches of the church. A short montage of drab landscape imagery is juxtaposed with the prayer, thus comparing the words of the priest to the empty state of a cold, greyish and deconstructed Swedish landscape, at least if we compare with the splendid imagery of *Guesthouse Paradise*. At the end of the montage, the final landscape image is here dissolved into a close-up of the priest, thus determining firmly in the audience his empty state of mind. In fact the whole introduction to the film has been described by Maaret Koskinen as being 'excruciatingly lengthy', as expressing 'the idea of religious faith as bad theatre' and that it is all 'nothing more than one long meaningless ritual' (2000: 216). But through the codes I have been trying to unveil, it seems to me that this emptiness is also expressing something general about Swedish society and culture.

In his autobiography, legendary Bergman cinematographer Sven Nykvist claims that Bergman's films changed drastically from *Såsom i en spegel* (*Through a Glass Darkly*, 1960) onwards (1997: 87–93). Gone was the *chiaroscuro* lighting of Gunnar Fischer in the 1950s, and instead Nykvist was, according to his own testimony, forced by Bergman to create a contrastless tone of 'graphite', extremely difficult to achieve technically. Nykvist himself explains this cinematographic style in terms of heightened levels of realism, and he furthermore underlines how it was perfected during his work on *Winter Light*, where an irritated Bergman forcefully made him 'learn the enormous significance of reduction, to reduce all artificial light, all light that is not purely logical' (1997: 92; my translation). It was partly due to this change of cinematographic practice, I think, that we here perceive the appearance of a post-utopian landscape in Bergman's films.

It was, as is so well known, on the island of Fårö in the Baltic that Bergman eventually found the perfect spatial metaphor for the condition of man in the modern Swedish welfare state. The landscape, often employed by Bergman all the way up to Liv Ullmann's *Faithless* (2000), is barren, lonely, even overtly hostile with its warped vegetation, yet, one has to admit, strangely beautiful. The profoundly anti-modern experience of the Fårö landscape to Bergman personally is emphatically expressed in various places in his autobiography *The Magic Lantern*:

In the middle of March, we moved out to Fårö, where the long struggle between winter and spring had just started, one day strong sunlight and mild winds, shim-

Bibi Andersson and Liv Ullmann in *Persona*. To the left and right the stony, hostile beach of

mering reflections on the water and newborn lambs scuttling about on the bare thawed-out ground, the next day stormy winds from the tundras, the snow coming in horizontally, the seas raging, windows and roads blocked, the electricity off. Fires, paraffin stoves and battery radio. (1988: 95)

The nostalgia is here signified by the syntactic juxtaposition between dramatic landscape description and the laconic praise of the absence of modern facilities. Later in the book, Bergman dwells poetically on his love for the little island:

My ties with Fårö have several origins. The first was intuitive. This is your landscape, Bergman. It corresponds to your innermost imaginings of forms, proportions, colours, horizons, sounds, silences, lights and reflections ... Other reasons: I must find a counterweight to the theatre. If I were to rant and rave on the shore, a gull, at most, would take off. On the stage, such an exhibition would be disastrous. (1988: 208)

To underline my argument, somewhat different from but still clearly related to Bergman's own point of view, I want to mention the famous scene from Bergman's antimodern, yet modernist *tour de force Persona*. Here, two existentially suffering women, played by Bibi Andersson and Liv Ullmann, walk on the stony beach along the menacingly warped vegetation, which is obviously metaphorically tied to the status of their 'twisted' minds. This is in turn, according to the rhetoric of the film, the result of a rationalist society gone psychologically berserk, or on the verge of a breakdown, which according to Robin Wood is both the 'theme and form' in *Persona* (1969: 145). In terms of the Swedish cinematic tradition, the landscape is also a 'breakdown', here represented by the famous tracking shot of the quarrelling women walking along the Fårö shore.

Of course, to regard this symbolic use of landscape as connected to social ills in Swedish society would be extremely rare. It is rather typical that no one interviewed in Birgitta Steene's book (1996) – the only major reception study ever devoted to Bergman in Sweden – emphasises, perceives or even notices any kind of social criticism in Bergman's films. Steene herself, however, underlines the difference between

Bergman and mainstream cinematic landscape depiction by stating: 'With the establishment of the Fårö landscape as the symbolic space of his characters in 1960s films like *Persona*, *Hour of the Wolf*, *The Shame*, *A Passion* and *The Touch*, he broke the last ties with the glittering and melodramatic summer landscapes of Swedish cinema' (1996: 173; my translation).

But generally, Ingmar Bergman has just not been understood in politically deconstructive terms in Swedish discourse, mostly, I would argue, since Swedish culture in the 1960s was much too involved in and connected to hierarchies inherently alien to the Bergman universe: that is, precisely, the more or less unquestioned belief in the moral and economic supremacy of the Swedish model of a welfare state.

Initially, Bergman's films were often – though certainly not always – met with outright malice in Sweden, particularly within literary circles or within the late 1960s new Marxist intelligentsia. In literary circles, there was clearly envy over Bergman's international success, as shown by well-known poet and Swedish Academy member Lars Forssell's slightly condescending claim that even if Voltaire had an extremely limited readership, his influence on his contemporaries by far exceeded that of Bergman (Forssell 1968: 605). What Forssell really seems to implicate in spite of his general praise for the director is thatVoltaire wrote books – literature – for nobles and royalty, while Bergman created films, entertainment for the international riff-raff.

Although it was never really articulated, I would argue that all this negative response to Bergman's films in certain circles was exactly because of their being at odds with life in modern Sweden, the welfare Utopia. Also, Bergman's critical stance was expressed at a time when few other Swedish filmmakers disclosed the severe existential problems of industrial modernity and affluence, even if this critical-existentialist dimension was clearly present in some contemporary literature, particularly in the 1940s and 1950s, as in the novels of, say, Stig Dagerman and Birgitta Trotzig. And in his creation of a cinematic landscape Bergman was certainly a social heretic, challenging – whether he was aware of it or not – a traditional cinematic discourse which had so far been clearly connected to strong nationalist sentiments.

The power of auteurism

Another reason for not regarding Bergman's films as representations of contemporary Swedish society is the extremely strong position of an old-fashioned auteurism – to regard film as the representation of the director's life – particularly in Swedish film culture, but also, of course, elsewhere. In a review essay, American scholar Mark Sandberg describes the tendency of Bergman courses at American universities to become '"embarrassing" because of their outdated emphasis on *auteur* instead of *culture*' (1997: 358; emphasis in original). Without wishing to dispose of the auteur theory entirely, Sandberg however proceeds to investigate research approaches and

A lonely Erland Josephson in the stone landscape of Fårö in *Faithless*

teaching methods that might organise itself 'along different theoretical and cultural axes than the one beginning with "Ingmar Bergman was the son of a Lutheran minister…"' (ibid.).

A typical case to study in this context would be Bergman's next to last cinematic venture, *Faithless*, for which he wrote the script. Here, we are once again on familiar Bergman territory: emotional chaos, adultery, a painful divorce, sexual blackmail, a horrendous suicide, deeply disturbed childhood, social malaise caused by the absence of moral values, disastrous interventions from, unsurprisingly, the welfare state and its engineers in the shape of an Ingemar Hedenius-style social worker and so on. And, the story is once again set against the backdrop of a barren Fårö landscape, which now and then turns up on the screen to remind the audience of the psychological torments so often suffered by Bergman characters in this setting. Even if the Fårö imagery shot by cinematographer Jörgen Persson lacks the extreme photographic stylisation of Sven Nykvist, the landscape still emphasises human loneliness and the essential lack of a coherent social context.

The film was directed by Liv Ullmann, yet it remains in public discourse a Bergman film, even if some reviewers, infested by the still so dominant *politique des auteurs*, became confused and did not really know how to handle the film as a Bergman movie without him having actually directed it himself. Hence, Kathleen Murphy claims *Faithless* to be the 'golden child of [Bergman's and Ullmann's] tangled liaison as lovers and collaborators. Its aesthetic DNA can be traced to fundamental forms and themes in the Old Master's lifework softened and redeemed by Ullman's remarkable faith in forgiveness' (2001: n.p.). Patrick Z. McGavin similarly concludes his review by expressing concern about the unclear authorship of the film:

Exterior and interior from a drab post-utopian city in *Show Me Love*

Ullmann has great instincts for a director, but if there's a weakness, she hasn't completely proven she has a clearly articulated personality of her own. Then again Ullmann has her own highly charged personal and professional association with Bergman, aspects which no doubt bring additional nuances and subtexts to this work. At a time when few films seem to have anything important to say about truthful, recognisably human emotional interaction, *Faithless* turns public spectacle into a very private anguish. (2000: n.p.)

There is certainly no question of any Barthesian death of the author in these pieces of mainstream cultural discourse. Neither is there any trace of Sandbergian embarrassment for unfashionable auteurism within contemporary academia. Instead, the problem seems to be whether we possibly have two great auteurs instead of only one.

Films do not, consequently, according to this theory, belong primarily to social or cultural discourse, but are the pure result of the elevated mind of artistic genius. On the other hand auteurism is in fact the only reason that there still exists a film industry in Sweden. Without the auteur, by tradition a necessary predicament for applying concepts of high art to film, there would certainly be no governmental support for domestically-produced films, and hardly any film can survive without part of its funding coming from the state. Also, as Swedish culture functions, there would be little ground for the creation of an auteur or reference to the discourse of high art, without a strong biographical legend, in Russian formalist Boris Tomashevsky's sense (see 1978). Without domestically-produced films, there would be much less press coverage and consequently no serious film criticism. Hence, the view of Bergman as isolated from his own social and historical context, a situation that has as much to do with Bergman himself – *the* auteur *par préférence* – as with other cultural discourses.

Yet, it should be noted that Swedish scholars and critics lately have been made aware of a tradition in Europe, aptly designated by Jennifer M. Bean as 'Post-Utopian European cinema' (2000: 62). Bean describes a loss of innocence in post-1989 European films, with depictions of social crises and resentment over governmental policies. In Sweden this can be clearly noticed in many films of the late 1990s, where the possible failures of the Swedish model welfare society are duly scrutinised. In the great Swedish hit movie of 1998, Lukas Moodysson's *Fucking Åmål* (released in English-speaking countries as *Show Me Love*), collectivism is typically condemned and individual initiative praised, here in the case of two young lesbians daring to face the scorn of the heterosexual mob. The film is about the cruelty of small-town mentality, set against the backdrop of drab landscapes and extremely ugly 1960s city-scapes, shot with the use of soft focus and a shaky hand-held camera. We are here very, very far away from the 1930s or 1940s style of glorious mountains, picturesque villages and romantic lakes shining in the midnight sun, and regarding semantic substance substantially closer to the angst-ridden, deconstructed landscapes of Berg-man's 1960s films.

Conclusion

To sum up my argument: traditionally, Swedish cinema chauvinistically hailed Swed-ish landscape as the basis of Swedishness, even employing it to stigmatise that which was considered foreign. In the 1960s, this tradition began to be deconstructed in the films of Ingmar Bergman, despite a culturally encoded unwillingness among audi-ences, critics and scholars alike, to read the new aesthetics in terms of a social cri-tique of modern Swedish society. In the 1990s, however, social and aesthetic develop-ment – with accumulated Swedish wealth heavily in decline – have made this insight more or less necessary.

And, at last, the study of social contemporary discourses, particularly those relat-ed to the Swedish model – at the very height of its existence in the 1960s – certainly represents a new and exciting challenge for Bergman scholars. It may even reveal hidden agendas, political controversies and cultural hierarchies in the dark corners of the history of Bergman country.

Note

1   Some writers have adopted a slightly more critical approach to the understanding of landscape in Swedish cinema history. In his study on the matter, Bo Florin scrutinises some of the critical clichés regarding Sjöström's *You and I*. Florin claims that instead of unambiguously creating harmonious beauty, the landscape imagery is dialectically related to man in Sjöström's film: that is, the Swedish landscape is in reality even depicted as a mortal enemy. Regarding the film's ending, Florin's reading is the following: 'The smiling landscapes of the valley or the sunlit days on the mountain are gradually and mercilessly left behind the refugees. In the final image of the film, the ice and the snow become the masters and there are no longer any traces

of human beings' (1997: 84; my translation). Thus, the traditional understanding of the greatness of landscape, encoded by various discourses, is drastically overturned.

References

Bean, J. M. (2000) 'Post-Utopian European Cinema', *Aura: Film Studies Journal*, 4, 3, 62–70.

Bergman, I. (1988) *The Magic Lantern: An Autobiography*, trans. J. Tate. New York and London: Penguin.

Bergom-Larsson, M. (1977) *Ingmar Bergman och den borgerliga ideologin.* Stockholm: Pan/Norstedt.

_____ (1992) 'Film som religiöst språk: Hedenius och Ingmar Bergman i livsåskådningsdebatten', in M. Bergom-Larsson, S. Hammar, B. Kristensson Uggla (eds) *Nedstigningar i modern film hos Bergman, Wenders, Adlon, Tarkovskij.* Delsbo: Åsak, Sahlin & Dahlström, 9–49.

Florin, B. (1997) *Den nationella stilen: Studier i den svenska filmens guldålder.* Stockholm: Aura.

Forssell, L. (1968) 'Film', *BLM*, 37, 8, 605–7.

Gervais, M. (1999) *Ingmar Bergman: Magician and Prophet.* Montreal: McGill-Queen's University Press.

Hedenius, I. (1949) *Tro och vetande.* Stockholm: Bonniers.

Idestam-Almquist, B. (1939) *Den svenska filmens drama: Sjöström – Stiller.* Stockholm: Åhlén & söner.

Koskinen, M. (2000) 'Ingmar Bergman and the Mise en Scène of the Confessional', in A.-C. Gavel Adams and T. Leiren (eds.) *Stage and Screen: Studies in Scandinavian Film and Drama. Essays in Honour of Birgitta Steene.* Seattle: DreamPlay Press Northwest, 209–28.

Lidman, S. (1968) 'Skammen', *Aftonbladet*, 6 October, 5.

McGavin, P. Z. (2000) 'Ullmann's *Faithless*, It's Bergman', *Indiewire.com.*, http://www.indiewire.com/movies/rev_00Cannes_000519_Faith.html (accessed 20 May 2005).

Murphy, K. (2001) 'Actions Matter. *Faithless* in the Haunted House of Bergman', *The Stranger.Com*, 10, 28 (29 March–4 April), http://www.thestranger.com/seattle/Content?oid=6918 (accessed 20 May 2005).

Nordin, S. (2004) *Ingemar Hedenius – en filosof och hans tid.* Stockholm: Natur och Kultur.

Nykvist, S. (1997) *Vördnad för ljuset: om film och människor.* Stockholm: Albert Bonniers Förlag.

Qvist, P.-O. (1986) *Jorden är vår arvedel: Landsbygden i svensk spelfilm 1940–1959.* Uppsala: Filmhäftet.

_____ (1995) *Folkhemmets bilder: Modernisering, motstånd och mentalitet i den svenska 30-talsfilmen.* Lund: Arkiv.

Sadoul, G. (1952) *Histoire generale du cinéma.* Paris: Denoel.

Sandberg, M. (1997) 'Tracking Out: The Bergman Film in Retrospect', *Scandinavian Studies*, 69, 3 (Summer), 357–76.

Steene, B. (1996) *Måndagar med Bergman: En svensk publik möter Ingmar Bergmans filmer.* Stockholm/Stehag: Symposion.

Tomashevsky, B. (1978) 'Literature and Biography', trans. Herbert Eagle, in L. Matejka and K. Pomorska (eds) *Readings in Russian Poetics: Formalist and Structuralist Views*. Ann Arbor: Michigan Slavic Publications, 47–55.

Wood, R. (1969) *Ingmar Bergman*. London: Studio Vista.

Wright, R. (1998) *The Visible Wall: Jews and Other Outsiders in Swedish Film*. Carbondale: Southern Illinois University Press.

Zern, L. (1993) *Se Bergman*. Stockholm: Norstedts.

WHAT SHOULD WE BELIEVE?: RELIGIOUS MOTIFS IN INGMAR BERGMAN'S FILMS

Astrid Söderbergh Widding

Bergman and religion – is that not the very prototype of a subject that has been discussed so much that one is sick and tired of it, and thus without any further interest? Birgitta Steene (1983) has rightly noted that the fame of Bergman, as a filmmaker, still relies not so much on his aesthetic contributions to the art of cinema, but rather on his psychological insights and his religious obsession. Maaret Koskinen (1993) shows in her dissertation on Bergman's cinematic aesthetic that within Bergman studies internationally, there exists a strikingly large amount of studies of philosophical or religious problems in the films. What, then, about the Swedish horizon?

Bergman studies in Sweden may still seem a bit underdeveloped in comparison with international approaches. Given the limited space that has been accorded to religion in Swedish society in general during the last decades, it ought to come as no surprise that comments on religious aspects in the films are rare. Christianity and culture have nothing to do with each other, have they? This rhetorical question by an anonymous Swedish feature editor is referred to in Hans Nystedt's book (1989) on Ingmar Bergman and Christian belief. The author has reacted precisely to this idea in his portrait of the director and his films, written from a very personal point of view, and mostly biographically related to Bergman. Nystedt looks for Christian symbols, not least from the Bible, and he finds them. But he also goes into polemics with earlier interpreters, like Jörn Donner (1962) who notes that even though the problems dealt with in the films often appear in the guise of religious questions, everything is still perfectly comprehensible to irreligious people. Religious motifs, even though they might be shaped in the form of criticism, must nevertheless be as much excused as possible. According to Donner, Bergman has succeeded in transforming his private observations into general ones, comprehensible to other people, in which his strength as an artist also resides. Religious questions are widened, so that they contain all of the painful experience that tortures people of our times.

However, this point of view of Donner's also creates a number of problematic consequences. For example, according to Donner it is more difficult to translate *Nat-*

tvardsgästerna (*Winter Light/The Communicants*, 1963) to a non-Christian problematic than many previous Bergman films – but on the other hand, Donner has already found the very essence of the film: that it is unimportant whether God exists or not (1962: 175–82). In his book on Bergman, Leif Zern notes that it might be possible to claim that Bergman is not a Christian, as no possible affirmation of Christian belief can be found in any of his feature films. Instead, Christianity appears as pure negativity, present only by its absence: 'Demoniacal and unreflected, it casts its long black shadows over the silver screen. The more invisible it is, the more visible it becomes. Bergman's God is internalised and speaks each time the director opens his mouth. If the actors have a mission in his films, it seems to be that of both evoking and dispersing these phantom images, evaporations, reflexes of the spinal marrow' (1993: 162; my translation).

I find the emphasis on this doubleness in Bergman's films, on an evocation which also seems to be a dispersion, remarkably pertinent. And Zern continues: 'Ingmar Bergman may be religious in the sense that he uninterruptedly deals with man's relationship to what is most high in existence, and even the one who sticks to the idea that the most high fails – or remains silent – is of course religious' (1993: 163; my translation).

The problem that I find in large parts of the Swedish critical discussion of religious motifs in Bergman, whether from a positive or a negative perspective, is its literal character. When there is talk about God, and only then, religion is seen as present in the films. And there is much Lutheranism and sin and guilt, but little by little, Bergman throws out this fatherly heritage – for better or for worse, depending on the critic's point of view. The air has become lighter, and it is easier to breathe. At worst, the repressed may return in the figure of an evil priest, like Bishop Vergérus in *Fanny och Alexander* (*Fanny and Alexander*, 1982/1983). I think on the contrary that it is particularly important, when it comes to a filmmaker as ambiguous as Bergman, to approach the question from a much wider perspective. From such a point of view, what is important is neither the question of tracing the presence of enough Christianity to allow for their interpretation as a living continuation of the heritage from the director's childhood, nor is it the idea to 'save' Bergman as a religious filmmaker in one sense or another of the word. It is not even Ingmar Bergman as a person who stands in focus any longer. Rather, it is about the films themselves and what they articulate – and to what extent they may be seen in relation to a religious or more specifically Christian tradition.

Such a wider perspective is adopted by the Canadian film scholar and Jesuit Marc Gervais in his book *Ingmar Bergman: Magician and Prophet* (1999). He tries to capture the poetic vision of the director with the development of contemporary culture as his particular point of departure. According to Gervais, Bergman is not just a passive witness to this culture in his films; on the contrary, it is incarnated there. But the book may also be seen as an encounter between Bergman's movies and what might be called a contemporary Christian sensibility. Gervais emphasises how the films both consciously and consistently express the most central questions in religious inquiry: life and death, hope and despair, evil, morality, forgiveness, grace, meaning and absurdity, eternal life and nothingness, and last but not least the question of art as redemptory or 'diabolic'. But Gervais makes an important point when he states that these questions are not posed in the films as timeless or eternal, but always anchored in a concrete landscape and in historical time, be it past or present, and often within the context of contemporary culture.

In the field of Bergman studies in Sweden, a similar attempt to widen the discussion is made by Maria Bergom-Larsson, Stina Hammar and Bengt Kristensson Uggla in their anthology on modern film, where they call for a renewal of the Swedish debate on ethics, religion and the philosophy of life (Bergom-Larsson *et al.* 1992: 9–22). They want to come to terms with Ingemar Hedenius and his central role within the post-war debate in Sweden, and not least with his belief in reason and reason only. They also claim that the main basis for Hedenius's unique position is the centrality of the power of words within Swedish tradition, not least due to the Lutheran heritage. Bergman on the other hand, who had reached international fame, had not even come close to playing an equally central role within his own country, neither as a thinker in general, nor as a critic of Christianity, even though his project – so the authors argue – was comparable to that of Hedenius, regardless of the fact that the focus of Bergman's criticism differs from his. Above all, it is different because Bergman expressed his view of the world within a symbolic language, and both images and symbols have largely been set aside, at least in public debate. When Bergom-Larsson and Kristensson Uggla plead for an introduction of the creative or symbolic dimension, with Bergman as a prominent representative, this is motivated both by looking backwards and forwards. They look back to the battle with the iconoclasts in the history of the early Church which led to victory for the advocates of the icon – it is the Christian conviction of the incarnate God that allows for an upheaval of the ban on images from Biblical tradition. They look forward to the society of the image which still to a large extent remains to be developed, and which they interpret from a postmodern point of view. Here, images have gained more importance than words. Here at last, there is enough room for various meanings.

From there, the discussion takes a leap to the camera in Bergman's films, which is interpreted as supplicant; through a description of the empathy of its look, the authors argue that it sees the world through the lens of love. The analysis is very beautiful, and doubtlessly it may function as a possible reading of the films that they discuss – among them *Prison* (1949), where the camera seems to show compassion for the main character, Birgitta-Carolina, and her destiny. However, I find this interpretive frame problematic in relation to Bergman, not least because I consider it more ahistorical than necessary. To me, it seems like a long way to go to anchor an interpretation of his films in the debate on iconoclasm in the Eastern Church of the eighth and ninth century, even though they also refer to a quotation from Luther where he expresses his dislike for the iconoclasts. Nor does it seem evident that the films should bear the mark of postmodernity.

Between sacred clutter and holy things

First of all, it might be wise not to be too hasty. It is impossible to ignore the explicit images of a god that remain so central in a number of his films. Between fascination and fear, or between idyll and panic – it is in such terms that Bergman describes his own childhood in Olivier Assayas's and Stig Björkman's (1990). This might as well function as description of the relationship to religion in his films, at least during the cinematically dense years around 1960 when the most violent religious settlement in Bergman's films takes place on screen. Joseph Marty, a Catholic theologian, links the motif of fear in Bergman to the first commandment in Luther's catechism: 'We shall fear and love God above all' (1991: 36). That God is fearful is a well-known reality in a Biblical context. And in Bergman, this does not primarily refer to the monstrous or grotesque aspects of the images of God that are so significantly expressed in the films, but rather on the contrary it is the question of a fear that overthrows the nice, harmless, domesticated images of God. Both Marc Gervais and Joseph Marty on one hand and Leif Zern on the other have an advantage in that they deal with Bergman's specific way of expressing religious matters from the outside, from a Catholic and a Jewish point of view respectively. This may be helpful in order to see clearly; to others, Swedish or Lutheran tradition may be all too familiar and block the sight, but to Marty or Zern on the contrary it has a certain quality of strangeness.

One of the most thorough investigations of the question of God may be found in one of Bergman's costume films – I avoid the label 'historical film' even though the film is situated in the Middle Ages, and it is, to a very large extent, a historical myth that is brought to the screen. Obviously, I am referring to *Det sjunde inseglet* (*The Seventh Seal*, 1957), which may seem to make spiritual drama easier to handle by placing it in another historical context, but at the same time it contains exactly the same conflicts as the films situated in a contemporary context. In Bergman's autobiography *The Magic Lantern* (1988) and quoted in *Images: My Life in Film* (1994), Bergman tells about his inspiration from his own one-act play *Wood Painting* (1954) which in turn was inspired by *Biblia pauperum*, the Bible for the poor – the expressive paintings from different churches in the countryside, which he had been studying during his childhood, while listening to his father's sermons.

In the film, Bergman portrays Jof and Mia, the clown and his wife, as a harmonic couple radiating love and confidence in life. Through his visions, Jof also enjoys an immediate and seemingly natural contact with a greater reality. But in the beginning of the film the more melancholic Knight, Block, who has played chess with Death and so far been successful, decides to go to confession. In the confessional sits Death instead of a priest, but the Knight is yet unaware of this. Under the sign of the tormented crucified, in the dark shadows of the confessional, to the faint sound of church bells, Block settles up with his God in a very Bergmanesque way, but in a manner that is also very characteristic of modern man:

Is it so cruelly inconceivable to grasp God with the senses? Why should He hide himself in a mist of half-spoken promises and unseen miracles? How can we have faith in those who believe when we can't have faith in ourselves? What is going to happen to those of us who want to believe but aren't able to? And what is to become of those who neither want to nor are capable of believing? Why can't I kill God within me? Why does He live on in this painful and humiliating way even though I curse Him and want to tear Him out of my heart? Why, in spite of everything, is He a baffling reality that I can't shake off? Do you hear me?
 – Yes, I hear you.
 – I want knowledge, not faith, not suppositions, but knowledge. I want God to stretch out His hand towards me, reveal Himself and speak to me.
 – But He remains silent.
 – I call out to Him in the dark but no one seems to be there.
 – Perhaps no one is there.
 – Then life is an outrageous horror. No one can live in the face of death, knowing that all is nothingness.
 – Most people never reflect about either death or the futility of life.
 – But one day they will have to stand at that last moment of life and look towards the darkness.
 – When *that* day comes...
 – In our fear, we make an image, and that image we call God. (Bergman 1960: 28)

Perhaps the most striking thing in this scene is the close linking of the concept of God to death. On one hand we have the will either to die or – temporarily – escape death; on the other we have the will to kill God, the eluding reality, that Block wants to master, to catch, to lay hands on, but in vain. Here we also meet with the silent God, and the idol created by man in order to conquer his own fear of emptiness.

In *Images*, Bergman has commented in considerable detail on the religious dimension of *The Seventh Seal*:

Since at the time I was still very much in a quandary over religious faith, I placed my two opposing beliefs side by side, allowing each to state its case in its own way.

In this manner, a virtual cease-fire could exist between my childhood piety and my newfound harsh rationalism. Thus, there are no neurotic complications between the knight and his vassals. Also, I infused the characters of Jof and Mia with something that was very important to me: the concept of the holiness of the human being. If you peel off the layers of various theologies, the holy always remains … I still held on to some of the withered remains of my childish piety. I had until then held a totally naïve idea of what one would call a preternatural salvation. My present conviction manifested itself during this time. I believe a human being carries his or her own holiness, which lies within the realm of the earth; there are no otherworldly explanations. So in the film lives a remnant of my honest, childish piety lying peacefully alongside a harsh and rational perception of reality.

The Seventh Seal is definitely one of my last films to manifest my conceptions of faith, conceptions that I had inherited from my father and carried along with me from childhood. When I made *The Seventh Seal*, both prayers and invocations to something or someone were central realities in my life; to offer up a prayer was a completely natural act. In *Through a Glass Darkly*, my childhood inheritance is put to rest. I maintained that every conception of a divine god created by human beings must be a monster, a monster with two faces or, as Karin puts it, the spider-god. (1994: 235–8)

Såsom i en spegel (*Through a Glass Darkly*, 1960) depicts the insane Karin waiting for God's visit: he will cross the threshold at any moment. First she wants to be alone on this occasion and tries to send her husband Martin away because he is an unbeliever and because she is afraid that he will ruin her moment with the god. But yet he stays in the room when she kneels down. Then she changes her mind and implores him also to kneel. Immediately after that the helicopter arrives to take her to the hospital. To Karin the shadow of the helicopter on the wall instantly becomes the concrete figure of a dreadful god who breaks into her reality. Her existence is torn to pieces; a calming drug is all that remains along with her story about the appalling spider god who has shown his face and tried to rape her.

In his notebook, Bergman wrote about his conception of the visit of the god, a passage that he cites in *Images*:

A god descends into a human being and settles in her. First he is just an inner voice, a certain knowledge, or a commandment. Threatening or pleading. Repulsive yet stimulating. Then he lets himself be more and more known to her, and the human being gets to test the strength of the god, learns to love him, sacrifices for him, and finds herself forced into the utmost devotion and then into complete emptiness. When this emptiness has been accomplished, the god takes possession of this human being and accomplishes his work through her hands. Then he leaves her empty and burned out, without any possibility of continuing to live in this world. That is what happens to Karin. And the borderline that she crosses is the bizarre pattern on the wallpaper. (1994: 252)

'I have seen God' – Karin's declaration is strong in its madness. God appears like abominable vermin, a raping spider that does not fall short of the worst horror film, even if it is visible only to Karin's inner sight; here the viewer perhaps meets with the most sombre of Bergman's concepts of God. The connection with violence, with outrage, that becomes so explicit when the hysterically shouting and struggling Karin gets her sedating drug, also places this god on the side of brutal power; this once and for all will ruin the foundation of the dialogue in the epilogue where David assures Minus that love is a feeling of certainty, in all its forms and versions, and that God and love are one and the same.

Is Karin's cruel spider god just the effect of a sick imagination? That Karin's image of God has considerably more strength and validity in Bergman's filmic universe is evident from the reference he makes to it in his next film, *Winter Light*. Here Bergman takes his next step in his banishing of the images of God and here the monstrous spider god also returns in the periphery. Theologian Jean Paillard writes about the film:

What [Bergman] has tried to do with his film is to obliterate our old image of God thus letting us conceive of a different one: the image of a God whom it is difficult to comprehend, explain and describe. To his horror the main character of the film, the clergyman and sceptic Tomas Ericson, discovers a false God. A God who is totally his own creation and who answers his own needs, but who is completely devoid of any relation to outer reality – an echo-God giving the replies you expect him to. (1970: 77; my translation)

This becomes evident not least in the nuclear scene in the film where Tomas is forced to confront his old image of God in meeting the fisherman Jonas Persson, who not only doubts but also is full of dread for 'the Chinese' – in other words an invasion from a foreign country. This is a totally absurd scene, where Tomas asks Jonas to come back to the church, to make it possible for them to talk in peace and quiet, to give Jonas the chance to speak his mind, but where Tomas's own anxiety and his eagerness to speak predominates; he talks incessantly, thus making it impossible for Jonas to say anything whatsoever. The conversation also has fatal consequences – immediately afterwards Jonas takes his own life:

I and my God lived in one world, a specially arranged world, where everything made sense ... Please, you must understand. I'm no good as a clergyman ... I became a clergyman and believed in God. An improbable, entirely private, fatherly God. Who loved mankind, of course, but most of all me ... D'you understand, Jonas? What a monstrous mistake I'd made? Can you realise what a bad priest must come of such a spoiled, shut-in, anxious wretch as me? Can you imagine my prayers? To an echo-god. Who gave benign answers and reassuring blessings? Every time I confronted God with the reality I saw, he became ugly, revolting, a spider god – a monster. (Bergman 1967: 84–5)

In the following scene, when Tomas staggers out into the chancel, Märta is waiting for him and he cries not without a certain triumph or at least relief that he has finally become free, free from the father God, free from falsehood. But it is to be a short relief: how free is he, in fact, you ask yourself – he begins to cough, and, ironically, he falls over on his knees in front of the altar. Evidently it was not as easy as it seemed to be. But still, the important thing in the film is less the echo-god that Tomas leaves behind than his own growth as the film advances, and the new development that is possibly hinted at when we reach the end of the story, where Tomas, in spite of his unbelief, still decides to hold the service in an empty church. Thus, to him, the service turns out to be a real sacred act, not a spectacle in front of a more or less devout crowd of spectators. This is probably as close as we can come to a renewed and mature image of God in Bergman's films, at least on the explicit level. After that the whole thing is eliminated.

In an interview with Vilgot Sjöman, Bergman has referred to Pär Lagerkvist's words from the novel *The Death of Ahasuerus*:

Beyond the gods, beyond all that falsifies and coarsens the world of holiness, beyond all lies and distortion, all twisted divinities and all the abortions of human imagination, there must be something stupendous which is inaccessible to us. Which, by our very failure to capture it, demonstrates how inaccessible it is. Beyond all the sacred clutter the holy thing itself must exist. That I believe, of that I am certain. (1963: 205)

Moreover, the words of Lagerkvist are not far from Bergman's own reasoning in the quotation above from *Images*, where he is talking about Man and the sacred. As a matter of fact, in his films Bergman preaches less of God's death – even if this may be his point of departure – than the death of the images of God. The images of God that are mistaken for reality, these childhood images that are often called upon, seem to be one of the chief antagonists in his films. Bergman makes a clean sweep of Christian imagery in order to be able to turn the page. The images have to be broken down, to be destroyed because they are fatal and untruthful. What will come after the iconoclasm is a different question. But Bergman's films have in common with

Praying to an echo-god: Gunnar Björnstrand in *Winter Light (photo © AB Svensk Filmindustri)*

the mystic tradition the idea that what is certain and articulate must make room for what is uncertain and inarticulate, and that comprehension and knowledge gradually must be replaced by total unknowing. It would be to betray the experience of the mystics to turn the perspective and assume that their negations are only rhetorical gestures meant to disguise a positive, affirmative image of God. The dark night where the images of God are dying and where man is confronted with his complete silence is a true, real night.

The aesthetics of redemption: faces and words

Already in her book on Bergman from 1976, Maria Bergom-Larsson deals with the road leading away from the father god in Bergman's films. She talks of the confrontation between on one hand the image of an evil god, the horrifying god in *Through a Glass Darkly*, and on the other the lame, impotent god of imagination, the private father god whom men invent for themselves. She describes how this father god is carried out from the scene in *The Silence* (1963) in the shape of the dead father: all that remains is a dead greybeard weighing 400 pounds, as Bergman himself has said to Vilgot Sjöman (see Bergom-Larsson 1976: 56–9). What is left? God's silence only? Or perhaps the other, unknown language existing in that film?

In a later book from 1992, Bergom-Larsson returns to the death of the father god, but now in a discussion that refers to the imagery of the films rather than to their ideological dimension. She then takes her starting point in Bergman's well-known anecdote of the cathedral in Chartres, how he wants to compare his own filmic work with that of the anonymous sculptor and craftsman, who is cutting out his pictures from the stone. She thinks that the new cathedral he is building is a cathedral of fraternity, which exists in a selfish communion on the warm, filthy earth under a cold and empty sky, as Bergman has phrased it (see Bergom-Larsson *et al.* 1992: 24, 48). Bergom-Larsson sees this as a confrontation between two images of God: the father god in Chartres and the brother god who has moved into the heart of man. She proceeds with the theme of deprivation and of returning home or reincarnation, starting from *Gycklarnas afton* (*The Naked Night/Sawdust and Tinsel*, 1953) and a series of other films. In her opinion, Bergman's films are in harmony with what she names the Christian basic pattern and she points out the Christ-like feature in many of the artists portrayed in the films. This is what she names the Christ pattern, which she observes breaking through in the films. This gives her interpretation an almost archetypical character.

In his book on Bergman, Leif Zern distinguishes between two methods to approach and explain the Christian trait in the director's films (1993: 163–4): the first is the search for symbols that theologians and others have been engrossed in, symbols that may or may not be biblically oriented. As a rule the interpreter is successful here, because Bergman's universe is so totally leavened with the Lutheran tradition that has been his starting point – I have already referred to interpretations that are so different from one another as those of Hans Nystedt and Maria Bergom-Larsson. But of course the vital issue is, as Zern points out, how this material is going to be interpreted. What has been explicitly formulated in generally accepted symbols does not tell us much about what meaning the Lutheran legacy actually gives to Bergman's filmic art.

The second method, which Zern himself makes use of, instead seeks for the Christian trait in Bergman's aesthetics. It is not really a question of direct symbols or religious state properties, but of something else, something much more difficult to lay hands on. Zern, who has Jewish origins, sees 'Bergman's scenery as something radically different. I very well knew, or felt, to be exact, that this was not my realm, but this was not due to Tomas Ericson, this unbelieving shepherd of the soul in the Lutheran church, but to what was written in between the lines; it was not the tangible but the intangible, not the denominations but what had been left without denomination that provoked me and shut me out; the glances, the special light upon an actor's face, the mood, the text below the text' (1993: 20; my translation).

Very often, Bergman's films have been summarised according to his way of filming faces, leaving man with his desire and his need to express it at the centre of his films.[1] This life is therefore to be divined in the faces, in the close-ups by which Bergman – according to his own testimony – is possessed, showing them in detail in his films: 'the human face is the starting point of my work … the closeness to the human face is without doubt the special characteristic of the film, its sign of nobility' (1959: 5). In this connection I consider the close-up of the face less as the first characteristic sign of illusionist aesthetics than as a kind of ethic imperative in the depiction of man in Bergman's films. The face is the screen where the inner life of man is both made visible and concealed, is made to appear and then disappear. The face can be made corrupt, distorted; it may become affected, false, conventional or hypocritical. But still, out of all these deformations a transformation may finally come into existence, a re-moulding of what is into something that is yet in the process of coming into existence. No matter how, you cannot pull off the mask to expose the truth that is behind. The truth about man is never visible. It evades representation.

Thus I think that in Bergman you may possibly look upon the face as the place where speech is born: by means of the face the words are brought forth from the heart, from the body. Also words can be falsified, they can lie, distort truth. But the lie is made visible by the face. In this way the face acts as a persona, a mask that exactly as in the theatre makes visible what is trying to hide itself by means of a distorted or locked-up speech. Joseph Marty writes that the creation of the face as the place where speech is born is a holy act, holy like the theatre and the prototypical mask so convincingly called forth by *Sommarnattens leende* (*Smiles of a Summer Night*, 1955), *Riten* (*The Ritual/The Rite*, 1969), *Trollflöjten* (*The Magic Flute*, 1975), *Fanny and Alexander* (1982/1983) or *Efter repetitionen* (*After the Rehearsal*, 1984) (1991: 46).

The redeeming character of the word, of speech, is touched upon at the end of *Through a Glass Darkly*, in the epilogue that has often been branded by the critics as loosely attached. In *Images*, Bergman notes that the criticism is just: 'I suppose that was written out of my need to be didactic. Perhaps I put it there in order to say something that had not yet been said; I don't know' (1994: 243). 'Father spoke to me', Minus somewhat theatrically exclaims. And surely these words are a bit awkward coming from him. The hope they give on the level of verbal expression is not really authentic and surely enough in the following films the words of the father have been replaced by the silence of God.

Leif Zern, again, has pointed out the important role of speech in *Winter Light*. In her letter to Tomas, a letter that he has read immediately before the scene referred to above – her face in close-up all the time – Märta writes: 'It is so difficult for us to talk to each other.' Yet speech is going on all the time: 'Why don't you say anything?' – 'Because you are speaking all the time.' Zern beautifully describes the film as a series of attempts at conversation and in the end he asks himself 'why [Bergman's] characters regard speech with such a profound anxiety. Why does Märta write a letter to Tomas whom she is still meeting every day? What is the meaning of titles like *The Silence* or *Cries and Whispers*? Why does the rapist in *The Virgin Spring* not have any tongue?' (1993: 131; my translation).

Zern's analysis ends up in the conclusion that 'Bergman's conception of God is a metaphor for the dialectics between silence and speech in his films. You need not be a clergyman in order to doubt. It is enough to have been born, and this magnetic field affects the characters of Bergman by linking them to two similar absolute magnetic poles: silence and the word' (1993: 166; my translation). In this there is an obvious dualism. Also the relation to the word – both God's incarnate word and words generally – is characterised by a stern, absolute relation: either belief or unbelief, acknowledgement or denial. And it is absolutely decisive which alternative a person is finally choosing.

Perhaps the mute Elisabet in *Persona* (1966) in her way communicates more, even at times in a perverted way, than her loquacious nurse Alma. But yet she has decided to lock herself up in silence, a provocative choice, hard to put up with for the people around her. Her doctor is scolding her:

You can keep quiet. Then at least you're not lying. You can cut yourself off, close yourself in. Then you don't have to play a part, put on a face, make false gestures. Or so you think. But reality plays tricks on you. Your hiding place isn't watertight enough. Life starts leaking in everywhere. And you're forced to react.

No one asks whether it's genuine or not, whether you're true or false. It's only in the theatre that's an important question. Hardly even there, for that matter.

Elisabet, I understand that you're keeping quiet, not moving, that you have put this lack of will into a fantastic system. I understand it and admire you for it. I think you should keep playing this part until you've lost interest in it. When you've played it to the end, you can drop it as you drop your other parts. (Bergman 1972: 41–2).

In *Viskingar och rop* (*Cries and Whispers*, 1973), the figure of the maid Anna articulates silence; combined with her self-sacrificing love for the dying Agnes this will make her a kind of mother of truth. Moreover, a parallel might be drawn with the Hymn to Love in the First Letter to the Corinthians: Anna does not take part in false speech. Also, in *Scener ur ett äktenskap* (*Scenes from a Marriage*, 1973) Marianne says that she is learning to speak. The emotionally illiterate are learning language a second time. This is hard learning, perhaps the most difficult of all, and it will take its time. Experience has got may faces: speech and silence, belief and unbelief, existence and non-existence.

In *Ansikte mot ansikte* (*Face to Face*, 1976), Tomas says that he is hoping that somebody or something will affect him so much that he will become real. He does not stop repeating to himself that he is hoping that one day he will really come into existence. But perhaps, he says to himself, reality is not at all what he imagines. Perhaps it only exists as a wish, as a desire. To seek and to communicate – this is finally

Articulating silence: Kari Sylwan as the maid in *Cries and Whispers* (photo © *AB Svensk Film-*

what man's pursuit pertains to in the films of Bergman. To listen and to express one-self – this is the way the films express the exchange of love. Love figures not least by means of the frequent – and disconnected – quotations from the Hymn to Love in the thirteenth chapter of the Letter to the Corinthians: *Through a Glass Darkly, Face to Face* and so forth; it also figures within the frame of *Scenes from a Marriage*. Love implies mutual speech – in other words to express oneself to another person who is listening, and vice versa.

Words, when they are true, allow man to be rooted in himself, in his body; this is also true of the silence of words, the space that is created in the pauses, in attentive-ness, in the rapidly stopped torrent that in the middle of the adjusted discourse, the prefabricated words of the lie of life, suddenly allows something new and unexpected to be born. But this mutual speech is also constantly threatened. Two things threaten it more than anything else. One is repetition where speech only becomes an empty reiteration or recitation. This is also something that you may learn from the theatre. It is unimportant that theatre itself is performance and pretence. But if the words are not reborn in every new performance there are only empty phrases and meaning-less gestures left. The moment after the repetition is thus one of the most central in Bergman's universe. The second threat is narcissism, that finally I am only talking to myself, am reflected into my own words, mistaking the other person for myself and the echo of my own words for the answer of the other. Finally, because of that, I am drowned in my own picture – and this is hell.

In *Fanny and Alexander*, on his deathbed Oscar says to Emelie that he is hoping that everything will continue as usual. One year later she admits that everything has continued as before – but everything has changed, and she adds that everything will go on as before. This will to keep or to preserve is, in fact, fatal. It was also the plan of the Devil in *Prison* that everything was to remain unchanged, static. And in *The Seventh Seal* Block says that his heart is empty and that emptiness is a mirror turned towards his own face. He is seeing himself and is seized with disgust and horror. Excluded from human communion he is living in a world of ghosts locked up into his own dreams and imaginations.

The dynamics of reciprocity finally turn out to be the original basis of speech. Maaret Koskinen has described how a dialogicity and reciprocity may come into existence in Bergman's films, paradoxically enough often in front of the mirror, which then in a way opens up, and ceases only to reflect one's own image (1993: 75–9). Only when speech is a real exchange in one way or another, when it is quite openly directed to the other person, can it tell something and so perhaps also liberate. Here the pattern of Bergman's filmmaking is strikingly close to the biblical myth of creation. The first human being who has been given the task to name all living creatures on the earth is yet not able to find a partner, his equal, among them. In vain he is looking for his own image among birds and other creatures. The consequence at the moment when the human being has become two and thus finally has found his equal is of vital importance: not until then is man speaking in direct speech, and so for the first time begins to speak in the first person. It is also this original speech that makes man into man.[2]

What, in fact, should we finally think about Bergman and religion? Naturally, there is hardly one, and only one, unambiguous answer to that question. But it is obvious that there is a love appearing in his films, a love with its foundation on earth, between human beings. Thus there is no religious love contrasting with a profane one. And the same thing is true about silence or speech; they may not be divided into profane and religious. What is explicitly religious is often expressed, hesitatingly, with an 'if': 'If I could only lead him out of his emptiness, away from his lie-god. If we could dare to show each other tenderness. If we could believe in a truth … If we could believe…', as Märta says in *Winter Light* (Bergman 1967: 104). Or the way the pastor is praying at the deathbed of Agnes in *Cries and Whispers*: 'If it is true that you have brought together our suffering into your poor body. If it is true that you have carried it with you through death. If it is true that you shall meet God away there in the other country, if it is true that he will turn his face against you, if it is true that you can speak a language that this god will understand. If so, pray for us.'[3] But this is an 'if' that simultaneously overcomes the contrasts and dualism. To be free from the god of lies, to show tenderness, to believe – this is on one and the same line.

What I have tried to do here is not to attribute to Bergman or his films a Christian religion with which he himself has explicitly claimed, once and for all, to have come to an end. Bergman, the iconoclast, on one level made a clean sweep. The only thing I have wanted to show is that in spite of these declarations that his own religious ideas disappeared completely, in the human experience that has been created in Bergman's films there are strong associations to God and man who appear in biblical traditions as well as in Christian mysticism.

Yet, the essential difference between Bergman and the mainstream in this tradition is the subjectivity of Lutheranism, which remains the basis of his thinking and his way of expression. Everything is finally dependent on the decision of the individual human being, on her act of belief or non-belief. And as it is only possible really to know something about what is within this world, the desperate struggle of the knight in *The Seventh Seal* to attain knowledge and assurance is doomed to failure from the very beginning. And this is why, as regards himself, Bergman finally decided to draw a subjective conclusion: 'That which had formerly been so enigmatic and frightening, namely, what might exist beyond this world, does not exist. Everything is of this world. Everything exists and happens inside us, and we flow into and out of one another. It's perfectly fine like that' (1994: 241).

Notes

1   For example, Gilles Deleuze refers to Bergman's films as his central example in defining one category in the affection image, where the close-up equals the face (see Deleuze 1983: 141–8).

2   I owe this reading of the myth of creation to the late French theologian Paul Beauchamp.

3   Quoted from the soundtrack; author's translation.

References

Assayas, O. and S. Björkman (1990) *Conversation avec Bergman*. Paris: Cahiers du cinéma.

Bergman, I. (1959) 'Varje film är min sista film', *Filmnyheter*, 14, 9–10 (19 May), 1–8.

_____ (1960) *The Seventh Seal*, trans. L. Malmström and D. Kushner. London: Lorrimer Publishing.

_____ (1967) *Three Films by Ingmar Bergman*, trans. P. B. Austin. New York: Grove Press Inc.

_____ (1972) *Persona & Shame*, trans. K. Bradfield. London: Calder & Boyars.

_____ (1988) The Magic Lantern: An Autobiography, trans. J. Tate. New York and London: Penguin.

_____ (1994) *Images: My Life in Film*, trans. M. Ruuth. London: Bloomsbury.

Bergom-Larsson, M. (1976) *Ingmar Bergman och den borgerliga ideologin*. Stockholm: PAN/Norstedts.

Bergom-Larsson, M., S. Hammar and B. Kristensson Uggla (eds) (1992) *Nedstigningar i modern film*. Delsbo: Åsak.

Deleuze, G. (1983) *Cinéma 1, L'image-mouvement*. Paris: Minuit.

Donner, J. (1962) *Djävulens ansikte*. Lund: Aldus/Bonniers.

Gervais, M. (1999) *Ingmar Bergman: Magician and Prophet*. Montreal: McGill-Queen's University Press.

Koskinen, M. (1993) *Spel och speglingar: En studie i Ingmar Bergmans filmiska estetik)*. Stockholm: Stockholm University Press.

Lagerkvist, P. (1962) *The Death of Ahasuerus*, trans. N. Walford. New York: Random House.

Marty, J. (1991) *Ingmar Bergman: une poétique du désir*. Paris: Cerf.

Nystedt, H. (1989) *Ingmar Bergman och kristen tro*. Stockholm: Verbum.

Paillard, J. (1970) *Quand Dieu est inutile*. Paris: Cerf.

Sjöman, V. (1963) *L 136: Dagbok med Ingmar Bergman*. Stockholm: Norstedts.

Steene B. (1983) 'Ingmar Bergmans mottagande i USA', *Svenska Dagbladet*, 3 June.

Zern, L. (1993) *Se Bergman*. Stockholm: Norstedts.

EPILOGUE

THE POWER OF SHADOWS
OR HOW WE STUDY INGMAR BERGMAN

Birgitta Steene

Let me begin by quoting from a work that has elicited more academic studies than any other Bergman film – namely *Persona* (1966). In a passage in the script (which was not included in the screen version) Bergman discusses the famous rupture of the film strip and suggests that his work may at that point begin to take on a life of its own. I quote from scene 22 in *Persona* in Keith Bradfield's translation:

> At this point the projector should stop. The film, happily would break, or someone lower the curtains by mistake; or perhaps there could be a short circuit [a premonition of what happens many years later in the film *Larmar och gör sig till* (*In the Presence of a Clown*, 1997)] – there could be a short circuit, so that all the lights in the cinema went out. Only, this is not how it is. I think the shadows would continue their game … Perhaps they no longer need the assistance of the apparatus, the projector, the film or the soundtrack. They reach out towards our senses, deep inside the retina, or into the finest recesses of the ear. Is this the case? Or do I simply imagine that these shadows possess a power, that their rage survives without the help of the picture frames. (1972: 93–4)

In this passage Bergman imagines both a breakdown of his artifact and a continued life for his created work, but he also couches his thoughts in a collective form of address – he uses the possessive pronoun 'our' in describing a multi-sensory reaction to the film we have seen. Its dynamic impact may live on in our minds as lingering shadows without the filmmaker's technical instruments. Bergman's statement harbours some fundamental premises in his view of the aesthetic experience, namely the mesmerising quality of the medium and the participatory function of the viewer. Judging by the sheer volume of studies that his work has elicited, we have indeed responded to those premises beyond measure.

Thus there are to date, around the world, some fifty book-length studies of Ingmar Bergman, in addition to more than thirty dissertations, most of them from the

Object of study I: on location (*Persona*) with actors Bibi Andersson, Gunnar Björnstrand and Liv Ullmann (photo: Bo A. Vibenius)

English-speaking world but also with contributions from Germany, Italy, Poland and the Scandinavian countries. Today when we look with hindsight at this huge wealth of material, we realise that a good deal of it consists either of introductions written for readers as yet fairly unfamiliar with Bergman or of studies motivated by their author's strong personal engagement in the subject – in that sense Robert Manvell's brief study *Ingmar Bergman: An Appreciation* (1982) might serve as a generic title. But what is it in Bergman's filmmaking that has elicited this global response? To begin with, his case is one where timing turns out to be talent's best friend. Bergman's scripted filmmaking with its Kafka-inspired brand of existentialism (reinforced by the metaphysical mood of the Swedish poets of the 1940s and, of course, his own religious background) was considered a novelty in post-war Europe and America. In addition, certain international discussions of the film medium, such as Astruc's arguments for a 'camera stylo' (written in 1948) had prepared the way for a response to Bergman's work as that of a scriptwriter/director. Post-war film critics were ready to shift the focus from big movie moguls with their film star cult back to the director as a central consciousness in the filmmaking process. What Bergman added to complete this shift was a personal vision framed in a visual style that was both new and yet familiar; it looked somewhat like film noir or a product of German expressionist cinema, but it was conceived within a personal, metaphysical context.

If one reads critical commentaries of Bergman's films from the mid-1950s when he had his international breakthrough, one is struck by their obliviousness to his dependence on a Swedish filmmaking tradition that combined outdoor shooting with high contrast, black-and-white studio photography. In the final analysis, however, it was the philosophical implications of Bergman's work that attracted most critical attention abroad. At least up to the 1980s, international studies on Bergman tended to focus on the thematic implications of his films and demonstrated that their thought content was of far more interest than his developing filmmaking style. It is no coincidence for instance that when the American film critic and sometime editor of the English-language edition of *Cahiers du cinéma*, Andrew Sarris, introduced Bergman to American viewers in 1959, it was as the first truly existentialist filmmaker in the history of the cinema, a director who gave a metaphysical and ethical dimension to the film medium. The end result was, internationally speaking, a cementing of Bergman's position not only as an *auteur du cinéma* but as a *directeur de conscience*. In other words, he was seen as both a new phenomenon in the cinema – the scriptwriting filmmaker – *and* as a moral voice in a post-war world. As such he would appeal to groups of viewers far beyond the cadres of film critics and students of the cinema.[1]

Bergman would, however, lose, from time to time, his status as a filmmaking pioneer and be relegated to the less prestigious class of 'middle-brow' filmmakers – too popular in the minds of cinematic purists to be truly ground-breaking artists. One can observe Bergman's decline among film critics in the 1960s and 1970s in such journals as the British *Sight and Sound*, the American *Film Comment* and the French *Cahiers du cinéma* and *Arts*. In their negative assessment, Bergman's commentators contrasted his 'middle-brow' status, often referred to as 'bourgeois', to new political and aesthetic trends favouring realism and social engagement in the cinema. This critical attitude was particularly strong in Bergman's own country. Yet at the same time he won recognition at home as an outstanding theatre and media director and doggedly pursued his filmmaking vision, which came to include such works as *Persona* (1966), *Viskingar och rop* (*Cries and Whispers*, 1973) and *Fanny och Alexander* (*Fanny and Alexander*, 1982/1983), films that today are considered central in his canon and have solidified his standing as one of the great filmmakers of all times. When he retired, first from filmmaking and later from the theatre, the world at large had long ago expressed esteem for his art by awarding him with every conceivable honour and recognition. In fact, few Swedish artists have achieved such international applause.

The foreign recognition of Ingmar Bergman is all the more remarkable as his world has always been rooted in Sweden, even during his years in exile (1976–83). His language – both in a linguistic and an artistic sense – is Swedish and this is reflected in the material deposited in the Ingmar Bergman Foundation Archive at the Swedish Film Institute. I kept thinking of this 'provincial' aspect of Bergman's life and work when reading Janet Staiger's fascinating analysis (in this volume) of two American interviews with Bergman in the 1970s. As Staiger points out, Bergman belonged among those artists who avail themselves of their personal background to transform autobiography into a self-fashioned legend. In noting that Bergman's remarks in public seem to follow 'generic formulae', a set of motifs that 'author-ise' the interview situation and tend to make it follow a given 'plot' pattern, Staiger brings to our attention its normative functions, such as the obligatory scene-setting in Bergman's modest and tidy office and, more importantly, its nature of an encounter between a directorial persona and his (interviewing) audience. What is particularly intriguing in Staiger's sampled interviews is that Bergman's 'plot-making', his setting of the stage, creates a dynamic where the interviewer loses his or her professional anonymity and seems compelled to reflect on their own self as he or she responds to Bergman's directorial pronouncements. The situation is remarkably similar to Bergman's descriptions of how, in his rehearsals of a play, he sought out an electrifying point on stage, where he and the actors could respond in such a way that the audience too would become involved, electrified (see Sjögren 1968: 291–3; Marker 1983: 251–61). What Staiger describes in her analysis of these two American interviews is perhaps as close as we can come to understanding the elusive concept of the famous Bergman 'magic' at work.

And yet, to return for a moment to Bergman's Swedish roots. Is an interview situation such as the one analysed by Staiger only a display of Bergman's self-fashioned controlling persona? Could he really, before the two American interviewers, have camouflaged the fact that when it comes to an English-speaking setting he was not very verbal or at ease? His command of English was always rather shaky and typical of a Swede of his generation, for whom the first foreign language learnt at school was German. To what an extent did the linguistic gap impact on the interviewers' assessment of the subject they faced? Did Bergman's hesitant enunciation in English shift their attention to his visual appearance and did it encourage them to drift back into their own preconceived discourse? These questions address the fact that a great deal has been written on Bergman in a language he did not fully master and often by scholars who do not read Swedish. Add to this that a good deal of valuable material on Bergman has been published by his own countrymen in their native tongue. Certainly this poses a particular problem for any student of Bergman who has to rely on translations, if they exist. To give a concrete example: there is, for instance, an excellent article on *Ormens ägg (The Serpent's Egg*, 1977) by Swedish film and literary critic Carl Johan Malmberg, published in the Swedish journal *Filmhäftet* in 1978, which, I am sure, would have been very useful to Thomas Elsaesser in his chapter on the same film in this volume. *Filmhäftet* became English recently (and is now known as *Film International*) and that may be the trend of the future, though I believe that this will simply shift the problem, since Swedish contributors will, in some cases at least, have to hand over their original texts to translators. My remarks are not meant to undermine Staiger's and Elsaesser's contributions here, for there is an implicit value in the way their chapters place Bergman's work in an international theoretical and/or film-historical context. Nevertheless, and in view of the opening of the Bergman Foundation Archive, it is necessary to ask the question of how to deal with Bergman's Swedish material and heritage in terms of future scholarship among foreign film, theatre and literature students. Should the onus fall on them to learn Swedish – as several contributors here have done – or is it not our responsibility to provide them with adequate translations?

A very different problem related to how we avail ourselves of Bergman material has to do with the voluminous media attention allotted to Ingmar Bergman over the years and the risk it entails that he may emerge as more of a *concept* than an *artist*; in other words, that his public persona overshadows his creative achievements. Bergman himself handled his celebrity status with a certain degree of level-headed humour. When his name became a conversation piece around the world in the 1960s, he once dismissed the phenomenon as a kind of virus which, though it might first cause a pandemic, would soon die out (in Moberg 1951: 42). Yet, despite such a disarming dismissal of fame, Bergman always possessed and exploited a certain PR skill, in part to promote his work and its crew, in part to help formulate his persona. Emphasising from the start the public nature of his artistic modes, he also recognised the value and necessity of *visibility*. Even when he was just a young amateur director at a youth centre in Stockholm's Old City, he engaged – with the assistance of Sven Hansson, his mentor at the time – in promotional activities concerning his chosen repertory or his amateur group's rehearsals, so that before long the daily press began to send reviewers to write, however briefly, about his productions. It is certainly remarkable that among the audience attending Bergman's pre-professional stage work one could see Strindberg's third wife, the actress Harriet Bosse, playwright in exile Bertolt Brecht and actors from Stockholm's Royal Dramatic Theatre.

Interarts Studies: an important approach to Ingmar Bergman

Now, how might academic studies of Bergman separate the media publicity around him from the work itself? I do not think it is a matter of just dismissing the media attention as journalistic trivia. Rather it is a matter of asking what prompted Bergman's early visibility and what it entailed. What did his spectators get to see when they came to his early stage productions? Indications are that audiences encountered the work of a young artist who, from the start, was aware of both the auditory and spatial dimensions of the production of a play. Bergman would often, on stage and also on screen, combine a variety of art forms, and in doing so would transgress their traditional borders. For that reason, his work has come to lend itself particularly well to interart studies – as Ann Fridén stated a few years ago in her editorial introduction to a special English volume on Ingmar Bergman and the Arts in the journal *Nordic Theatre Studies* (1998: 5–6). Some of the contributions in this volume can be seen as an extension and continuation of such studies and of earlier conferences on related topics, one of them in 1995 resulting in a collection of essays juxtaposing Bergman's filmmaking and theatre work, titled *Film och teater i växelverkan* (loosely translated as *The Cross-Fertilisation of Film and Theatre*), edited by Margareta Wirmark (1996). The interest in interart studies manifested itself in the formation, in the 1990s, of the Nordic Society for Interart Studies at Lund University. Two of the contributers in this study, Ulla-Britta Lagerroth and Erik Hedling, co-edited a collection of papers from the Society's first meeting, a volume that appeared in 1997 under the title *Interart Poetics: Essays on the Interrelations of the Arts and Media*. More extensively, the research into the interplay of film and theatre in Bergman's work became the focus of a book by Maaret Koskinen in 2001, *Allting föreställer, ingenting är* (*Everything Represents, Nothing Is*), while yet another Bergman scholar, Egil Törnqvist at Amsterdam University, has authored two books on the interaction of stage and screen in Bergman's career. Especially worth noting is Törnqvist's volume published in 2003 under the title *Bergman's Muses: Aesthetic Versatility in Film, Theatre, Television and Radio* which addresses some of the pragmatic and aesthetic problems that faced Bergman in his presentation and transformation of various forms of dramatic expression. In sum: we can really assert that the interart and intermedia approaches to Bergman's work is a flourishing field, and several essays in this volume have chosen such an approach. Marilyn Johns Blackwell, building on Koskinen's work, in particular in terms of Bergman's use of different kinds of theatre stages and stage-like filmic configurations, focuses on Bergman's ritualisation of beds to project a sex-death-theatre

Object of study II: on location (*From the Lives of the Marionettes*) with cinematographer and long-time collaborator Sven Nykvist (photo: Ingmar Bergman Foundation)

matrix, while Ulla-Britta Lagerroth broadens the interart scope to include the theoretical and creative framework of 'musicalisation' in four of Bergman's Shakespeare productions. She notes his meaningful use of music in the theatrical *mise-en-scène* in terms of 'framing' a scene, of creating or shattering a mood, of raising spectator awareness. Though Lagerroth's essay focuses on Bergman's theatre work, it also points to interesting parallels in his filmmaking, where he has only rarely used music in the conventional Hollywood manner of intensifying or foreshadowing an emotional moment and, instead, has made music an active narrative component or psychological comment on a scene. Both Blackwell and Lagerroth reinforce the image of a multi-art creative persona who has always worked with coordinating set design, lighting, costumes and sound, so that verbal and auditory text and visual space are reinforced by various interart sensations.

One could say that music was not only a link between word and image in Bergman's work but was an essential aspect of his creative method, what might be termed its 'musicalisation process'. Bergman referred to it in a radio talk with Mikael Timm, later published in Timm's book *Ögats glädje*:

> All art has to do with breathing in and breathing out. Because our whole life consists of rhythms: day and night, light and darkness; black and white, breathing in and breathing out – and in this we live. If we do not inscribe rhythm in every interpretation, every recreation – swiftly, slowly, holding back, you let loose, you make a pause, you maintain the whole time a tension to give the public a possibility to breathe along – if you don't do that, well, then it doesn't work. (1994: 129; my translation)

Ingmar Bergman – self-modelling as a strategy

In another radio talk – this one from 1947 – Bergman criticised modernist Swedish poets of his own generation for writing thin volumes of poetry for a readership of some fifty people within their own inner circle. Artistic activity, he stated, is not a form of exclusive inbreeding but an interplay between an artist's search for contact and an audience ready or challenged to respond. But the artist himself should be anonymous, a cog in the big wheel of performance. The idea is expressed in Bergman's essay 'What is Filmmaking?' ('*Det att göra film*') from 1954, where Bergman cited an anecdote about the cathedral of Chartres when the dome had been hit by lightning and burnt to the ground:

> What happened was that people in the thousands flocked together from all directions; it was like a gigantic trek of lemmings from all the corners of the world, representing all kinds of people. And together they began to build up the cathedral from its old base. They lived their lives with their immense building project until it was finished … but they remained anonymous, no one today knows the names of those who built the cathedral at Chartres. (1954: 8–9; my translation)

Here Bergman fantasised about constructing a work of art where his role would not be that of a master builder but a member of a collective, a small part of a group enterprise. This is clearly a very different attitude towards his artistic undertakings than the construction of a self-fashioned persona discussed earlier. Not unexpectedly, Bergman's attempt to present his position as a member of a larger team was complicated by his ready acknowledgement of the subjective basis of his filmmaking and its element of self-projection, albeit behind a mask. Quite early, Swedish commentators addressed this matter. In reviewing the film *Ansiktet* (*The Magician/ The Face*, 1958), a journalist asked the question: Ingmar Bergman, do you have a face? (Schildt 1958). In her chapter here 'Self-Projection and Still Photography in the Work of Ingmar Bergman' Linda Haverty Rugg implicitly asks the same question by discussing Bergman's understanding of selfhood as representational, constructed *and* projected. Referring to these various functions of selfhood both in Bergman's films and in his autobiographical texts, Rugg's analysis, based on neuro-physiological research, throws a different light on Bergman's employment of the still photograph as a gateway to his use of doubling and self-projection. Rugg's approach brings to mind an essay on *Persona* by Andrew Hobson, titled 'Dream Image and Substrate: Bergman's Films and the Physiology of Sleep' (1981). Hobson distinguishes between the classical psychoanalytical presentation of the dream sequences in *Smultronstället* (*Wild Strawberries*, 1957) and *Persona*'s linkage to experimental neuro-physiology. Unlike Rugg, however, he does not pursue the cinematic, narrative and psychological consequences of this. Instead he shifts his attention back to *Wild Strawberries* and classical psychoanalysis. So Rugg is indeed to be congratulated for venturing into relatively unexplored territory. Interestingly enough, Thomas Elsaesser has made use of similar material as Rugg in his chapter on *The Serpent's Egg*. Here then are two discussions which, though using very different film material, both touch on Bergman's self-modelling as a human strategy aiming at integrating inner and outer worlds: himself as a Consciousness and himself as the Other. There also seems to be a parallel between such outer and inner layers of directorial or authorial self-representation and Bergman's use of an actor in his theatre productions in both an active role and as a silent witness on stage. Future studies might pay greater attention to Bergman's use of groups of specific actors and the double role he often assigns them as both a play text character and a symbolic presence, that is, as both speaking role player and voyeuristic Other.

Janet Staiger's chapter 'Analysing Self-Fashioning in Authoring and Reception', referred to earlier, suggests yet another variation on the theme of self-projection and Otherness. James Baldwin's and Mary Murphy's separate encounters with Bergman create their own dramatic scenarios, in which both parties can claim authorship *and* performative roles. But one could also say that these interviewer/director encounters constitute a kind of archetypal scene, a Bergman *urscen*, demonstrating his artistic method at large, a psychological set-up that finds its technical counterpart in the visual structure of his filmmaking and theatre work, where intimate close-ups and long-distance takes oscillate. In the interview book *Bergman on Bergman: Interviews with Ingmar Bergman*, one finds the following self-revealing passage:

> Long shot versus close-up arises out of an ambivalence in the director himself ... Suddenly, one morning ... you're seized with a sudden need to get to grips with your devils, challenge them, force them up against a wall. In the best of humours you want to torment them until they yield their last possible ounce of expressiveness. Sometimes you feel a violent urge to burst all bounds, both your own and the actors'. To force them to burst their bounds. Sometimes in close-ups ... But some days you feel nothing, just a huge revulsion and fatigue. Most of all you'd like to go home, or bawl everyone out, or just stand in a corner and whimper. Then suddenly, you feel – 'Ah, now I want to make long shots, now I want them at a distance, far, far away' ... You must use your ambivalence as something fruitful, something functional. (in Björkman *et al.* 1973: 206–7)

Bergman's statement is much more than a description of a director's psychological mood swings. It is a work method: *You must use your ambivalence as something fruitful, something functional.* It also applies to the situation he sets up with many interviewers, though judging by their ambivalent, even irritable, response it is doubtful that James Baldwin and Mary Murphy experienced their situation as either fruitful or functional. But Staiger's choice of interview situations is far more revealing than those exemplified by John Simon in his book *Ingmar Bergman Directs* (1972) or Dick Cavett's television talk with Bergman where the interviewer is a polite, almost ingratiating listener and Bergman a lacklustre respondent.[2] An interview that is not conducted on Bergman's premises tends to be lifeless.

Bergman and reductionist studies

From the very start Bergman emphasised the sensuous and aggressive power of the film medium. In an early visit to Bergen, Norway, in 1954 he stated that 'film must assault people emotionally' (Anon. 1954; my translation) rather than appeal to their intellect. This does not mean that Bergman was an anti-intellectual, but philosophical ideas for him were neither the essence of the creative act nor the essence of experiencing a work of art. Ideas very easily become ideologies to Bergman and were in his mind very close to the attitudes of repression that he encountered (or felt he was exposed to) as a child and that he thought he recognised in the exponents of socially-conscious art in the 1960s and 1970s, an ideological position embraced by his most severe critics. Considering how much Bergman emphasised the creative importance of intuition and emotional impulse rather than intellectual discussion and theory, it is ironic that so much scholarship has focused on the thought content in his work. This is particularly the case in foreign studies of his filmmaking. The dominant subject matter discussed was its Christian context, often reflecting an author's very personal engagement with Bergman's films. Such is the case with Arthur Gibson's book *The Silence of God: Creative Response to the Films of Ingmar Bergman* (1969), Father Robert Lauder's study *God, Death, Art and Love: The Philosophical Vision of Ingmar Bergman* (1989) and Marc Gervais' work a decade later, titled *Ingmar Bergman: Magician and Prophet* (1999). The problem with many of these studies lies in the fact that they tend to be *reductionist* in kind; that is, their purpose is to relate and reduce Bergman's work to the author's own ideological position. There are two other major areas where Bergman's filmmaking has been used in such a fashion: political ideology and psychoanalysis. In the first area, a good example is the Italian reaction. Throughout the 1950s and 1960s two Italian factions, la critica catolica and the agnostics, both claimed Bergman as their mentor. As for psychoanalytical approaches they are, not unexpectedly, most dominant in American studies. They function best when focusing on a single film, for example Don Fredericksen's recent monograph on *Persona* (2005), but they tend to be problematic in works that address Bergman's entire oeuvre. Frank Gado's voluminous study *The Passion of Ingmar Bergman* (1986) is a case in point. Though very well written and knowledgeable, Gado's persistent focus on Bergman in the light of a psychoanalytical father-mother-son matrix makes his analysis of every film more or less predictable.

In this volume, Paisley Livingston's contribution on Bergman and philosophy questions Gado's way of making a direct connection between a specific, exemplifying detail in Bergman's *Wild Strawberries* and the filmmaker's familiarity with psychologist Eino Kaila's book *Psychology of the Personality* (1934). In order to examine its thesis, namely that man lives according to his needs, paraphrased by Bergman in a statement from the 1950s, Livingston examines Kaila's work and raises questions that reflect our scepticism today of the creative process as a simple correlation between an artist's reading habits and his own finished work – or as Livingston phrases it in one of his questions: 'How did Kaila's specific ideas make their way into Bergman's films and, if so, how – and here's the rub – how were they *transformed, adapted or revised in the process?*'] That Bergman should be attracted to Kaila's thesis, which questions the human being as an enlightened rational animal and focuses on motivational forces that tend to produce various forms of irrationality, is hardly surprising. Livingston's chapter gives examples of 'Kaila-esque' reminiscences in Bergman's filmmaking, yet also suggests the director's *departure* from Kaila's purely subjective conception of values in favour of an implicit moral perspective and a creative curiosity about the world. The problem is that Bergman describes his curiosity as a purely subjective drive and not as a curiosity about the outside world, thus confirming rather than departing from Kaila's thesis. In his famous 'Snakeskin' essay he describes his creative motivation, his 'curiosity', as follows:

Object of study III: from the set of *Wild Strawberries*, with actor Gunnar Sjöberg getting ready for the nightmarish school sequence (photo: Ingmar Bergman Foundation)

If now … I assert that in spite of everything I wish to continue making art, it is for one very simple reason (I will discard any purely material considerations).

This reason is *curiosity*. An unbounded, never satisfied, continuously renewed, unbearable curiosity, which drives me forward, never leaves me in peace, and completely replaces my past hunger for fellowship (1970: 14).

The cultural persona of a Swedish filmmaker at home and abroad

To follow a highly visible and prolific artist's production is to partake in the making of a creative persona who may undergo different metamorphoses over the years, depending upon the kind and degree of mythmaking that particular cultural contexts help formulate. To the image of a self-fashioning artist we must add the image of that same artist as created in the public mind. The view of a young Ingmar Bergman in the emerging Swedish *folkhem* of the 1940s differs from the view of him in the politicised 1960s or the portrait of him as an ageing cultural giant in later years. In addition, the foreign conception of Bergman has often differed quite markedly from his reputation at home, so that it is relatively rare to find a foreign and Swedish consensus of his work, especially in terms of its significance as a representation of Swedish society and mentality. Generally speaking, foreign commentators have tended to view Bergman's universe as emblematically Nordic while Swedes have denied, rather vigorously at times, the relevance of his work as a reflection of a Swedish psyche or a portrayal of life in his own contemporary welfare state. The foremost representative of Bergman as a prototypical Swede is Vernon Young's book *Cinema Borealis: Ingmar Bergman and the Swedish Ethos* (1972), from which we might extract the following illustrative passage:

> So often when trying to summarise Ingmar Bergman's idiosyncracies, I have been met by the Swedish comment: 'But Ingmar Bergman is not a typical Swede!' Of course, he is not typical; he has genius and no genius is typical [sic]. Yet no man can wholly transcend his culture and in his stress as in his grasp, in the nature of his rejections and in his fleeting discoveries, Bergman is quintessentially Swedish … [He] falters to our surprise when arraigned or snubbed by regional criticism, even though he has the rest of the world at his feet. We should not be surprised, for he is Swedish and the *pueblo* of his world. (1972: 116)

At the opposite end in discussions of Bergman's 'quintessential Swedishness' we find someone like filmmaker Bo Widerberg whose rather forceful repudiation of Bergman's cinematic vision charged him with having fabricated a false image of contemporary Swedish values in order to perpetuate existing foreign fantasies about Swedish culture. In *Visionen i svensk film* (1962), Widerberg wrote:

> Bergman's export items are faraway legends, mystical light, unabashed exoticism … He obliges the crudest myths about us and our society; he underlines the sort of misconceptions about us that foreign countries love to hold on to. He turns away from questions that occupy most of his colleagues; his films have only one perspective; inwardly, towards the North. (1962: 29; my translation)

Perhaps because Widerberg's timing of his critique of Bergman was just right in terms of the cultural climate that developed in Sweden between the early 1960s and the early 1980s, a time that witnessed the final transformation of the Swedish *folkhem* into a modern welfare state, there has been relatively little interest among Bergman's own countrymen to discuss the historical factors behind his art or to relate his film-making to a Swedish cinematic tradition – other than paying lip service to his repeated recognition of Victor Sjöström. Among the few exceptions are an article by Maaret Koskinen (1995) in which she compares certain links between Bergman's screen works and motifs in older Swedish cinema.

The essay that comes closest to addressing the 'Swedishness' of Ingmar Bergman is Erik Hedling's 'The Welfare State Depicted: Post-Utopian Landscapes in Ingmar Bergman's Films', included in this collection. Vernon Young in his aforementioned, rather dystopian study *Cinema Borealis* already saw Bergman as a half-hearted defector from the welfare state's ideals. Hedling's more specific focus is to identify a cinematic landscape in Bergman's filmmaking that reflects his departure from earlier Swedish films depicting an idyllic or utopian society. To this purpose he juxtaposed two clips, one from the Swedish film *Pensionat Paradiset* from 1937 and the other from Bergman's Fårö landscape in *Persona*, nearly thirty years later. It would perhaps have been more revealing to examine how, quite early in his career, a rather young Bergman transformed a Swedish idyll into a post-utopian world of angst. In a sequence from *Sommarlek* (*Illicit Interlude/Summer Interlude*, 1951), made more than fifteen years before *Persona*, Bergman punctures the iconic summer motif that constitutes a generic feature in the *folkhem* film by infusing it with his own sombre mood and personal brand of symbolism. The main character in *Summer Interlude*, Marie, a ballerina at the Stockholm Opera, boards the same type of small steamer as in Hedling's sampled shots from *Pensionat Paradiset*. Marie's trip into the archipelago begins traditionally enough with sunny shots of water splashing against the boat's prow, a sky filled with white cumulus clouds and popular indigenous music on the soundtrack. But what is depicted is really a tragic flashback, and the moment Marie disembarks alone on an island the music, lighting and mood darken. On a pathway, she is passed by an old woman dressed in black, an obvious figure of morbidity related to Death in *Det sjunde inseglet* (*The Seventh Seal*, 1957). It is an emblematic Bergman vignette signalling the direction of his future filmmaking.

In a review article on *Jungfrukällan* (*The Virgin Spring*, 1960), Jörn Donner once suggested that Bergman's filmmaking up to that date might be divided into three landscape periods: the Stockholm period, the Skåne period and the Dalecarlia period – all landscapes with which he had had personal or professional contacts. Each landscape gave a specific contour to his filmmaking style, from the flat Skåne topography and the urban setting of Stockholm or its sunlit summer archipelago to the romantic landscape of Dalecarlia with its birch trees, lakes and undulating hills.

As Donner's suggestions indicate, there is not one but several landscapes in Bergman's pre-Baltic filmmaking, each one with different connotations. The difference between the pre- and post-Baltic landscapes can also be related to Bergman's change of cinematographers, from Gunnar Fischer (and before him Göran Strindberg) to Sven Nykvist. Both from the point of view of artistic temperament and professional training, Fischer and Strindberg were much more rooted in the traditional Swedish projection of idyllic summer landscapes and *clair obscure* (from French literature, meaning 'obscure light'; associated earlier with *camera obscura* and the painting of the Düsseldorf School) or backlit studio lighting, while Nykvist was instrumental in developing Bergman's starker 'island' milieu that is to be understood not only as a physical setting but as a state of mind.

Bergman was an iconoclast and angry young man from the start, someone who sought to depict counter-images of the utopian and idyllic *folkhem*. As Hedling points out, this was noted in 1972 by Maria Bergom-Larsson in her study, *Ingmar Bergman och den borgerliga ideologin* (translated as *Ingmar Bergman and Society*), and some twenty years later in a co-authored essay with Ulf Kristensson Uggla that discusses the cultural impact of philosophy professor Ingemar Hedenius.[3] Hedenius's atheistic attack on Sweden's religious establishment was bound to impact on the rebellious son of a Swedish clergyman but also served as a catalyst in defining the rational mentality that was to epitomise the policies and values of the Swedish welfare state. Hedling's reference to the Hedenius debate is therefore a crucial acknowledgement of an important factor during Ingmar Bergman's formative years.

It is interesting to juxtapose a discussion of Bergman's 'Swedishness' to the cultural ramifications analysed by Thomas Elsaesser in his aforementioned piece on the production of Bergman's first film in exile, *The Serpent's Egg*, set in Germany during Hitler's attempted coup in 1923. While sweeping references to the German expressionistic cinema have been common in Bergman literature, Elsaesser's framework is much more specific as he relates *The Serpent's Egg* both to the 'retro-mode' of historical films made by Bergman's contemporaries, and to Bergman's production situation in Munich and the political situation in West Germany at the time. Such referential material avoids limiting the background of *The Serpent's Egg* to Bergman's personal exposure to Nazism in his teens or to his own cinematic universe in other films of his, an *intratextual* procedure dominant in both thematic and aesthetic studies of Bergman's filmmaking. Yet at the same time – and like Livingston in his discussion of Kaila's impact on Bergman – Elsaesser's analysis, though pointing out common motifs between *The Serpent's Egg* and the retro-historical films, also suggests a certain independence on Bergman's part *vis-à-vis* the referenced material. Bergman chooses moral positions that question the values and ethical dichotomies of the genre, revealing a personal vision that in the final analysis constitutes the uniqueness of his art even in a somewhat mediocre product like *The Serpent's Egg*. I believe that discussions of Bergman's cultural context, whether Swedish or international, will always, in the final analysis, reveal his strong artistic and moral persona. That may also be one reason why we have few comparative studies of Bergman and other Swedish artists, except for the lip-service paid to Victor Sjöström in the cinema or Olof Molander in the theatre. Bergman's position is reminiscent of the strong dominance of Henrik Ibsen in Norwegian culture. With a reference to the Boyg, the monster who blocks the way in Ibsen's play *Peer Gynt*, one could say that Bergman, like Ibsen, filled the space by his very presence. In his book *Filmen i Sverige*, Leif Furhammar suggests that this came to polarise Swedish film criticism, at least up until Bergman's exile in 1976:

> Regardless of his choice of style, there is in almost all of Bergman's films a deadly personal imprint that in a strange way provoked and polarised the contemporary corps of film critics. With the victory in Cannes of *Smiles of a Summer Night* in 1956, the world was wide open to Ingmar Bergman...
>
> For the first time since the days of Sjöström and Stiller, Swedish cinema was again considered among the most interesting in the world. The only problem was that Swedish cinema came to be identified so completely with one single figure. After 1956 it's practically only Ingmar Bergman that counts. (1991: 246; my translation)

It will therefore be a special challenge for future students of Bergman to try to argue that he was and remains nevertheless part of a Swedish cultural syndrome. Bergman may have been the Nordic Protestant, presumably someone typifying the lifestyle of Scandinavia, to someone like James Baldwin, but what was he and what is he still to us and to the Swedes? The homage paid to him by everyone at the symposium that resulted in this collection is a sign of respect, but what is Bergman to our younger filmmakers?

Bergman scholarship today

The Ingmar Bergman symposium and this volume have presented a wide spectrum of topics. Perhaps we might now sum up three different components in Bergman's aesthetics that have been touched on: (i) the importance of the audience as a participatory element; (ii) the striving for an interart synesthesia in his work on both stage and screen; (iii) artistic creativity as a pendulum between collective act and self-projection. But an equally noteable subject here has been the cultural implications – Swedish and international – of Bergman's work.

We can see that the contributions organised themselves into three subject areas: (i) interart discussions; (ii) psychological analyses of a director's self-modelling and self-projection; (iii) juxtapositions of cultural or philosophical concepts and cin-

Object of study IV: inspection of a miniature model for a stage production of 'The Castle' in 1953 (photo: Ingmar Bergman Foundation)

ematic motifs in Bergman's filmmaking. What these contributions confirm is that we have come a long way since the days when Bergman was primarily treated as an auteur with a religious concern – his Christian hangover as one Swedish critic called it – but also that we have probably put behind us the Bergman backlash that first appeared in France around 1960 and then spread to Sweden and to film critics in the Anglo-American world, where Bergman was demoted to a middle-brow artist who appealed to Woody Allen and a coffee-house clientele, and was considered an outdated modernist whose motifs (such as the silent God syndrome or the 'corroded' artist paradigm) had become a tedious mantra. At the same time, however, there was always a kind of muted, ongoing scholarship on Bergman. As he abandoned the cinema for theatre, television work and writing after his return from exile, he also stimulated many to continue their research on his work, research that began to reflect theoretical and topical shifts in humanities studies in general and in theatre arts and cinema studies in particular. Religious and psychoanalytical studies gave away to feminist readings, such as Marilyn Johns Blackwell's book *Gender and Representation in the Films of Ingmar Bergman* (1997). With Bergman's publication of *Laterna magica* in 1987 and subsequent works exploring his family background, the director has become a fascinating example of the ambiguous autobiographical self, explored in postmodernist literary studies. At the same time greater attention has been paid to Bergman's theatre and media work. In addition, the material in the donated Fårö library has already produced scholarly results as we can see in Maaret Koskinen's study *I begynnelsen var ordet* (*In the Beginning was the Word*, 2002), which traces central motifs in Bergman's films back to his diaries and notebooks.

What has been the collective impact of the writings presented in this volume, and their origins at the symposium? Well, first they have cemented the fact that words and images, verbal expression and visual style have to enter into partnership in studies of an artist whose creativity embraces a multifarious use of literature, cinema, radio, television, theatre and opera work. But to me personally, this work is especially valuable in showing the great vitality and variety of academic discourses on Bergman today. I believe this is more important than prescribing an exact future course for Bergman research.

With that in mind, I want to return to Bergman's Chartres essay which I quoted earlier, where, in hinting at his own posterity, Bergman suggests how he would like to view his own artistic contribution and our present or future assessments of it:

> Thus, if someone asks me what I would like the purpose of my work to be, I would answer: I want to be one of the artists in the cathedral on the vast plain … I never need to worry about the verdict of my contemporaries or the judgement of posterity, I consist of a given name and a surname … which will disappear when I myself disappear. But a small part of myself will nevertheless survive in the triumphant, anonymous totality. A dragon or a devil or perhaps a saint – it does not matter which. (1954: 9; my translation)

Notes

1 For the early reception of Ingmar Bergman outside of Sweden, see my reference guide (2005: 887, 904–8, 910–20). For a study of the Swedish reception, see my monograph (1996).

2 Dick Cavett Show, ABC/TV, 1 August 1971. Also on National Educational Television (NET), 12 April 1972.

3 See also my own discussions of the Zeitgeist (Steene 1984: 592–5; and in Steene 2000: 493–9).

References

Anon. (1954), 'Interview with Ingmar Bergman', *Filmjournalen*, 8 (April), 3.

Astruc, A. (1968 [1948]) "The Birth of a New Avant-garde: 'le caméra stylo'", *The New Wave*, ed. P. Graham. London: Secker & Warburg, 17–23.

Bergman, I. (1954) 'Det att göra film', *Filmnyheter*, 9, 19–20, December, 1–9.

_____ (1965) 'Den fria, skamlösa, oansvariga konsten – ett ormskinn, fyllt av myror', *Expressen*, 1 August, Culture page.

_____ (1966) *Persona*. Stockholm: Norstedts.

_____ (1967) 'The Serpent's Skin', *Cahiers du cinéma in English*, 11, September, 24–9.

_____ (1970) 'The Snakeskin', *Film Comment*, 6, 2, Summer, 14–15.

_____ (1972) 'Film and Creativity', *American Cinematographer*, 53, 4, April, 378–9.

_____ (1972) *Persona and Shame*, trans. K. Bradfield. London: Calder & Boyars.

_____ (1987) *Laterna magica*. Stockholm: Norstedts.

Bergom-Larsson, M. (1977) *Ingmar Bergman och den borgerliga ideologin*. Stockholm: Norstedt/ Pan.

_____ and S. Hammar (1992) *Nedstigningar i modern film hos Bergman, Wenders, Adlon, Tarkovski*. Delsbo: Åsak, Sahlin & Dahlström AB.

Björkman, S., T. Manns and J. Sima (1973) *Bergman on Bergman: Interviews with Ingmar Bergman*, trans. P. B. Austin. London: Secker & Warburg.

Blackwell, M. J. (1997) *Gender and Representation in the Films of Ingmar Bergman*. Columbia: Camden House.

Donner, J. (1960) 'Jungfrukällan', *BLM*, 19, 3, March, 254–9.

Fredericksen, D. (2005) *Bergman's Persona*. Poznan: Adam Mickiewicz University Classics of Cinema Series.

Fridén, A. (ed.) (1998) *Ingmar Bergman and the Arts*. Nordic Theatre Studies, 11, 5–6.

Furhammar, L. (1991) *Filmen i Sverige. En historia i tio kapitel*. Stockholm: Wiken/SFI.

Gervais, M. (1999) *Ingmar Bergman: Magician and Prophet*. Montreal: McGill-Queen's University Press.

Gibson, A. (1969) *The Silence of God: Creative Response to the Films of Ingmar Bergman*. New York: Harper and Row.

Gado, F. (1986) *The Passion of Ingmar Bergman*. Durham: Duke University Press.

Hobson, A. (1981) 'Dream Image and Substrate: Bergman's Films and the Physiology of Sleep', in V. Petric (ed.) *Film and Dreams. An Approach to Ingmar Bergman*. South Salem, NY: Redgrave, 75–95.

Koskinen, M. (1984) 'Det typiskt svenska hos Ingmar Bergman', *Chaplin*, 5–6, 221–6.

_____ (1995) 'The Typically Swedish in Ingmar Bergman', in Roger Oliver (ed.) *Ingmar Bergman. An Artist's Journey*. New York: Arcade Publishings, 126–36.

_____ (2001) *Allting föreställer, ingenting är. Filmen och teatern – en tvärestetisk studie*. Stockholm: Nya Doxa.

_____ (2002) *I begynnelsen var ordet. Ingmar Bergman och hans tidiga författarskap*. Stockholm: Wahlström & Widstrand.

Lagerroth, U.-B., E. Hedling and H. Lund (eds) (1997) *Interart Poetics: Essays on the Interrelations of the Arts and Media*. Rodopi: Amsterdam and Atlanta.

Lauder, R. (1989) *God, Death, Art & Love: The Philosophical Vision of Ingmar Bergman*. Mahwah, New Jersey: Paulist Press.

Malmberg, C.-J. (1978) 'Bergman ansikte mot ansikte med historien', *Filmhäftet*, 15–18, May, 106–16.

Manvell, R. (1982) *Ingmar Bergman: An Appreciation.* New York: Arno.

Marker, L. (1983) 'The Magic Triangle: Ingmar Bergman's Implied Philosophy of Theatrical Communication', *Modern Drama*, 26, 3, September, 251–61.

Moberg, R. (1951) 'Framgången, gosse, är en kviga med såpad svans', *Se*, 17, 27, April, 42, 44–5.

Schildt, J. (1958) 'Brev till Ingmar Bergman', *Vecko-Journalen*, 49, 15, April, 22, 44.

Simon, J. (1972) *Ingmar Bergman Directs.* New York: Harcourt, Brace, Jovanovich.

Sjögren, H. (1968) *Ingmar Bergman på teatern.* Stockholm: Almqvist & Wiksell/Gebers.

Steene, B. (1984) 'Det sjunde inseglet. Filmen som ångestens och nådens metafor', in J. Donner, S. Grönberg and L. Åhlander (eds) *Svensk Filmografi* V. Stockholm: Svenska Filminstitutet, 592–5.

_____ (1996) *Måndagar med Bergman.* Stockholm/Stehag: Symposion.

_____ (2000) 'Från subjektiv vision till tidsdokument och arketyp: Ingmar Bergmans *Det sjunde inseglet i mentalitetshistorisk belysning*', in J. Marnersdottir-Cramer (ed.) *Nordisk litteratur och mentalitet*, Annales Societatis Scientiarum Færoensis XXV, Torshavn, 493–9.

_____ (2005) *Ingmar Bergman. A Reference Guide.* Amsterdam: Amsterdam University Press.

Timm, M. (1994) *Ögats glädje. Texter om film.* Stockholm: Carlssons.

Törnqvist, E. (1995) *Between Stage and Screen: Ingmar Bergman Directs.* Amsterdam: Amsterdam University Press.

_____ (2003) *Bergman's Muses. Aesthetic Versatility in Film, Theatre, Television and Radio.* Jefferson, NC: McFarland.

Widerberg, B. (1962) *Visionen i svensk film.* Stockholm: Bonniers.

Wirmark, M. (ed.) (1996) *Ingmar Bergman. Film och teater i växelverkan.* Stockholm: Carlssons.

Young, V. (1972) *Cinema Borealis: Ingmar Bergman and the Swedish Ethos.* New York: Avon Books.

FILMOGRAPHY

American title/UK title if different/Swedish title and year of first release

Crisis/Kris, 1946
The Man With an Umbrella/It Rains on Our Love/Det regnar på vår kärlek, 1946
A Ship to India/The Land of Desire/Skepp till Indialand, 1947
Night is my Future/Musik i mörker, 1948
Port of Call/Harbour City/Hamnstad, 1948
The Devil's Wanton/Prison/Fängelse, 1949
Three Strange Loves/Thirst/Törst, 1949
To Joy/Till glädje, 1950
This Can't Happen Here/High Tension/Sånt händer inte här, 1950
Bris (nine 1-minute Bris soap commercials), 1951
Illicit Interlude/Summer Interlude/Sommarlek, 1951
Secrets of Women/Waiting Women/Kvinnors väntan, 1952
Monika: The Story of a Bad Girl/Summer With Monika/Sommaren med Monika, 1953
The Naked Night/Sawdust and Tinsel/Gycklarnas afton, 1953
A Lesson in Love/En lektion i kärlek, 1954
Dreams/Journey into Autumn/Kvinnodröm, 1955
Smiles of a Summer Night/Sommarnattens leende, 1955
The Seventh Seal/Det sjunde inseglet, 1957
Wild Strawberries/Smultronstället, 1957
Brink of Life/So Close to Life/Nära livet, 1958
The Magician/The Face/Ansiktet, 1958
The Virgin Spring/Jungfrukällan, 1960
The Devil's Eye/Djävulens öga, 1960
Through a Glass Darkly/Såsom i en spegel, 1960
Winter Light/The Communicants/Nattvardsgästerna, 1963
The Silence/Tystnaden, 1963
All These Women/Now About These Women/För att inte tala om alla dessa kvinnor, 1964
Persona/Persona, 1966
Stimulantia ('Daniel' episode, home movie documentary)/*Stimulantia*, 1967

Hour of the Wolf/Vargtimmen, 1968
Shame/The Shame/Skammen, 1968
The Ritual/The Rite (TV play)/*Riten*, 1969
The Passion of Anna/A Passion/En passion, 1969
The Fårö Document (documentary)/*Fårödokument*, 1969
The Touch/Beröringen, 1971
Cries and Whispers/Viskingar och rop, 1973
Scenes From a Marriage (feature/TV miniseries)/*Scener ur ett äktenskap*, 1973
The Magic Flute (TV opera)/*Trollflöjten*, 1975
Face to Face (TV miniseries)/*Ansikte mot ansikte*, 1976
The Serpent's Egg/German title: *Das Schlangenei/Ormens ägg*, 1977
Autumn Sonata/German title: *Herbstsonat/Höstsonaten*, 1978
The Fårö Document 1979 (documentary)/*Fårödokument*, 1979
From the Life of the Marionettes/German title: *Aus dem Leben der Marionetten/Ur mari-*
  onetternas liv, 1980
Fanny and Alexander (feature/TV miniseries)/*Fanny och Alexander*, 1982/1983
After the Rehearsal (TV play)/*Efter repetitionen*, 1984
The Blessed Ones (TV play)/*De två saliga*, 1985
Document Fanny and Alexander (documentary)/*Dokument Fanny och Alexander*, 1986
Karin's Face (documentary)/*Karins ansikte*, 1986
The Last Scream (TV play)/*Sista skriket: En lätt tintad moralitet*, 1995
In the Presence of a Clown (TV play)/*Larmar och gör sig till*, 1997
Saraband (TV play)/*Saraband*, 2003

Screenplays written by Ingmar Bergman and directed by others:

Torment/Frenzy/Hets (director Alf Sjöberg, 1944)
Women Without a Face/Kvinna utan ansikte (director Gustaf Molander, 1947)
Eva/Eva (director Gustaf Molander, 1948)
While the City Sleeps/Medan staden sover (synopsis; director Lars-Eric Kjellgren, 1950)
Divorced/Frånskild (director Gustaf Molander, 1951)
The Last Couple Out/Sista paret ut (director Alf Sjöberg, 1956)
The Pleasure Garden/Lustgården (director Alf Kjellin, 1961)
The Lie/Reservatet (TV play; director Jan Molander, 1969)
Good Intentions/Den goda viljan (director Bille August, 1991)
Sunday's Children/Söndagsbarn (director Daniel Bergman, 1992)
Private Confessions/Enskilda samtal (director Liv Ullmann, 1996)
Faithless/Trolösa (director Liv Ullmann, 2000)

INDEX